Starting Points in Critical Language Pedagogy

A Volume in Contemporary Language Education

Series Editor

Terry Osborn
University of South Florida

Contemporary Language Education
Terry Osborn, Series Editor

Spirituality, Social Justice and Language Learning (2007)
edited by David I. Smith and Terry Osborn

Identity and Second Language Learning (2006)
edited by Miguel Mantero

Early Language Learning: A Model for Success (2006)
edited by Carol M. Saunders Semonsky and Marcia A. Spielberger

Teaching Writing Genres Across the Curriculum:
Strategies for Middle School Teachers (2006)
edited by Susan Lee Pasquarelli

Teaching Language and Content to Linguistically and Culturally Diverse
Students: Principles, Ideas, and Materials (2006)
edited by Yu Ren Dong

Critical Questions, Critical Perspective:
Language and the Second Language Educator (2005)
edited by Timothy Reagan

Critical Reflection and the Foreign Language Classroom (2005)
by Terry Osborn

Starting Points in Critical Language Pedagogy

By

Graham V. Crookes
University of Hawai'i at Mānoa

and

Arman Abednia
Murdoch University, Australia

INFORMATION AGE PUBLISHING, INC.
Charlotte, NC • www.infoagepub.com

Library of Congress Cataloging-in-Publication Data

CIP record for this book is available from the Library of Congress
http://www.loc.gov

ISBNs: 978-1-64802-491-7 (Paperback)

978-1-64802-492-4 (Hardcover)

978-1-64802-493-1 (ebook)

Printed in the United States of America

DEDICATIONS

Graham dedicates this book to Ikaika and Hildre

and

Arman dedicates it to Ahdieh

CONTENTS

PREFACE

In this prefatory section, we, the authors, will speak quite directly to you, the readers, about the book itself, why we've written it, and some of its features. (And in the Introduction, we'll go into the structure and logic of the book itself.)

It's a little unusual for academic books to adopt a style in which the authors say "We" and frame their remarks directly, addressing a reader as "You." Nevertheless, we will do that explicitly here in the Preface, and quite often in the rest of the book. We believe this is an appropriately direct and simple way of writing, to foster good communication between authors and readers. It also reflects a theoretical position important for us, that is, the idea of "dialogue." (We'll write much more about that in the body of the book.)

So who are we?

Graham Crookes: I'm a White male—I am originally from England but have lived in Hawai'i since 1982, where I am now a professor and language teacher educator at the University of Hawai'i. I have been teaching English as a second or foreign language (ESL/EFL) since I was in my early 20s. I lived and taught in Malaysia and Japan before coming to Hawai'i to get my master's degree in the disciplinary area associated with my teaching. Even though my MA was completed in what was then a fairly conventional department, I had always been interested in alternative schools and non-mainstream ways of teaching, but it wasn't until I heard about critical language pedagogy in the early 1990s that I realized there was something

Starting Points in Critical Language Pedagogy, pp. xiii–xv
Copyright © 2022 by Information Age Publishing

that would bring together my personal values as a teacher with an actual applicable set of practices (and theory) in language teaching.

Arman Abednia: I am an Iranian man, 40. I am a language teacher, teacher educator, and researcher. I have been teaching EFL/ESL most of my professional life, mostly in Iran, and lately in New Zealand and Australia. I first became aware of what we are calling in this book "critical language pedagogy" when I started teaching undergraduate students of English In Iran. It seemed to offer some conceptual solutions to some of the less than desirable experiences I had when I was a student.

Continuing with introductions: One of the slightly unusual and good points about this book is that besides our (authorial) voices, it also carries and reproduces the voices of teachers. The teachers you'll hear from, in direct quotes, are language teachers who have taken part in a couple of courses that we have offered recently on the topic of this book. We are particularly grateful to them for their bravery in explaining their actions to teach towards social justice, for being willing to ask questions, to share and explore their ideas, sometimes quite experienced, in other cases, quite beginning, in this area. We have included their names when we quote them or include their accounts of practice. Some of them have chosen pseudonyms. For you to easily identify when we are quoting one of our teachers rather than the literature, we have used a smaller font size for the quotes. The smaller font size by no means implies that our teachers' ideas and experiences are any less worthwhile than the authors' whose works we have cited. Without them, the voice of ordinary teachers would not appear anywhere in this book and it would manifest few aspects of dialogue. It's important for teachers to talk to each other, to talk back and question the mainstream, to engage with the professional literature (some of which is represented in articles that teacher educators like Arman and Graham curate for them). It's important for teachers who are reading this book to see people much like them already (in some cases) manifesting the ideas indicated by the book, or in many cases see language teachers grappling with them, or questioning them.

And you? We think that you, the readers, are mostly English language teachers with an interest in equality and social justice, perhaps people who've heard the term "critical pedagogy," but haven't had the opportunity, the conditions, or the support, to start exploring this in your classrooms. You might be new teachers; more likely, you are somewhat established teachers who are looking to shift your teaching in the directions favoring social justice. You probably also have a sense that this is not a simple matter, and one that requires care and forethought.

And the topic of the book: *Starting points in critical language pedagogy*. Most of the time we will be dealing with English language teaching— teaching English as a second or foreign language, though most of what we say applies to other languages, particularly powerful ones. And probably it's obvious, but in brief, we mean teaching a language (English or any other) for social justice; specifically, how to *begin* to do that. We'll save further discussion of the book's topic to the first chapter.

The book itself can be thought of as vicarious experience. We, along with our teachers, are sharing with you a concentration of experiences and reflection, worries, concerns, and small successes, in beginning to teach language with the idea of social justice in mind. Some of the time we are writing from our own experiences; part of the while we will hear from teachers we have worked with; and of course, we are mining the published literature having read many reports *for* you, and we share our notes and thoughts arising from them in this book.

Another thing about the book: the role of theory. We have not loaded up this book with theory and theoretical terms to the extent that we could have (though we certainly have included plenty of academic references) because we want to emphasize practice, and indeed, the *beginnings* of practice in the area of English language teaching for social justice. But theory is a tool with which to think about practice. So, as you read the book, recognize your already-existing capacity to theorize, that is, to reflect on the bases or principles you adhere to in your teaching—those are "theories in action." Your own theorizing is very important. And of course, we want to assist in the development of this in a critical direction. We have written the book based in an understanding of teachers which includes their interest in theoretical pedagogical knowledge, and imagines them as actively reading publications on teaching when they can. Although we deliberately write in a personal style, we have consciously avoided a simplistic, minimally, or solely practical language in the book to avoid unintentionally insulting teacher readers' intellectual capacity. In this way, us getting "academic" at times in the book is justified.

We should make it clear that while our main audience in this book is teachers, we have not adopted a narrow definition of teachers as those who are not interested in reading and expanding their knowledge. Rather, we believe our readers do have that exploratory attitude. But in addition, that means, incidentally, that although we refer to the published litera-tures of critical pedagogy and its language component, we don't assume that readers can find this material or already are familiar with it. This is a situation that has perhaps improved, though is still not good. We will have something to say about "accessing the literature" near the end of the book.

Here at the end of the preface, we'd like to thank our families and loved ones for support (this is a conventional part of such sections, but we mean it just the same).

ACKNOWLEDGMENTS

Many thanks to the teachers who participated in our online courses and allowed us to have their voices in this book. Their names (real names or pseudonyms) are as follows:

Elaheh, Fereshteh, Hoda, Jaleh, Jing, Kourosh, Mahsa, Masoud, Mitra, Mohtaram, Mowla, Samaneh, Shuang, Soodabeh, Susan, Theresa, and Zahra.

CHAPTER 1

INTRODUCTION

THE RATIONALE OF THE BOOK AND ITS STRUCTURE

In this chapter, we will explain the overall rationale of the book and its structure. We have written this book because despite the increasing size of the literature on critical language pedagogy, there is a shortage of introductions to it—that is, material written for the teacher beginning to explore this area. Most of the literature is still in the form of academic journal articles, which means it is written for specialists. There is comparatively little that focuses on the practical realities faced by would-be critical language teachers in international English language classrooms. Overall, almost none of us teachers have experienced an apprenticeship of observation—that is, the many years we spend in classrooms as students, during which time we observe, in a sense, our teachers—that included any classes taught by a teacher who had a critical pedagogy philosophy of teaching. So almost all of us are in a sense beginners in this area. And then in addition, many discussions of critical pedagogy in general, or the narrower literature of critical language pedagogy, are written as if every teacher has favorable teaching circumstances, high degrees of professional autonomy, and lots of easily available supplementary materials, when that is far from what is normally the case.

Starting Points in Critical Language Pedagogy, pp. 1–12
Copyright © 2022 by Information Age Publishing
All rights of reproduction in any form reserved.

As this is an introduction, let's get straight away to defining a few terms we're going to need immediately. First, we will use the phrase "English Language Teaching" and its acronym ELT to cover all teachers we address in this book, who are teaching English as a second, foreign, or additional language. We will also sometimes refer to English as a second language (ESL) contexts or countries, as distinct from English as a foreign language (EFL) contexts or countries. The former are places where there is relatively easy access to English, probably because it is a dominant or official language, and the latter are places where most students will not hear the language on the street and only easily engage with it through web or internet resources, besides the classroom. But we'll come back to this almost immediately.

We'll use the word *pedagogy* a lot. In the context of critical pedagogy, this is not just a synonym for teaching practices, but is understood to also include the theory behind them, which is a curriculum theory, that includes theoretical positions on society, education, learning, and the nature of the individual. And by theory we don't mean theories proposed by established scholars only. Instead, we wish to acknowledge teachers' theories-in-action—that is, their theoretical understandings of their own contexts, that they themselves develop—as equally credible.

And then for us, *critical language pedagogy* is teaching languages for social justice. The English teachers whom we address in this book are mostly those who, like us, are concerned about issues of equity, democracy, and social justice, but have not yet had a chance to act on these interests. At least some of them are using conventional conceptions of language teaching: the four skills and associated components like grammar and vocabulary. They are probably working with comparatively limited resources and limited professional discretion. We want to start at these points and positions and that is what our chapter headings reflect. Most of the time we will be talking about students as adults and adolescents, because most of our teacher participants have taught these age groups and they have reflected mostly on students who are intermediate or higher-level learners.

We have tried to keep our writing style relatively simple and direct. So for example, we use the first person as much as possible, and often write directly to you, the reader. We, together with you, will nevertheless engage with matters of intellectual challenge and ethical importance.

As mentioned in the Preface, we also draw on the writing of ELT teachers we have worked with recently in several teacher development courses on critical language pedagogy. Most of the teachers in our most recent courses have been EFL teachers, and in this book we are particularly interested in their concerns, because questions continue to be asked in the area of critical language pedagogy concerning the difficulty of using this approach in EFL contexts.[1] But we work with ESL teachers as well on a regular basis. So let's just talk about that a bit. First, the diversity of circumstances of ELT is increasingly obvious now in the early 21st century, given globalization and the continuing power of English. We do have countries (as just mentioned, those which are often called "EFL countries") where contact with and use of English is quite limited (Japan and Korea, for example). And at the other end of a spectrum there are true "ESL countries," like the United States and the United Kingdom, where English is extremely important and learned by most immigrants to those countries. But between those extremes are places where English is an important official language and widely used by elites or major sections of the populations (India and South Africa are good examples) as well as other countries where it was once an official language and remains important (for example, Malaysia), and languages where it is powerful and relatively accessible though not official (some South and Central American countries, with Mexico at one end of a continuum here, and poorer countries not so impacted by the United States, like Bolivia or Guyana, at the other). And there are European countries where very large sectors of educated society have high or intermediate levels of English competence, as in Denmark. So saying EFL or ESL is quite inadequate, which is one reason for using the catch-all term "ELT."

With that degree of diversity in mind, it does not make sense to just assume that critical language pedagogy is somehow easier in places where access to English is greatest. The local culture, of a specific school or institution, could override access; administrative constraint could overcome teacher initiative. We should be honest and share our opinion that critical language pedagogy is not easy *anywhere*. In this context, we should perhaps lower unreasonable expectations. Critical pedagogy is rare. It is no more Western than Eastern, and overall, it is not found significantly more in any one culture than another, though admittedly it is probably less rare under conditions of freedom than oppression. With this book we hope to bring out more obviously the point that wherever dedicated critical language teachers are, they will find a way to have their say and deliver language lessons that orient towards social justice.

Now let's tell you about the structure and organization of the book. If you have already looked at the Contents page, you will have seen the sequence of topics by chapter. After this initial phase of the Introduction, we will go through some of the history and key concepts of critical pedagogy. But if you want to get a more immediate sense of what is involved, it is not necessary to treat this book linearly. You might jump immediately to the next chapter or indeed look anywhere and move back and forth through the material.

In Chapter 2 we start with the implications of running a second language classroom that's going to be less teacher-fronted than conventional classes. A central idea of critical pedagogy is that in the classroom the learners have an active role, working together with each other and the teacher, with the view that this is consistent with their desirable role in society too. This means that in many cases, for many teachers around the world in what we are calling "conventional" classrooms, to begin a critical pedagogy implies gradually making a shift in classroom interaction practices, which raises classroom management questions.

In Chapter 3, the topic is "what can critical language pedagogy classes refer to or be about?"

We use grammar and the old (and not entirely satisfactory) division of language into the "four skills," to organize the next four chapters. So we have Chapter 4 on reading, Chapter 5 on writing, Chapter 6 on grammar, Chapter 7 on listening and speaking, and Chapter 8 on pronunciation. Across those chapters, we have broken topics up (to fit them into chapters) that really should go together. We chose this structure because we think it will make it easier for us to explain things with the intention of starting with typical or mainstream concepts commonly in use in our field. However, ideally at least some of these skills go together (as signaled by the use of terms like "oracy" for listening and speaking, and "literacy," for reading and writing).

Aspects of the important matter of the place and role of English in the world are taken up in Chapter 9. Testing and assessment are always important but doubly so when power is a central concern, so that is the focus of Chapter 9. And the main part of the book closes with two forward-looking chapters: Chapter 10 on how we as teachers may continue to develop, and Chapter 11 on the critical pedagogy world outside the classroom.

Finally, we (Graham and Arman) are always on the look-out for very concrete examples of practice to share with you. This is because it's really difficult to imagine alternative classrooms in the face of so much conventional experience. In several chapters of the book, we share classroom tasks and minimal lesson plans that provide concrete examples of what can be done with quite basic conventional material.

THE HISTORY OF CRITICAL PEDAGOGY AND THE LITERATURE OF CRITICAL LANGUAGE PEDAGOGY

Education has often been implicated in social changes, and since the earliest times, there have always been educators trying to find ways of improving the well-being of their students and of society, and people who learned and used second languages for personal and societal improvement. One of the clearest early examples of an educator with such an orientation is Confucius. After a not entirely successful career as a provincial administrator, in a period of exile he unsuccessfully sought positions advising political leaders to promote good government. In the final phase of his life, he turned to teaching those who would enter government. He was critical of the state of governments around him. By teaching at his school, through a strongly ethics-focused curriculum, he hoped to educate young adults[2] for goodness, who (because of their character and understanding) would make government work well for all (cf. Zhao, 2013).

As civilizations expanded, the dominant language of one cultural area became the second or foreign language of another, or more likely, in ancient times, the second language of the elites of areas affected by the civilization in question. As Chinese influence expanded into the contact zones of what is now Korea and Japan (from the first century AD on), local elites learned Chinese for trade and diplomacy purposes. The spread of Chinese Buddhism from the fourth century or later, and Confucianism, was seen by some scholars and administrators as likely to lead to improved lives and possibly government. Some would have learned a second language from societal or personal improvement motives.

In ancient times in Europe, the Roman empire was run as a bilingual operation. Romans learned Greek, and at least part of what they learned was intended to make them better individuals than they would have been had they depended solely on Roman culture (e.g., Feeney, 2016)

Coming closer to modern times, consider Comenius. In the 17th century, as one of the most famous language teachers and textbook writers of early modern Europe, Comenius promoted first language literacy out of dissatisfaction with the way things were, and with a vision of his countries of origin and those in which he worked that included a school in every town (Howatt, 1984).

Or consider the Classics movement of the 19th century, and the role of foreign language literature teaching that followed. In the British account of this (e.g., Arnold, 1868, as cited in Connell, 1950, p. 179), England at that time was a culture badly in need of humanizing civilization, requiring a moral commitment to the elimination of poverty through the schools, in need of better government and a better elite to run it. The ideals of Greece and Rome, embodied in Greek and Latin languages and literatures were to pave the way for this[3] (Goldmark, 1918). Greek and Latin therefore were studied as second languages in elite schools for that reason. In this period, in many European countries and the United States, the best literature in modern languages was taught for similar reasons (see Clark, 1987, on "classical humanism").

On the other hand, in those early times, most people simply didn't receive any formal education at all. The interests of ordinary people, then, whether or not seen as distinct from those of the elites or the gradually-developing middle classes, did not show up in education systems until those systems became extended to the masses. This did not start until the age of the Enlightenment in Europe, and the political revolutions that accompanied it, in what became the U.S. and in France. Both bourgeois as well as truly radical ideas show up in schools from the 1700s on. American voices argue for mass education to serve the needs of democracy (e.g., Jefferson, 1785/1954); European voices argue for radical forms of education to reflect the Romantic conception of the child (e.g., Rousseau, 1762). Radical democrats wanted radical schools (such as the New School of Ferrer (during 1901–1906; Avrich, 1980). Those very much concerned with freedom wanted free schools (e.g., Neill, 1927). The progressive movement for both science and social reform advocated for progressive education in the United States (and *l'education nouvelle* in Europe, for example). These ideas were taken further during the Great Depression and social reconstructionists advocated for more and better democracy both in the schools and in society. (For further discussion: Crookes, 2013.)

But as *language* teachers interested in a form of education that would improve our societies, where should we start our history? The radical tradition we've just sketched in the previous paragraph eventually produced one specialist who placed more emphasis than before on language, and that was the Brazilian teacher and philosopher of education, Paulo Freire (1972). As an L1 literacy specialist, and one who worked with adult learners[4] from the middle of the last century on, he is closer to us than those broadly radical educators (mentioned in the previous paragraph) who went before. Built upon by others during the last 50 years, in a time of heightened attention to languages of immigrants and the development of a powerful world language (English), his ideas have become the local, comparatively immediate (rather than historically distant) starting point for discussions of a perspective on second languages that would be strongly democratic and based in a critique of mainstream society, having the intent to improve it.

As a young university teacher, Freire became involved in socially-progressive movements backed by local provincial authorities in Northeastern Brazil to promote literacy (first language literacy) among the poor. This was adult education, informal, developed in different locations, with short-term literacy campaigns whose content was designed to reflect the concerns and interests of the downtrodden, in a country wracked by poverty, racism, and machismo, and with considerable potential for revolution. When revolution came, it was from the right, not the left, and Freire was exiled (to Chile, and then to Switzerland, by way of the United States). As a result, his ideas spread more than would have been the case had he stayed in Brazil; a couple of his early books in particular circulated widely and the ideas were taken up by educators in search of alternatives during the turbulent years of the 1960s.

For teachers of English as a first language in the United States, the work of Shor (starting in 1980) made Freirean ideas practically visible for the community college classroom. For what we used to call foreign language education,[5] in the U.S., Crawford's dissertation (1978) extracted principles from what Freire had published up to that time and explored how they could be manifested in the teaching of languages such as French or Spanish in the U.S. high school setting. For ESL education, Wallerstein and then her colleague Auerbach drew on Freirean ideas in grant-funded work with adult immigrants, providing an ESL version of Freire. Looking back on the developments that occurred during this period, Auerbach (1992, p. 18) commented

> For the past three decades, educators around the world have been working to put Freire's vision of "education for transformation" into practice. Early attempts often focused on struggling to transpose Freire's pedagogy into different contexts in a literal way; however, because his work grew out of specific conditions, took place in a third world country, was developed for a syllabically regular language, and was part of a movement for social change, this kind of literal translation was often not possible, causing some practitioners to become discouraged or to question its applicability to their situation. However, over time, it became clear that this kind of transposition of methodology was neither the intention nor the spirit of Freire's approach. Rather, practitioners realized that they had to constantly reinvent Freire for their own contexts, taking from his work the underlying outlook but developing tools to implement it according to their own situations. Thus, over the past twenty years, Freire's vision has been adapted for second language, workplace, health, and peace education internationally.

In a related passage, Auerbach (1992) also refers to the practical extensions of Freirean classroom and curricular practices. We will come back to a number of the concepts she mentions in subsequent chapters, but it is important at this early stage to emphasize the development, and the continual change and improvements and extensions, that have been made through practice in this area. Auerbach says,

> Key among these [developments] is expansion of the learner's role in the curriculum development process: specifically, where Freire suggested that the educator undertake a period of investigation and identification of themes before instruction begins, others have moved toward a process of identifying themes through dialogue with participants, as part of the instructional process. In addition, rather than focusing on a single method (moving from code to dialogue to generative word to syllabification to creating new words and moving toward action), others have expanded the range of tools and processes for exploring issues, with student involvement in the production of material. Further, many have questioned the notion that the teacher's role is to facilitate conscientization and analytical thinking because it implies that the teacher has a more developed understanding than the students. The process of trying to redefine roles in the

classroom has been as much a learning process for teacher-learners as for student-learners. (p. 49)

On the academic side, Freire's work was extended and brought into contact with other radical curriculum theories by Giroux (e.g., 1981) and made its way into the academic field of applied linguistics through teacher education and research programs, notably one in Canada (at the Ontario Institute for Studies in Education, University of Toronto, associated with Simon, (e.g., 1985). A turn to the critical has become increasingly visible across applied linguistics and Teaching English to Speakers of Other Languages (TESOL), and is also to be found in approaches to world language teaching. For TESOL specialists, one question has been how to take the ESL version of critical language pedagogy and explore its practicality (or limits) in EFL settings, and that is one of the central concerns motivating this book.

KEY CONCEPTS OF CRITICAL LANGUAGE PEDAGOGY

Before we put down some basic ideas to get us going, let's be certain to make the (often repeated) remark: "there is no one critical pedagogy." In a way, the following question could and should be posed to each prospective teacher operating from a critical language pedagogy viewpoint, and a different answer obtained for each and every (different) location. That is, "In your circumstances, given your professional values which favor democracy and equity, and given your desire to direct your professional energies such that they work towards an increase in social justice in your classroom, school, and society, how should you teach a second language?" There could be no one, singular, answer.

However, the way some critical language teachers have answered that question give us possible "key concepts" of critical language pedagogy.

First, critical pedagogy is democratic, and intended to lead to increased democracy in society. A focus on democracy leads to a number of things—for example, democracy in the classroom. While the teacher is certainly an authority, how could there be democracy in society yet at the same time autocracy in school? If that is an obvious contradiction, what are the implications of having some, or at least more, democracy in one's classroom? Critical language pedagogy specialists would answer in terms of a participatory approach to syllabus or curriculum.

If we would like to see more social justice in our society, doesn't it follow that some emphasis should be placed on it in the curriculum, too? Isn't curriculum (and school) an integral part of society, after all? How that is played out from a critical point of view usually involves some focus on social problems, either those of the students themselves, of the school, or those they see in society. This may lead to some action to address the most immediate ones.

Second, but arising out of this, a critical pedagogy classroom is dialogical: broadly, it's exploratory and discussion-oriented. This arises out of a democratic and negotiated understanding of knowledge. It doesn't mean that we get to vote on what *is* knowledge, or on whether English is an S-V-O language or an O-S-V language! It is an implication of the view that knowledge arises out of social processes, and that as a result, knowledge continues to change, as well. Thus an inquiry-based orientation to what passes for knowledge of language is legitimate and necessary; this means that the teacher doesn't have to be all-knowing but can work with students to find things out where necessary. And besides the class as a whole searching for information, the class should (to the extent possible) explore, debate, discuss, or dialogue among its members, and between teacher and student, to also attempt to construct knowledge, solve problems, and develop curriculum. We will have more to say about the key term *dialogue* in Chapter 2.

And third, equally definitional in a sense but also difficult in many conditions of practice, critical pedagogy is action-oriented. This again arises from the centrality of a democratic perspective. Critical pedagogy theorists and practitioners align themselves with a desire for truly democratic environments, and such environments are relatively rare. Most societies would benefit (according to this perspective) with an increase in democracy in most aspects of people's lives, whether at home, at work, or beyond, in the surrounding cultures and political systems. So there is an implied desire to work for social and personal improvement through a focus on democracy, in the classroom and beyond. That cannot always happen; often just working on the classroom is challenging enough. But the desire, and the goal is there. Critique should not only be negative; ideally we can say also what constructive solutions might be provided, based on the initial critical analysis. And a strong hint of this is embedded in the term *praxis*, which refers to the unification of theory and practice that critical pedagogy seeks. If it's only theoretical, or if it's action without theory and reflection on practice, then it will not be adequate or consistent with the long tradition of critical pedagogy.

If much of the above sounds too challenging and very far indeed away from conventional classroom practices or what your school administration would stand for, please remember that this book is intended to provide points of entry and suggest baby steps. So articulating some basic but broad and general key concepts does not mean that they somehow have to be brought in immediately and completely. Far from it. On the other hand, you (dear reader) are entitled to immediate answers to a question such as "what is this all about?" to which we are replying in terms of some key implications that we believe arise from the focus on democracy, on social justice, and on the inquiring and active student that critical pedagogy would like to see eventually turn into the inquiring and active citizen.

Much more could be said, and longer lists of key concepts could be (and have been[6]) developed. But as this is an introduction, perhaps this will suffice for now.

THE ROLE OF THE (DEVELOPING) TEACHER IN CRITICAL LANGUAGE PEDAGOGY

From the beginnings of critical pedagogy, Freire was clear and explicit that because of the dialogical and inquiry-oriented nature of critical pedagogy, it is not the case that the teacher knows everything and the students know nothing. Far from it—and as a result, in his writings he often referred to "teacher-student" and "student-teachers". The terms are a bit clumsy but the point he was making is that the students have plenty to share with, indeed teach, both their peers and implicitly the teacher, and the teacher has plenty to learn, from and with the students. In a critical pedagogy classroom, very often material, realia, a picture, and so forth, is the focus of part of a class, but it is presented either by students or the teacher as a question or a problem: "What is our view about this? What do we need to find out (whether involving language or content) about this?"

This could be even more important to bear in mind if one is just starting to develop a self-image, an identity, and associated practices as a critical language teacher. If you have favorable circumstances in regard to a good rapport with your students, you could be honest with them and tell them, "I am trying out some new ideas in my teaching". Or if that degree of self-disclosure will threaten students' trust in you, at least you should be on the look-out for pitfalls. It should not be the case, in critical language pedagogy, that students are seen in a deficit light, as knowing little or nothing, and that the teacher is somehow "enlightened" or will "empower" students.[7] Rather, the critical classroom should have an atmosphere of working together and helping each other fulfil our potential and flourish, with the teacher providing additional support as part of his/her professional role.

This is particularly important because it enables critical pedagogy to address the charge of imposition. We ourselves may be worried; we may say "if I honestly express my opinions in class to my students, is that a form of imposition?" The most typical view in the critical pedagogy literature is, if students are put in the position of themselves actively finding out information, leading class sometimes, collectively investigating and discussing issues, then the teacher ought to be able to engage with them on a more equal footing. Not completely equal by any means, but not the sole authoritative source of information. Whenever there is a controversial topic on which students and teacher, or students and other students, are engaged with but don't agree with, critical pedagogy perspectives indicate the teacher can suggest, "Let's investigate this together." This kind of shared student and teacher inquiry puts the students in an active role, and also prevents the teacher from being charged with imposing her or his ideas.[8]

Here, as elsewhere, an interactive, dialogic process is called for which reflects the multiple roles of a critical teacher. That is central to critical language pedagogy, and also what we are hoping to indicate in this book, as we share the dialogic interactions we've had with other teachers. To conclude this Introduction, let us restate our central theme. In this work, we are trying to address second language teachers who are intrigued by and beginning to consider engaging with critical language pedagogy. Their teaching conditions may not be altogether favorable. And, it is inevitably difficult to move towards a critical pedagogy from a more mainstream position. Consequently, in most circumstances, cautious first steps may be needed. In what follows, we will try to pull apart numerous areas of language teacher practice, and sketch those steps, and offer our suggestions, concerning how these initial moves or development in one's teaching practices can be made.

NOTES

1. Although more publications than ever before address this area (e.g., Sung & Pederson, 2012).
2. Though men, not women, in the patriarchal culture of his time.
3. As a highly influential inspector of British schools, Arnold also believed that other European countries were using the Classics to do this, but with better effect.
4. There is much more that could be said about writers whose work is interesting or inspiring to read in what we'll call "mainstream" curriculum areas (i.e., not language teaching). Given the comparative shortage of L2 treatments of this approach for young learners, we would like to mention the account of practice in a first language elementary class run by a critically-minded teacher, Mary Cowhey, in Massachusetts, United States (Cowhey, 2006).
5. The term "world languages" is now rightly preferred.

6. We often turn to the early critical second language studies of Crawford (1978, 1981), just mentioned above, for a long list of principles. See Crookes (2013) for discussion.

7. These particular inverted commas are scare quotes, and indicate our distrust of the terms enclosed!

8. This has been advocated at least as far back as Dewey (1910a, 1910b).

CHAPTER 2

FIRST STEPS TOWARDS A CRITICAL ELT CLASSROOM

INTRODUCTION

Under most circumstances, shifting to a critical pedagogy from a mainstream pedagogy means shifting to a more interactive classroom where students have more say about what goes on and have more to do. Of course, you don't have to make that shift across all classes you teach, or across all meetings or modules or units of a single course, even. However, this shift has immediate classroom management implications, and we would like to address them as a first order of business, the first item on our agenda.

Specialists (both teachers and academics) who have written about critical pedagogy have not said much about how to *transition* to the more interactive, dialogical ways that they favor; even the more practical authors have mostly just described the activities they use and how they organize them. And as usual, we have very few accounts about doing this sort of thing, or transitioning towards doing this sort of thing, that come from conventional EFL settings, in which students and teacher often have very little freedom and there are other forms of strong social control. In order to make that transition, a teacher will have to engage with what might seem to be alterations in the control aspects of the classroom. Now, any time we are talking

Starting Points in Critical Language Pedagogy, pp. 13–36
Copyright © 2022 by Information Age Publishing
All rights of reproduction in any form reserved.

about control in the classroom, or helping students have a controlling role in the classroom, we are in the area of *classroom management*. So, the classroom management needed will be different from what we have usually done, because classroom interaction, and the content of the class, will generally have to be more negotiated between teacher and students, in a classroom where critical language pedagogy is being attempted.

Overall, in the advisory literature of our field, classroom management is rarely treated systematically as an area of practice to be engaged with (one book-length exception: Wright, 2005[1]). And within the literature that exists on critical pedagogy in general, the topic is also not extensively treated, although comprehensive discussions are to be found elsewhere (Kohn,1996; Hoover & Kindsvatter, 1997) by specialists who seem to be sympathetic to critical pedagogy. A key piece of advice that allows us to break a large topic down into smaller pieces from which to find places to start is the remark of Australian teachers Murdoch and Le Mescam (2006, p. 44):

> In considering greater negotiation with students, many teachers worry about potential chaos or loss of structure in the classroom. From what we have experienced, negotiating can be much more purposeful and meaningful if structures, routines and record keeping are tightly in place. Essential skills such as questioning, time management, self-assessment, decision-making and critical thinking need to be explicitly modelled and discussed. In addition, successful teachers actively work on dispositions that accompany independence-persistence, risk taking, patience and having the confidence to seek assistance and receive feedback.
>
> Such skills and dispositions are clear in this reflection from a Year 6 student who revealed, "I have found my confidence has deeply improved, and I am amazed at the organisation skills I have developed. I now feel confident about conferencing with my teacher ... and I know that I am interested in my topic, and really enjoy it. I think it's great to learn about (negotiating) because what you learn pretty much stays with you forever."

So if we take our lead from these specialists, we will identify one aspect of the classroom manifestations of critical pedagogy—for example, students' responsibility to choose a topic, say—and plan carefully what is needed for that to happen, in terms of class time, language needed, and possible homework assignments. We will explain carefully in class what is to happen and why, as well as allowing time for students to discuss this. We will allocate appropriate amounts of class time to preparing for this new departure, as well as to the activity itself, and after the first implementation, review (preferably with the class) the extent to which this went as planned, and the extent to which this new classroom practice needs to be fine-tuned.

Even when conventional classrooms are apparently managed by the teacher effectively, what is actually happening is that years of training of the *students* (in conventional, authoritarian classroom practices) are paying off, as the well-disciplined students enable the teacher to easily lead, apparently unilaterally. Obviously for a teacher and students new to any kind of more dialogical or even-handed classroom practice, on neither side can there be recourse to years of practice. But when this sort of classroom management becomes routinized, it is much easier. As Murdoch and Le Mescam (2006) again say: "Students who are empowered to contribute to the conversation about their learning from the outset become highly skilled in the process as they move through the school" (p. 43). That is of course what we are aiming at—developing students who are highly skilled with a form of pedagogy that places them in a more active role than the conventional teacher-fronted one does. That takes time. In addition, it usually cannot be achieved completely in all aspects at once.

In the rest of this chapter, what we will try to do, with the help of the voices of our students—teachers who have already been thinking about critical language pedagogy—is draw on the bits and pieces in the critical literature and the books on classroom management just mentioned to convert them into suggestions for practice that the beginning critical language pedagogy teacher can work with. After some general discussion, then, we will extract some principles from this literature, suggest ways of starting to implement them, and supplement this with comments from "our" teachers who are trying this.

ESTABLISHING YOUR AUTHORITY AND THEN BEGINNING TO MANAGE THE CLASS IN A MORE CRITICAL PEDAGOGY WAY

Beginning teachers are usually worried about two things and can't think about much else—these things are (a) establishing their authority and (b) commanding their content. They know that it is important for them to manifest the role of teacher in ways that will be recognized by students. Particularly in traditional classrooms,[2] some students will challenge the teacher's authority if the teacher fails to conform to their conventional expectations of the teacher's role. And also, the teacher has to be seen to be in command of the material, which is not always easy for the beginning teacher. A regular experience of mine (says Arman), as a beginning critical teacher, was that when I taught a new group of students, many of them initially found it difficult to engage in negotiation. They were not used to having a say in the classroom content and procedures since most of their previous teachers had everything sorted out for them. So they sometimes thought the reason I asked them to have a share in classroom decisions was that I didn't have the knowledge necessary to make those decisions independently.

While these challenges are inevitable, they can be lessened if we start with a reasonable base of conventional practice and build a good rapport with our students before getting into practices and content more associated with critical pedagogy. We need students who mostly trust our capacity to teach, even if they are about to be surprised or challenged by the upcoming new developments in our teaching style. Regarding the students I (Arman) just talked about, I think things could have been smoother if I had actually started off with a more conventional teaching style rather than throwing the class in at the deep end of critical language pedagogy from the very beginning.

While establishing our authority in the classroom is of immediate importance, we should also try to win the school's (and our colleagues') trust. One of our teachers who took a course with us, Kourosh, believes this can happen through patience and maintaining a balance between following school rules and practicing our own critical style:

> I've realized one way to establish one's credibility in a [school] is to be patient and do what one believes in, as much as it is possible under the supervisor's rules, and it will pay in time.... [W]hen I started my job as a primary school teacher some years ago, I remember they were very skeptical toward my methods and classroom management at first (and they were right since I didn't have any experience teaching at any schools prior to then). I didn't like it, but I played by their rules (bending and breaking the unnecessary ones whenever I could). It took less than two months to gain the trust of all the experienced teachers and the administrators, and from then on, their rules were not written in stone anymore. They wanted good results from the class and happy students and parents. When they received it, I was free to choose the method I thought suitable for each class. I left the school to continue my studies at university a year later. When I did, it felt as if I was leaving my family behind. I think a critical pedagogy teacher must consider (while not necessarily accept) the school's point of view but at the same time the school should also respect each teacher's personal traits.

As our quote from Kourosh indicates, when teaching young learners, in addition to students, colleagues, and supervisors, we should consider students' parents' views. A substantial example of this is provided by Bruneau et al. (1991), who were "whole language" teachers working at a U.S. kindergarten. The "whole language approach" (like critical language pedagogy) presents challenges to conventional expectations of language teaching. Particularly designed for L1 young learners, it capitalizes on first language learners' natural ability to acquire language as a social practice if exposed to enough opportunities to use and communicate with language. So young children are given lots of opportunities to write (and draw) their own stories, sometimes dictating to the teacher, choosing their own simple picture story books to read, and writing, using their own spellings and sometimes made-up words. The latter usually are not to be corrected by the teacher. It is expected that with enough exposure, invented spellings will move towards the spellings students see in the books they read. However, this and other aspects of the approach must be properly communicated to parents. In the case reported, the authors not only talked about their teaching at parent evenings, they in due course composed and sent a letter about their teaching to parents.

Once you have established your authority, and as a matter of practicality, it is usually important to make a topic like "rules of classroom participation and interaction" become explicit rather than implicit. What we mean by implicit is this. As teachers, we are usually very rushed, and don't have time to reflect on our practice. So usually we take it for granted that we and the students know what is normal (locally, or in a specific institution) concerning classroom practices, and we don't mention what is normal practice, what the rules of the classroom are, unless something goes wrong. Most teachers are unlikely to negotiate the rules with their students. As teachers, we may even simply reproduce the rules explicitly in a written syllabus (copying the usual rules about attendance, lateness, and grading, perhaps). However, in critical pedagogy these things should be reviewed and discussed with students so that they can play a democratic role in the organization and planning of the class.

One of the things I (Graham) usually do in this area is to draw attention to interaction patterns, potential or actual, in the class (these days it is usually a teacher education class that I am running). In the United States, despite its apparently democratic character, men in mixed classes are, I think, more likely to "take the floor" (that is, speak up, and self-select to speak) than women. And of course, if you have a classroom where expertise in the language of instruction is not equally distributed, that inequality can play out negatively. So, I usually make reference to my values-based position, that the whole class should think about this sort of thing—imbalances in classroom participation. If the course has good technological support, e-mail, and course management software, then chat rooms can be used as additional means of communication, besides merely oral participation in class. That will allow students who are not so orally confident to have other means, for equal or better class participation. I tell the students that I will restrain those who (in my judgment) talk too much. I provide resources that can be used so that students will "call out" their peers who abuse their right to the floor. In a patriarchal society, women may have less opportunity to have a voice, be heard (even if speaking) than men, so it is equitable for classroom discourse (in my classroom) to be unequal in favor of women, since it is unequal against them in the wider society. Equality is not the same as equity!

The resource I (Graham) use is a couple of extracts from a pamphlet on group process in mixed gender discussion groups (Moyer & Tuttle, 1983, in Crookes, 2003, pp. 36 & p. 39). This, for example, lists 14 types of undesirable group participation that those having more social power may use when participating, without sufficient consciousness, in group discussions. They include *Hogging the show* ("talking too much, too long, and too loud"), *Defensiveness* ("responding to every contrary opinion as though it is a personal attack") and *Restating* ("especially what a woman has just said perfectly clearly").[3] While these can be associated with gender in conditions of patriarchy, they can also be associated with confidence or fluency in use of a second language in mixed language groups.

USE OF THE L1

Let's start this section with excerpts from two of our teachers, Theresa and Hoda:

Theresa: I believe that the use of L1 in the classroom is important because it is students' thinking language. If you prohibit the use of the language that they are most comfortable with and are able to use in order to discuss another language, so that they can learn the L2 then it does not allow them the optimum environment in which to learn.

Hoda: When I learn a new word, I am interested to know what it exactly means in my L1 and I think the students have the right to know the meaning of new words in their mother tongue. To me, it does not mean that the teacher is responsible for providing the meaning of every word in the students' L1, but when the teacher and the students have the same L1, it can be helpful.

We think that for critical language pedagogy to work, even-handed and careful use of the students' first language is important. Use of the students' first language is also consistent with the values behind critical language pedagogy. So perhaps this is one of the first issues within "critical language classroom management" that a teacher coming newly to this area might need to think about.

First, with our official academic hats on, we can say that "the literature" and "the experts" have shifted, over the last 15 years. Prior to that, whichever dominant "Method" you looked at, whether communicative language teaching or audio-lingual method, or even earlier, say, the direct method, maximum use of the target language was emphasized. These days (and in what has been called a post-method era), the expert position is one in which the use of the L1 is seen as a choice that should be based on a number of things. In particular, newer psycholinguistic research supports use of the L1, because it is now clear that within the mind of the second language user, the languages are not actually really separate (e.g., Cook, 2001). Since Cook (2001), there has been a wave of change by L2 teachers and researchers calling for a multilingual understanding of the learner at all levels. Among many experts we increasingly see the view expressed strongly, that monolingualism is not normal, and there is talk of a "multilingual turn." This term reminds us that most countries around the world actually involve more than one language and perhaps most people have some command (productive or receptive) of more than one dialect or variety.

Partly because of the realities of language use in contact situations, and also inheriting one language pedagogy tradition, the newer term "translanguaging" has come into use in this area. Critical language teachers who are advocating the legitimate use of the L1 in their classrooms for practical purposes should be able to use this concept. The historical language pedagogy part of the story is simply that in the domain of minority L2 teaching in Britain, the teaching of Welsh as a heritage language has received official support for a long time. This kind of L2 teaching was intended to foster bilingualism. During the 1990s, a particular approach to the use of both languages in the classroom was developed by Williams (1996, p. 64), who called it "translanguaging." He states, "Translanguaging means that you receive information through the medium of one language (e.g., English) and use it yourself through the medium of the other language (e.g., Welsh). Before you can use that information successfully, you must have fully understood it." And also, "translanguaging entails using one language to reinforce the other in order to increase understanding and in order to augment the pupil's ability in both languages" (Williams, 2002, p. 40). To some extent this overlaps with the older term "code-switching," which is what happens in multilingual contexts (like Singapore, for example) where some speakers may move freely between one or more languages in the same utterance. But translanguaging, as the quotes from Williams indicate, has a more explicitly pedagogical and bilingual education context. The term was taken up by U.S.-based applied linguists working with the very large Spanish-speaking communities in New York and elsewhere. This is also a situation where some speakers move freely between two languages, and where heritage language teaching may be aided by the use of both.

Garcia (e.g., Garcia & Wei, 2013) in particular has promoted and popularized the use of the term and associated instructional practices.

Use of the first language is going to be helpful if we want students to be able to talk about matters that are important to them in the second language. As critical language specialists, we can say that indeed, as critical pedagogy strongly values the importance of discussion and dialogue, and as indeed some of things critical teachers and students would like to talk (and perhaps write) about require vocabulary and grammar (at least) beyond what a conventional language syllabus provides at first—then it will be helpful if *some* use of the L1 is possible in the classroom. If students shift to the L1 at times of difficulty, it will prevent discussion breaking down and ceasing altogether. If the L1 is used to allow preliminary reflection or even content input (as Williams's quotes imply), this will support rather than hinder good learning all round. Of course, we will want the classroom language to subsequently shift back to the L2. What the appropriate balance between languages is, is a matter for the teacher, in his or her official role as language learning expert, to provide firm guidance about. But since critical pedagogy espouses a democratic viewpoint, the "votes" or voices of the students on this matter should also be heard.

As we said earlier, critical language teachers did not have an "apprenticeship of observation" in critical pedagogical practices. In fact, we may have been brought up in quite authoritarian educational cultures. So, in starting to do critical language pedagogy, we may have to work against, or question, our assumptions and accustomed practices. That is to say, critical teachers have to exercise "self-criticality"; reflexivity we have to be critical of ourselves. In this case, our own schooling and teacher training background may have led us to believe that the L1 does *not* have a place in L2 instruction. Jing, one of our teachers, said:

> When I was still a student in college, absorbing the teaching and learning theories, I held the ideal that my class in the future will and must be presented in English, and English only, no Chinese or mother tongue allowed. And I practiced this theory or ideal when I did my teaching training in two different senior highs. What I found was that ideal is what you wish for the best to happen and reality is what you need to think about down to earth. While I was talking enthusiastically in class in English, only few of the students can follow me. It is not because I speak too fast, sometimes I would repeat more than three times to make them understand. Then I started to realise that there were some problems in using L2 only in class. Then when I taught them grammar, pronunciation, language skills, I found that it was even more difficult to do so.
>
> As I am teaching the first year of senior high now, I am particularly concerned about this problem. Sometimes, I can use simpler English to ex-

plain the complex one, such as explaining "vet" as "doctors for animals," so that students are still exposed to an English learning environment. Sometimes, however, when it is too difficult to paraphrase it in simpler language, I choose our L1 to make us both easier.

Jing's experience helped her observe challenges involved in using the L2 when the L1 is also an available tool. But, if you as a teacher work in a school with an English-only policy, this matter could present another challenge to be engaged with right from the beginning. Jing went on to say:

> The institutional policy in China advocates pure English teaching in class, but at schools, we all know it's impracticable. So we are actually "dancing with chains", balancing standards with our practical situations.

Samaneh made a similar comment:

> I think almost all language schools in Iran favor the English-only policy. Whenever I had an observer I tried to be myself but at times I tried to run the class monolingually. They warned me about that but I'm still doing my job. I think some observers are not too strict about this issue which is promising.

Although institutional policies probably always limit our L1 use, as these two teachers' comments show, there are opportunities available in specific classes to use the L1 to facilitate learning, if teachers are willing to exploit them or work carefully within their specific circumstances and constraints. It is likely to be found used more explicitly than before in EFL settings as well (to judge by very recent work, e.g., Miri et al., 2017).

FIRST MOVES TOWARDS A DIFFERENT ROLE FOR THE TEACHER

In traditional classrooms, the teacher is the single authority figure, having (in most students' eyes) the final word on classroom procedures as well as classroom content. In critical pedagogy, we want the students to be active in the classroom and with regard to the course; we want them to have input into class content; and we (as teachers) want to be able to challenge them and engage them in dialogue. Additionally, and perhaps just as important, we want to get them to discuss matters with each other as well. All of this is because we hope to prepare our students to be active members of their societies, both within school and outside it.

Now, for students socialized into a traditional form of education, when a teacher asks for their opinion or input, they might think the teacher is incompetent. First moves in this area could be both difficult and important. So to start with, the teacher must be credible, in their traditional role. This applies both to their relationships with their students and their colleagues. Only when that is established, can one be confident about introducing unconventional teaching practices. Arman's experience of a challenge resulting from his not establishing sufficient initial credibility with his student teachers was as follows:

> I had a teacher training course at a language center cancelled halfway through because the teachers thought I did not know enough (since I would ask them for their opinions and wouldn't give them the "right" answer at the end myself). The same happened in classes at [a place I worked at] where the students had said "he is asking for our opinions" meaning "he does not have the knowledge necessary to run the course."

Another of our teachers, Zahra, had given her students a choice regarding whether to first go to the supplementary materials or do the workbook. The supervisor who had observed her had told her:

> that the students had already gone to the department and had asked to change me because they didn't consider me a teacher. She explained that in that school a teacher's word was the word of the gospel and couldn't be challenged, and that a teacher herself shouldn't create room for it. She said democracy doesn't work at this school and the students don't have capacity for it.... Later I realized I wasn't as strict as other teachers in classroom discipline and the amount of assigned homework and this was the problem.

Having noted this, let us ask "What is a good first move?" Theresa points out an extremely simple way to start:

> A simple question to individual students, a hands up or hands down class vote or a written note they write anonymously to the teacher are some ways students can provide us with feedback.

One way for teachers and students to get "on the same page" concerning this aspect of interaction between teacher and students, which concerns student input into the content and form of the class, is to have the students express their views about their school (and/or past schools and teachers) early on in a course. Many students' experiences with school will, overall, have been negative. Oppressive dimensions of mainstream schools put students under pressure to conform and become something other than they were, as dominant (racist, classist, ideological) cultures hold sway over others (minorities, women, the poor, working class, etc.).

Speaking out (or writing down) those experiences is a way to clear the decks for at least sometimes having some different attitudes and practices in the classroom. This is something that Ira Shor (1987), a very experienced critical pedagogy specialist, has described. In a writing class, he reports using a variety of initial writing topics, including "what is a bad teacher?" (p. 132) or asking students to list what should be done to improve school, right at the beginning of his writing course (Shor, 1996, p. 43. This is also the sort of thing that Zahra reports doing:

> A few years ago I had a class at a high school with a bunch of 16–17-year-old girls. It was the first time I taught there and I wasn't aware of their unwritten rules. As usual I gave a choice to the students. This time it was to first go to the supplementary (which were some reading texts assigned by department) or do the workbook (which was emphasized to be covered). Students hated both but were free to choose which one to do first. I usually added some taste to either by including a quotation, anecdote, or joke to sugar the pill. Once, after reading one of the texts implying good points about adults advising and leading the young, I wrote on the board the expression "to be a sage on the stage or a guide on the side," explained it a little bit, and asked their ideas. This raised a hot conversation and students got it all off their chest regarding control from their parents, school, and society, lack of understanding between generations.

Our overall suggestion here is to help students understand the benefits of and the rationale behind democratic classroom management and how it works. We have to explain that the fact that we ask them for their ideas does not mean we don't have a clue!

Of course, some teachers have been doing this sort of thing in a small way for a long time, possibly not thinking about this as an integral part of the value-based perspective that is critical pedagogy. Theresa wrote

> I often allow my students to choose which text they would like to study. For example, if according to the program they are to study autobiographies, then I would make a list of suitable texts and students can vote which one we should do in class. The voting needs to be done anonymously, however, so that students are not influenced by peer pressure.

> Another example of negotiating classroom content is by asking students what they would like to do next lesson. If this is too open, then I would suggest them to choose from 2–3 options. I am often surprised by how mature and responsible they are. Sometimes what they suggest to do next lesson is something I hadn't thought of and it really allows students to think about what they would like to work on more in class.

The same, although less likely to work in the short term, can happen with program administrators, principals, and other teachers. It is all about helping them understand what democratic education could mean and how it can happen. Of course, you as teachers who are trying out critical pedagogy have to use your judgment concerning what is, and what is not, a workable situation. Certainly not every situation will allow even this much movement. But if we don't try, we will not make any progress.

DISCUSSION, COOPERATION, AND DIALOGUE

A critical language pedagogy class is one where the language is used actively by all. Or to put that in a more theoretical way, we could say that in such a class, participation by whatever means (writing, texting, e-mail, online participation, if not always speaking) is equitable. Unfortunately, most conventional classrooms, and perhaps too many language classrooms around the world, are situations where one person talks (usually the teacher) and others, the students, listen. This results in passive forms of learning and doesn't encourage students to take an active role. If they don't take an active role in the classroom, the argument goes, they won't take an active role in the wider society (and then nothing will be improved). And for any understanding of language learning which places importance on actually using the language, a classroom where the teacher only talks and the students merely listen is also not effective.

Students taking an active role, through using language actively with others in the classroom and with the teacher, is important. Most experienced second language learners know this is important for learning. For critical pedagogy it is also important because it is felt that through interactions in which participants question each other's ideas (that is, not just talk for its own sake) students and even the teacher can push their knowledge of situations and concepts forward and come to think up possible solutions to problems. These in due course should be tried out in action. However, if a teacher is starting to move towards critical language pedagogy in a conventional setting, the move from the sage on the stage to the guide at the side[4] may be contrary to student (or parents') expectations.

In this area, we can refer loosely to dialogue and discussion. Critical pedagogy places theoretical weight on the concept of dialogue, which it takes as going far beyond discussion. But let's take *discussion* first.

We think that the ability to hold or take part in a discussion (relatively calmly, without being rude, belligerent, or brow-beating) is important. What things are needed, from a classroom management point of view, to enable discussion to begin? And even before we get to think about doing these things in the L2, can they be done in the L1? It is not even a question of language needs. It is a question of students' mutual respect, tolerance, patience with each other, and the local cultural expectations or typical practices concerning the expression of opinion on potentially sensitive topics. We are also assuming that the teacher him- or herself can also engage in discussion in an appropriate way! Teachers should reflect on their own practices as they begin to foster discussion among their students. Are we teachers able to participate in a discussion appropriately in a social setting and model this behavior for our students in the classroom?

At a simple level, the following is the sort of thing we have in mind. In a report on introducing critical literacy in a class for immigrants in Australia, teacher Eastman (1998, p. 25) writes:

> I noticed that some students lacked the language knowledge to make appropriate choices of register, particularly in relation to politeness. An early example was "Shut up. I don't understand you." This led to my introducing explicit discussion about what is considered polite or not polite and acceptable or not acceptable in the students' own languages and in English.

At the same time, the potential of strong emotion or at least serious interest in topics should not be dismissed as inherently dangerous in a language class. In fact, it can provide valuable energy. We agree that if students are not prepared for a shift in practices, a teacher new to this area can experience classes that "don't work" by conventional standards (in this case because of too much emotion) and the students may end up unhappy or confused. On the other hand, students' passionate interest in a topic can provide valuable energy.

So yes, you have to figure out if your students have the necessary skills and dispositions to discuss things, even perhaps contentious topics, in a satisfactory way, whatever language (L1 or L2) they use. So, you might have to discuss ground rules for discussion in the first language first, and even try this out! And then you would need to introduce or review appropriate phrases for doing discussion in English (addressing politeness, ways of interrupting or keeping the floor, discourse markers, and so on). Ideally this too should be done in a democratic way, so that the class as a whole arrives at and agrees to some basic rules for discussion.

Let's reemphasize that having "shared inquiry" is really important, from a critical point of view, for a couple of reasons. One is that the teacher should not be imposing his or her point of view. In some cases, s/he really doesn't know the facts of the matter. And if s/he behaves as if s/he does know, once again s/he is cutting away the active role and responsibility from the student and jeopardizing the dialogical atmosphere being created. It is much better and also weakens the charge of indoctrination, if the teacher, in response to a topic raised or a challenge made by the students says, "Let's investigate this together." And then that investigation may be in the form of a decision to bring in material after a search of the internet (assuming adequate connectivity), or to proceed based on the information that is collectively held by the class members, and also their different views of the subject. Also when presenting his/her own views, the teacher should explicitly avoid "being a teacher" while expressing that view and, instead, be a co-discussant at a similar level of control and knowledge to the students.[5] At that point we are clearly moving into the genre or interactional mode of *discussion*.[6] And with a moderately cooperative student group, or class, that can engage in discussion, it is possible to move on to dialogue.

DIALOGUE AND CRITICAL DIALOGUE

To start with, let us point out that, for obvious reasons, we do want dialogue as opposed to monologue. Teachers talking about "critical" things doesn't make the class critical, even if this concerns topics of importance to the overall (critical) thrust of the course. Zahra commented,

> Years ago, when I was a student at a language school I had a teacher who frequently lectured on controversial issues and touched upon politics, religion, crime, social norms, etc. He looked at things from his own point of view that was not completely accepted by us in one way or another. Even in the classroom discussions he asked fixed questions and there wasn't much interaction between us. The discussions followed in the way he would lead, and we didn't have room to think for ourselves and ask our own questions. He was very brave to open up many issues, and he received many warnings from [the administration], but I don't consider him that critical because he dictated his thoughts and values instead of encouraging a way of thinking at the beginning.

Dialogue, then, is both a central practice of critical pedagogy and an important theoretical concept.[7] An early exponent of Freire's ideas for L2 instruction, Wallerstein (1983, p. 15), explains as follows:

> To Freire, dialogue means much more than conversation; it is an exchange between everyone in a class, student to student and teacher to student. The term involves action—students initiate discussions, lessons, and activities to fulfill their educational needs.

> Dialogue differs from the traditional lecture and seminar methods where the teacher determines the scope of discussion and students remain passive objects of learning. A Freire approach to dialogue assumes students equally determine classroom interaction. As adults, they bring their concerns and

personal agendas to class. These concerns determine what's important to discuss

Among other things, that means that students should be encouraged to question each other's views. Also, it means that the teacher should feel that s/he doesn't have to appear neutral. While fostering student-student inter-action, the teacher also has an important role to politely challenge ideas, in a non-authoritarian way. Unless circumstances are quite unfavorable, the critical language teacher, having developed good rapport with students, can make it clear that s/he has views and positions on topics that come up or are brought into class.

Since Freire and other critical pedagogues make repeated use of the term *dialogue* and often imply a range of meanings, let us open the matter out a bit more. We'll draw on the ideas of another specialist in learning through dialogue, Burbules (e.g., 1993). He refers to dialogue as (1) con-versation, (2) inquiry, (3) debate, and (4) instruction.

His first sense of the term, conversation, is good for mainstream language instruction purposes, but his second, inquiry, serves a critical language pedagogy class better. Inquiry is certainly one of the foci of Freirean dia-logue, and Burbules quotes Freire saying that when this happens, people are "attempting, together, to learn more than they now know" (Freire, 1970, p. 79, as cited in Burbules, 1993, p. 116). Participants in this form of dialogue, says Burbules (1993), are "directed toward determining the reasons, evidence, and experiences that underlie [issues and problems], as a way of understanding and assessing them more accurately" (p. 116). In fact, Burbules points out several other forms of this kind of dialogue. It can involve problem-solving.[8] It might involve working to achieve a political consensus. It could involve coordinating actions for a common purpose; and it could involve "adjudicating moral differences" (p. 116). That last would be when people with very different views discuss to seek a basis for mutual tolerance.

His third sense of the term, debate, is fine, too, says Burbules, but it can harm dialogue (because the two debating sides may take positions very firmly, leaving no room to compromise, explore, or understand the other's view). Let's look at his fourth and final understanding: dialogue as instruction. Readers may be familiar with "Socratic" dialogical instruc-tion. In a famous example, Plato provided a written account of how the ancient Greek philosopher Socrates led the slave boy Meno, by way of patient and simple questions, through some steps in geometry, so that the untutored boy could learn and demonstrate his knowledge of a problem in geometry. But this kind of leading, in which the teacher has a set plan and knows to where s/he wants the student to go, is not consistent with critical pedagogy. An increasingly common term in education, *scaffolding*, signals this fourth understanding of dialogue. In this case, "the teacher not only models a process, but intervenes actively to provide just sufficient structure and guidance to allow the student to apply strategies effectively.... This support is gradually withdrawn over time" (Burbules, 1993, p. 123). It is not the teacher's view that is the target, but rather the internalization of the strategy of inquiry, so that the student can him/herself engage in critical review of matters either alone, internally reflecting, or with other students, in the future.

Because Freire's unmodified term *dialogue* has special differences between it and the everyday use of the term, some specialists in this area have started using the term *critical dialogue* (e.g., Shin & Crookes, 2005). This is consistent with Freire's use of the term dialogue but emphasizes the special features of dialogue in critical pedagogy. As the discussion so far has indicated, this includes inquiry, for which exploration is necessary. Burbules's (1993) reference to determining reasons, evidence, experience, which pertain to problems, issues, and important concepts, should surely be a major part of critical dialogue. It remains to be determined, and is an area of ongoing investigation, what the (second) language requirements for, and key linguistic features of critical dialogue are (see Wilson, 2010).

With that, we now move on to the slightly vexed but relevant topic of learner autonomy.

FIRST STEPS IN LEARNER AUTONOMY

Because the student in a critical pedagogy classroom has far more responsibility than the typical student in a "non-critical" classroom, we should consider the topic or concept of learner autonomy here. Basically, what we think is that students should be told the equivalent of "in our classroom you have more freedom which means you also have more responsibility." Or, depending on the students' age and previous experience, the teacher will work towards that position, articulating a view like, "we have discussed this and you understand why I think you should have more responsibility, and we are now in agreement that this will include making decisions about certain aspects of the class." Students will, after all, be encouraged to choose topics, possibly negotiate assignments, and ideally have a say in how they are assessed. If they have never had the chance to do any of these things before, it will all come as a bit of a shock! How can we be explicit, not implicit, about what we have in mind? One way to do this would be to specify *learner autonomy* as something that you will talk about early in the course.

Learner autonomy has been a big topic in applied linguistics ever since the early 1980s (having appeared earlier in the field of education, during the late 1960s). For our purposes here, all that is necessary is to mention again that critical pedagogy teachers want to foster active learners and active citizens. So, they will expect learners to take a greater than usual amount of responsibility for their own learning, as well as develop an active role to promote their own learning in the course through their exercise of choice and their having a role in directing the content of the course. Critical pedagogy is clear that the content of learners' lives should have a substantial effect on the content of education (Shor, 1992). However, learner autonomy is probably usually thought of in terms of the individual learner. It could certainly apply to the learner who is studying a language by themselves. When critical pedagogy specialists approach the topic, they want the social aspects of autonomy not to be ignored (Pennycook, 1997). That is, they say that a person's autonomy is not achieved alone, but also draws from others who support that person. (As the poet John Donne wrote, "No man is an island, entire unto himself.") Through mutual aid, teachers and learners working together can assist in a general improvement of learners' autonomy. So here we are emphasizing a balanced focus on the individual and social aspects of autonomy or, autonomy as both independence and interdependence (Smith, 2008), also highlighted in Dam (1990) definition of autonomy as "a capacity and willingness to act independently and in cooperation with others, as a social, responsible person" (p. 102).

Pennycook (1997) in fact says that we should see the emphasis on learner autonomy in critical classrooms as part of a struggle to rethink the culture of the classroom (as part of the struggle to redevelop the wider cultures of our countries or societies). So this means that the learner has a voice in the classroom (as opposed to being silenced), that local, culturally-relevant understandings of autonomy are involved, and above all, that autonomy is not reduced to some individualistic, psychological matter but also encompasses the social aspects of learning.

BEGINNING TO THINK ABOUT SYLLABUS NEGOTIATION: CRITICAL NEEDS ANALYSIS

So far, we have talked about learner autonomy, students having a voice and a say in the class, and the students and teacher engaging with topics and problems they think are important. But what do the ideas about learner autonomy, students having a voice and a say in the class, and the students and teacher engaging with topics and problems they think are important, mean in practice? There are a number of places to start. First, though, as we mentioned earlier, the teacher must have established his or her position and credibility. That is, if you are going to try out some new ideas that you know your students will be unfamiliar with, and perhaps find unusual or even not appropriate for a teacher, then you had better make sure the students trust you to carry out the regular roles of a language teacher first. That is, do not bring in challenging new ideas on the very first day if you are not extremely sure of yourself and your students.

However, once the class is off and running, shifting to a practice in which students have more of a say means, most obviously, having at least some class periods, or a section of the course, in which the topics or content are not already decided. These can then be decided closer to the period in question. They cannot usually be decided on the first day! So, this means that (typically) class time must be allocated to the decision-making process, and it must be discussed and explained as part of the course. If necessary, the language needed to negotiate course content must be taught. If some of this will be done in the students' first language, you as the teacher may have to explain and justify this. For lower level or younger age students, the teacher may need to make use of checklists and simple worksheets.

So learner autonomy is a target that the class as a whole moves toward, in answering a question like "What are we going to learn together?", or "what do we want to study in English?", or even "What are our goals as language learners?" Putting these questions in play, and working with the class to answer them, is often loosely called "negotiating the syllabus."[9]

No special materials are needed for this, though some simple forms or worksheets to foster individual reflection and group discussion would be useful. And if you are not already in the habit of making an explicit course syllabus or schedule, one will probably be needed to record class discussions and decisions, and also to record what responsibilities (if any) individual class members will have to, for example, lead discussion, or make presentations, in that part of the class that they may have greater responsibility for.[10]

So far in this book we have not made much of a distinction concerning how we teach depending on the age ranges of students we are working with. But maybe this needs to be addressed when we are talking about negotiating the syllabus. A distinction can be made between needs and interests, in regard to age range perhaps. That is, adults, and perhaps in some cases teenagers, might have identifiable needs for certain aspects of the language being learned. That is a basic idea behind conventional notional-functional syllabus design, part of the bedrock of communicative approaches. On the other hand, younger children are curious about the world and have interests they can express, though it's unlikely that they need specific aspects of English in the way that an adult working in contact with the tourism industry, or travelling to another country, or engaging in any kind of international trade, might have. So that said, we can consider that conducting a needs or interests analysis should be a common step in implementing a language course, unless it is staying with a pre-set, institutionally-imposed, probably structural syllabus.

So if there is any possibility that your students can identify things they really need the language for, or things they need to do with it (including passing exams), or the topics they are interested in, then a basic sense of having a democratic classroom would lead the teacher to ask students, at some point near the beginning of a course, "What actually do you need to do with English?", or a question like, "If you had a choice, what would you like to read and talk about with English in this class?" So clearly this is part of negotiating a syllabus. (The alternative requires a more well-resourced environment than we are usually experiencing, in which a needs analysis is done by outside or local experts prior to syllabus and materials development or selection.)

But critical language pedagogy goes beyond ordinary understandings of needs analyses to think in terms of a "critical needs analysis" (Benesch, 1996). The point here is not to take for granted the power contexts in which often instrumental needs for English, or for certain aspects of a language, are identified. Rather, we should probe the concept of "needs" further. A critical perspective leads us to notice that such needs are usually seen as only instrumental, and often decided by more powerful figures than the students or even the teacher themselves. A step further is to ask, "What are a student's human needs, in the school or classroom?" We believe that this question has answers like "good teaching," "respect," or "having one's views taken into consideration." Benesch (1996) goes a step further and turns from needs to rights. Not only do the learners need a good education, in most institutional contexts they have a right to one, as well. So, we should consider the students as having rights to a decent education, and then work further on what that actually implies concerning what should go into the course content and be specified in the syllabus. Another possibility is to recognize that indeed, sometimes the teacher is handed a syllabus, even one that is apparently based on some consideration of student needs, but this should be critiqued, looked at skeptically, and indeed turned over to students with the question, "Is this what you *really* need?" And then negotiation becomes important and can lead to a more respectful (indeed, more ethical) course in which the students have a stake and a role, and (we might hope) greater commitment.

Negotiation also heads off the imposition problem. Critical language pedagogy is rightly concerned about this. We don't want to be accused of forcing our views on students. And indeed, not only do we not want to be accused of this, we are concerned to find techniques that will actually prevent us from doing this. It was fortunate that a useful exchange between three of our students and us (from a synchronous chat session) sets this out clearly, so we can close this section with this set of comments[11]:

Soodabeh: The teacher should be careful not to force his/her way of thinking onto the students. Let them freely express their ideas without any judgement. I remember one of my English teachers who would come to the class every session with interesting topics (which mostly dealt with moral issues) to discuss but the problem was that he always wanted to force his ideas onto us and he sometimes annoyed the students. Therefore, now I as a teacher respect my students' ideas to keep my relationship with them positive, in addition to helping them to get rid of thinking in a biased manner.

Theresa: Yes it is important not to force our ideas onto our students. Sometimes, however, when we know that students' thinking are morally/ethically wrong, then other beliefs that I have had to better educate my students is about not stereotyping other students. For

example, they will tease the Asian student in my class for not being smart enough, following the stereotype that all Asians are smart.

Soodabeh: Yes my friend you are right, but how can we intervene to have an effective and morally right approach to our students?

Theresa: By critical pedagogy—expose them to texts and getting students to read them critically. Texts include advertisements that use men and women in different ways and analysing the race of subjects used in ads.

If I hear students talking then I tell them straight away on the spot that their thinking is wrong. I then use the opportunity to educate the class on why their thinking is wrong. For example, if they said that Asians have to be smart then I would say to them, "well you are not Asian that means you are dumb?" In my experience, questioning them as soon as you hear or see morally incorrect behaviour is the best way to intervene and change their thinking.

I will then do a lesson on stereotyping. For example not all Australians wear singlets, thongs, like to drink beer or like watching Australian football.

Students will not change straight away however, that is why it is important that we always choose the correct texts and know how to critically read dominant texts, so that our students understand where their wrong thinking might have come from.

Arman: I am sure by intervention Theresa does not mean "forcing" our opinions onto students, although it may involve the teacher's direct (not very friendly) feedback, as sometimes the situation entails it. For example, as Theresa said, if students stereotype their classmates, then the teacher should jump in and tell them what they need to hear. Yet this is not forcing our opinions. Instead, all we can do is "help" them change their way of thinking through bringing relevant content to the classroom and providing space for their critical reflection on their own and others' attitudes.

Susan: I do agree with Arman. Teachers have got an important role for students. Most of the time students follow their teachers as a model. Because of this, we can help them change their way of thinking through bringing relevant content.

Graham: This is a valuable exchange and helps us focus on a very important concept and associated practices in critical language pedagogy. Sometimes people think that critically-minded teachers should not express their opinions, lest they be seen as attempting to indoctrinate their students. But founding figures in the field, such as Freire, would certainly encourage teachers to challenge students' ideas, but to do so tactfully and respectfully, basing any such exchange in dialogue. Or even better, in a joint investigation. If one is lucky enough to have a syllabus which can flex a bit, then for any area of important disagreement, it is possible to say, "shall we look at this more closely?" And thanks to the internet, it is not too difficult for us (and/or students) to bring in relevant material in the target language. And also, to some extent, we could discuss the matter in the students' first language first, before moving on into the L2.

OUTSIDE CLASS

One less conventional option is the use of out-of-class meetings of one sort or another to continue or develop second language learning. These are called "co-curricular activities," on the understanding that they do relate in some way to the regular, in-classroom curriculum, even though they may have little formal teaching in them (but in our case, do probably involve the use of the target language). A teacher beginning to operate from a critical (language) pedagogy standpoint might keep to a more conventional teaching style and content in the classroom but start up some co-curricular or out-of-class activities. (These too of course have management challenges.) When the in-class context is just too challenging to do anything with at first, given that student-teacher relationships are very important, perhaps they could be established outside of class in legitimate educational activities. Such activities might also provide a forum in which non-mainstream content could more easily be introduced.

This of course depends again on the availability of teacher and students' time and energy, as well as a cultural context which sees such arrangements as plausible. In many EFL contexts over the years, an English language club which organizes after-school events centered on English has been a common phenomenon.[12] In mainstream (non-language) education, critical pedagogy teachers Duncan-Andrade and Morell (2008) write about how they agreed to coach their students in an after-school basketball team. This allowed them to carry forward their critical pedagogy practices as coaches supporting and extending concepts and practices that the students could use in their content classes. However, to the best of our knowledge, there are as yet no reports of language clubs with a critical orientation.[13]

CONCLUDING REMARK

So, in this chapter, we've introduced a number of concepts and initiatives that need to be thought of as you are starting out on this journey. Do please note the phrase in our chapter heading, "first steps," and also that it has taken us quite a few pages to even get through those first steps, with eight sections. It is not easy to start doing, or moving towards, critical language pedagogy. These preliminary moves, their importance, and the time (and planning) needed to undertake them should not be underestimated. Now we'll go on to answer the question, what's a critical language class about?

NOTES

1. And a chapter in Crookes (2003).
2. For a general review of "traditional" second language classrooms, that sees them as having their own positive qualities, in context, see Jin and Cortazzi (2011).
3. The latter term has become notorious in English-using popular culture in recent years, under the newer term "mansplaining!"
4. Or more accurately, in Freirean terms, a co-learner.
5. In the online course associated with this work (mentioned in the Preface), around here we referred to Edelsky and Johnson (2004). In that article, Johnson (that was the teacher's name) has a view of what is "good" critical discussion, and it includes directly acknowledging another's comment, being able to disagree "respectfully," and implied rules of participation which made it possible for all students to feel safe in articulating a position, while at the same time everyone has to feel that it is to be expected that their opinions may be disputed, whether by other students or the teacher. We also referred to Brookfield and Preshkin (1999).
6. We are assuming that students will naturally share a joint activity, perhaps both in the classroom and outside it (the latter as preparation for classroom work, mainly). But this too may be an assumption that flies in the face of conventional classroom practice. In many cultures, classrooms are highly individualistic places where there is student-student competition. Perhaps it will not be natural for students to work together. In that case, the teacher may also need to refer to the substantial literature which has occasionally been taken up in applied linguistics, concerning cooperative learning. So the techniques and dispositions identified by cooperative learning specialists (e.g., McCafferty et al., 2006) are also relevant.
7. The term "dialogue" has a very broad range of meanings in ordinary use and even in language studies (cf. Weigand, 1994). By comparison, critical pedagogy makes the term highly-loaded theoretically, including everyday senses of the term but going beyond them.
8. However, Freire prefers teachers to problem-pose (not solve). It is not the role of the teacher to solve problems that students bring up. Dialogue in critical pedagogy is not the teacher solving problems for students; rather, it is teachers and students investigating them jointly.
9. Many case studies on the subject (only one of which is from a critical pedagogy point of view, however) are gathered in Breen and Littlejohn (2000). See also Clarke (1991) and Nation and Macalister (2009a).
10. If you have good technological facilities, a Google Spreadsheet that all the class can share is great for this sort of record-keeping and updating a syllabus that is negotiated more than once.
11. Fortunate, because it means we don't have to present this just from our side. Teachers must think things out for themselves, about this and other important issues in critical pedagogy. Having other teachers to talk to is really important for this! See Chapter 10.

12. A recent survey of this area from Nigeria is Ajoke et al. (2015); a recent re-view from Malaysia is Pereira et al. (2013).
13. Kärkkäinen (2013) provides some suggestions, but no actual implementation.

CHAPTER 3

CONTENT IN CRITICAL ELT CLASSROOMS

INTRODUCTION

All classes have content, though the significance of this point is sometimes overlooked in a language course. Content is most likely to be neglected in a course with a structural syllabus, where there is an exclusive focus on grammar. In a structurally-focused lesson, it is the grammar of a sentence that we pay attention to rather than what the sentence is actually saying. Even if the teacher focuses students' attention on some aspect of the meaning of a sentence, it is often meant overall to facilitate the class's focus on particular grammatical forms.[1] Even in communicative classes, which do not have an exclusive focus on form and instead have an increased focus on meaning, the meaning aspect of the content is often treated superficially and in a context-reduced manner rather than in an in-depth manner and as part of a larger discourse. The idea that we build on in this chapter is that "language" in the language classroom should not be taken as devoid of a meaning which matters (especially to our students) in the real world. Even a single sentence is about something. Even a paragraph that has been written to practice a grammatical structure still has to be about something. Therefore, it should matter to us teachers (and our students) what content we are expected to teach, and what content we incorporate into the classroom and how. These points are the major foci of the present chapter.

Starting Points in Critical Language Pedagogy, pp. 37–52
Copyright © 2022 by Information Age Publishing
All rights of reproduction in any form reserved.

TEACHER AUTONOMY WITH RESPECT TO CONTENT

The content of what we are expected to teach may or may not be under our control. The professional literature of our field generally fails to address the reality of most teachers' working conditions,[2] and here we want to refer to the general implications of those conditions as concerning teacher autonomy. Unfortunately, many of us do not have professional working conditions—we don't have much control over what we teach, our schedule, our tests, choice of syllabus and textbooks, and so on. At the risk of depressing our readers, but also with the intent of dispelling some misconceptions, let us list some of what we know.

First of all, it is not the case that language teachers in the North, that is, in rich countries, always have discretion concerning what they teach, or how they can adapt it, or what they can supplement. In some states in the United States, teachers have to use "scripted" material (cf. Dresser, 2012). In many countries, much power in regard to state education resides in inspectors, who make visits to schools (sometimes unannounced) to see if, for example, they are conforming to the national curriculum and other official guidelines (see e.g., Janssens & van Amelsvoort, 2008; Rosenthal, 2004). In rich EFL countries like South Korea, state-sector teachers are considered (at least by the government) to be individuals who are government workers, that is, civil servants, and they are expected not to express any political views. (Relatedly, the main union for teachers in South Korea has in various periods been designated an illegal organization by the government: cf. Synott, 2007). Many other similar examples could be provided.

However, we have to focus on those cases where there is some discretion, otherwise we will indeed get nowhere. And if you are reading this book and would like to try some of the ideas considered in it but are convinced that you in fact have no discretion and will be fired if you engage in the smallest aspect of critical language pedagogy, we would not really encourage you to try it. By all means simply wait; bide your time; perhaps search for alternative classrooms; and find someone near or far to confide in. This way of approaching critical language pedagogy under unfavorable conditions is in fact what Freire (1972) encourages in *Pedagogy of the Oppressed*, where he says do it but "not in the open" (p. 65).

Critical pedagogy is hard to do if teachers and students have very limited discretion concerning what is to be studied and what content they work with. And while it is true that in some circumstances teachers have some control, or even extensive control, over content, it is also true that in many situations teachers, not to mention students, are tightly controlled by educational administrations. In many cases, language teachers are obliged to use just the textbook. Sometimes they are not even allowed to supplement it.

Given how institutional (and sociocultural) limitations may impact classroom content and teachers' share in them, let us face up to this matter and indeed analyze it a little bit. Although this is the truth, it is rarely alluded to in our professional literature (but see Ayers et al., 2010[3]). Indeed, in this literature, we don't encounter the voices of teachers very much at all, so we don't find teachers giving an account of their constraints, or opportunities either. Those that we do hear from are the exceptions who have done something interesting or unusual, despite their conditions. And our professional literature is mostly written by professors, and it addresses teachers as if they had the same comparatively large amount of discretion that professors have. But many teachers are working within substantial institutional constraints and are teaching in settings which are not favorable for innovations (e.g., large classes, students from different proficiency levels put in the same class, under-achieving or under-prepared students, general lack of resources, etc.). They may be struggling to cover the assigned content effectively. Therefore, these teachers may not find their daily tasks innovative and interesting enough to share with others through writing or even talking about them. A middle ground exists though, where teachers, while working within constraints, use any existing opportunities to introduce changes in the teaching-learning process and content.

So, it is clear that language teachers work under different levels of constraints, and that these are insufficiently discussed in our literature. On the one hand, we can note that unprofessional working conditions, commonly found in poorer areas, sometimes result in an absence of supervision, but this in itself will not lead to a critical pedagogy. For an example, see Sayer's (2012) study of English teaching in rural Mexico. "Carlos [the teacher] believes the administration doesn't support the English teachers by providing even minimal materials and equipment to work with. There have been no curriculum development efforts, and each teacher is left to his or her own devices to put together a course" (p. 44). Given the students' and the teacher's poor conditions, the potential for a critical pedagogy is there in the context, but does not develop. Even though this teacher has been provided with "excellent topics for peer-training workshops" (p. 46) done by Carlos's peers in his BA TESOL program, there is little development because of the total absence of resources, and also "corruption, especially in the form of bribing teachers and administrators for grades" (p. 47).

On the other hand, in a recent account of English teaching in provincial China, Hartse and Dong (2015, p. 19) refer to the fact that "English teachers are … required to submit their teaching plans to the department, though sometimes foreign teachers, who more often than not do not confine themselves to using textbooks in the classroom, are exempt from that. In fact, foreign teachers here, as in many Chinese colleges, enjoy more freedom in their pedagogy, which sets many of their Chinese counterparts to envy." Hartse, reflecting back on a typical teaching day, casually says "I teach oral English…. We have a textbook, but I try to vary the activities and bring in current events: something about a Chinese NBA player, a Hong Kong film star scandal, or a current political news story" (p. 34); not critical pedagogy directly, but a degree of autonomy within an otherwise supervised language teaching environment that might allow for the beginnings of one (depending on the teacher).

One example from teachers we have worked with is considered in the following exchange:

Hoda: I was thinking about how we can teach grammar critically while we may not be able to take the materials to the class. Lately, I had interviews with some Iranian teachers and I asked them if they take their own texts or movies to the class and they are told that they are not allowed. This is what I was faced with in some classes I taught. How can we teach grammar from the coursebook critically without any extra materials?

Theresa: Please explain why you are not allowed to bring extra materials to class.

Jing: Great question.

Hoda: Because the institutes believe that the priority is teaching the book.

Theresa: Who will know what happens in the class? Teach it along with the book? You are not going to throw it out all together.

Hoda: Sometimes the supervisors introduce some extra materials which do not let the teacher have enough time to cover anything else. Since the class time is limited and the institutes insist on covering everything in the book, the teacher won't have time to teach anything else. [Even] If we can make the time, we have to show the materials to the supervisor one session beforehand and [only] if it is confirmed, we can teach it.

Jing: Focus on the book, but at the same time when you have time and have the right topic, use CP.

Hoda: Actually I sometimes take some texts without asking for permission, but not all the teachers are eager to do so.

Hoda is brave enough to acknowledge that the severe constraints she is working under do in fact challenge our somewhat optimistic hope for critical language pedagogy. However, at the same time, her supportive interlocutors encourage her to recognize that sometimes she does buck the system, bringing in some supplementary texts or handouts without asking for the permission that she knows she won't get. Here are some other examples of teachers implementing under conditions of variable autonomy and discretion.

In Sadeghi (2008), the teacher-researcher reports on the possibilities of negotiating content in "a free discussion class" at an EFL center in a provincial capital in Iran. "Aware and proud of their traditions, beliefs, [and] priorities" (p. 277), the teacher and the students used a problem-posing approach to select topics related to how social justice is practiced in the context where they lived. Some of these topics were gender discrimination, cultural invasion, and prohibition of indigenous dress, music, and dance, mostly radical and forbidden in the kind of cultural and political context where the study was situated. In addition to the type of content, what further gave the class a critical direction was materials brought to the class by the students, including texts, pictures, and audiotapes, which were used as the basis for discussions. These measures enabled the teacher and the students to engage in critical reflection and discussion about topics derived from their own life experiences.

One more example from the same context is an undergraduate reading course that Arman taught in a state-run university in Tehran (Abednia & Izadinia, 2013; Izadinia & Abednia, 2010). Despite the considerable impacts of international English proficiency tests on the teaching-learning process, the monolithic political discourse dominating the Iranian educational system, and the traditionally teacher-fronted nature of this system, Arman was able to implement several aspects of critical pedagogy in this course. The critical procedures he applied were inviting the students to provide most of the passages themselves, encouraging them to pose critical questions about them, and basing the classroom process mainly on small group and whole class discussions prompted by the students' questions. He also asked the students to write reflective journals following the classroom discussions and entering into written dialogue with them within those journals. Finally, he asked the students to evaluate the teaching-learning process they experienced in a number of self- and class-assessment essays. The authors reported several ways in which the students engaged in critical reflection throughout the course, such as drawing on one's own and others' experiences and defining and redefining key concepts.

In light of these examples of the possibility of implementing critical pedagogy in the classroom, in the next section we further focus on what options we have with content to practice critical pedagogy.

OPTIONS WITH CONTENT AND TOPICS

As both published accounts and informal reports and anecdotes, like those mentioned above, make clear, in some cases teachers *can* shift the content of a class so that it would allow for raising or discussing issues that the class (teacher, students, or as whole) are concerned about or see as problematic, or locally or globally important, and which are of interest to critically-minded individuals. Having an effect on content is one conceptually simple possibility that is often suggested as a way for a teacher to move their practice in a critical direction (Vandrick, 1994). And note immediately, when we mention issues or topics that are problematic—critical pedagogy doesn't require *you*, the teacher, to solve your students' problems! It urges you to reflect them back to the students so they remain in an active position, potentially solving their own problems. This is called "problem-posing." More generally, you could engage your students in the very process of identifying problem-situations.

Commercially-produced textbooks usually contain relatively unchallenging topics, that is to say, topics which are about the happy sides of life, do not prompt thought about important matters of personal or social significance, and do not raise doubts about the way dominant economic and political agendas negatively impact individuals' lives and societies. Some typical examples of these topics are weather, entertainment, food, and hobbies (though actually all of these could be addressed in a less happy or more critical way). It is just that these topics lend themselves more to a safe treatment of life. Authors and publishers are reluctant to incorporate themes which are controversial, revolve around uncomfortable facts, or question current conditions, in the content of textbooks. Consequently, topics like poverty, addiction, prostitution, or capital punishment are rarely found in ELT textbooks, because they are assumed to decrease the likelihood of the books' being accepted or widely used. This avoidance has even been institutionalized—there are guidelines given by publishers, to textbook authors, as to what not to include in the books they are writing. According to Gray, a critically-oriented L2 teaching materials specialist, there is even a mnemonic—an acronym to help materials writers remember this! It's PARSNIP, which stands for Politics, Alcohol, Religion, Sex, Narcotics, Isms, and Pornography (Gray, 2001)—all the things mainstream ELT materials writers are supposed to avoid. Also, mainstream materials may not represent everybody equally well. Women and minorities may be stereotyped. (There have been many studies of this, but it still continues: see, for example, Tajeddin & Enayat, 2010.)

We mentioned a range of "edgy" topics just now. Perhaps we should specify this more formally and indicate how the critical pedagogy specialists summarize or group themes. Freire wrote in terms of major themes characterizing the state of the world.[4] Commonly, *critical* is thought of primarily in terms of class, gender, and race. In the literature of critical applied linguistics, Brazilian ELT specialists Pessoa and Freita (2012) summarize Pennycook (1999) as saying "more recently, these three domains have been broadened to encompass sexuality, ethnicity, and representations of otherness, orientations that seek to explore multiple ways in which power may operate in social life" (p. 759). In the teacher research study of critical language pedagogy Pessoa & Freitas report, their content was organized in terms of five themes: English in the age of globalization, Race and racism in Brazil, Culture and identity, Gender and sexuality, and The power of the body.[5]

The examples of critical topics given so far may suggest that critical content always focuses on ugly realities of life, such as racial discrimination, sexual discrimination, and identity crisis. Although reflection on these topics should include a focus on how they should be dealt with and resolved, this to us is still an inadequate, and perhaps too negative, treatment of what happens in society. Critical pedagogy, as a pedagogy of hope, should also celebrate what we have achieved so far in our pursuit of social justice and democracy. If a lesson is on drug abuse, for example, in addition to a critical examination of its negative impacts on individuals' life and how social factors are partly to blame, there should ideally be a focus on contributions of community centers and other (non)governmental bodies, or any possible actions, towards eradicating this problem.

All these issues mentioned in the above paragraphs show that for many L2 teachers who would like to adopt a critical approach in their teaching, an early step concerns making existing materials work to support this approach. That is, while it is true that critical language pedagogy allows for the possibility of materials being developed by teachers and students, this is perhaps too challenging a first step. Busy teachers are accustomed to relying on existing materials or indeed may not be allowed to dispense with them. Hence a possible first step is for teachers to become familiar with practical possibilities or constraints pertinent to adapting existing materials in terms of content. We'll focus on this first. Then in a subsequent section, we will consider next steps on materials.

STEPS TO TAKE, OR POINTS TO CONSIDER, IN ADAPTING MATERIALS WITH CRITICAL ELT IN MIND

Principles and practices for materials development are to be found in our mainstream professional literature, with an increasingly substantial line of work appearing in the last two decades (e.g., Tomlinson, 1998, 2012), but accounts and advice on textbook adaptation are few.[6] In an earlier review of this area (Crookes, 2013, p. 35), I, Graham, extracted the following six points from suggestions from previous specialists in this area. These are the ones that are particularly consistent with a critical philosophy of teaching.

1. **Who takes the initiative?** Teachers should assist the students in developing an active role in responding to, presenting, or modifying, materials. For example, when working through a textbook exercise with numbered items or questions, ask the class which ones have to be discussed in detail, or treated. If not all chapters of a book have to be covered, have a vote on which should be done, or done first. Thereafter, encourage the students to initiate a vote, propose options, and so on, whenever any opportunity for choice is present. In a grammar class, for example, Arman did the simple thing of bringing in to the class two volumes of a grammar series (at two different proficiency levels) and asking the students to have a look through them, in groups, and deciding which would suit their language level better. On another occasion, in a reading course, he asked the students each to write a list of topics they were most interested in reading texts about. Then he conducted a simple frequency analysis of the topics and collected passages about the most frequently mentioned ones, which then became the classroom content. In a listening-speaking class, his students brought movies to the class and briefly explained what they were about and why they thought they were suitable for the course. The class, guided by Arman, selected some to work on their content and language during the course.

2. **Personalize the materials.** In a grammar exercise, every sentence which both refers to individuals and also needs to be studied and, say, transformed, can have personal names appearing in it changed to those of class members, by the students themselves. Any actions, objects used, topics and so on can be replaced, *at the choice of the students,* by things more personally, locally, or culturally relevant. The point here is that students get used to exercising agency over the materials, instead of the textbook and teacher controlling every aspect of the classroom. Here's an example from Zahra.

[The students] didn't like the topic "sports" since it focused on some athletes' lives if I'm not mistaken.... They said we want to talk about our own problems as Iranian girls. So I asked "why don't we see what problems Iranian female athletes have, especially when they go to Olympic or other international sport events?" So most of the topics they chose through discussing them together, finally turned out to be close to the book's topic but addressed from the students' viewpoint.

3. **Dramatize the materials.** If we say "read with feeling," dry materials can sometimes be energized. Perhaps a tone of voice, an intonation pattern, can be brought to a passage, that questions the content. Once dramatized, a dialogue can be rescripted, with an alternative, perhaps more critical or personally-satisfying ending.[7] This is consistent with the next step.
4. **Encourage alternatives.** That is, seek divergent or generally creative answers to questions, as opposed to requiring only one correct answer or accepting the materials/ textbook's provided "correct" answer.
5. **Interrogate the materials.** That is, allow the class as a whole to discuss why we are using these materials and not others; what they (and you) like and don't like about them; talk back to the materials, write (though not necessarily send) letters to the authors and publishers pointing out the materials' limitations.[8]
6. **Ask critical questions about the way the materials treat a topic.** The teacher might be better able to do this (in English) at first, but we expect students will catch on if this is repeatedly modeled. This is in line with what we referred to above as problem-posing. We can, that is, make the content of the required materials *itself* be the subject of critical investigation and the basis for discussion or dispute.

Depending on the content of the materials, our students can develop and ask numerous critical questions. However, at the early stages of approaching classroom content critically, our students may not have enough confidence and insight to pose critical questions autonomously. Therefore, it may help for us as teachers to provide them with sample questions early on in their experimenting with critical pedagogy. Classic critical questions include "who benefits?", "where did this come from?", and "who or what is missing here?" In this case, we or students could ask questions like "what kind of student do these materials seem to be written for?", and "what kind of people are not visible in these materials?" For a much longer list, see the next chapter.[9]

Insofar as a critical analysis often is prompted by a gradual recognition that matters that seemed neutral actually have a moral or ethical dimension, this too is a stepping stone that should be recognized. One of the resources we have made use of in working with teachers in this area, to promote discussion among our teachers, is Sokol (2004). In it, the author (a medical ethicist) explains how to use ethical issues to foster discussion in the L2 classroom. Sokol is thinking of constructed cases, in which we have to decide whether it is right or wrong. But almost immediately, as we were discussing this, one of our teachers, Shiva, refocused the matter on ethical issues which arise from one's own context, which is indeed what has been a standard position all along in critical pedagogy. She wrote,

> Bringing ethical issues to classrooms could be a very effective way to motivate students to be engaged in classroom discussions and tasks. But the way that a teacher deals with ethical issues is also very important. Teachers can simply ask students' ideas on ethical issues when they are brought up in course books. Asking questions may draw students' attention to ethics, but to raise their consciousness, teachers need to go through the issues more deeply. So, it is better to think about the topics before the class, have a tentative lesson plan in mind, and design some tasks like what was offered in the article. I found the task very interesting. I also think a good way for teachers to find cases of ethics is to search for them in the community they are working in.

In other words, if the teacher is alert, the assigned, mainstream textbooks can be utilized to move towards more critically-oriented lessons.

We have referred to exercises, chapters, and even volumes as things which could be the focus of modifications, but rather briefly. A longer example contributed by one of our teachers, Theresa, who modified a mainstream lesson to make it critical by drawing upon some of the above-mentioned steps is as follows.

This lesson is the modified version of the reading part of a lesson called "Time Management" in *Four Corners 3* (Richards & Bohlke, 2012, p. 60). The part starts with the warm up question "Do you have a busy schedule? What's the busiest day of your week?" followed by the reading passage which provides time management tips, a few comprehension-based questions, and a speaking activity directed by the question "Which tips do you think are very useful? not very useful? Why?"

In the changes she has made to this task, Theresa has aimed to help students "understand that time is a cultural construct, and can be measured differently, and that time management is not required in all societies."

Teacher adds the following questions to the warm-up questions in Section A

- What is time?
- How do you measure time?
- What is time-management?

After doing sections B, C, and D, the teacher does as follows.

1. Conduct a class discussion based on the following questions

- Why would time management be important?

- What would be the consequences if time was not managed properly?
- Who is in power to give us these consequences?

To draw students' attention to the fact that time discipline is prevalent in societies where people have to work to provide commodities and services such as in mainstream countries, and that particular people have the power to enforce time management and discipline others:

2. Ask students to look at the introduction of the text under the title (i.e., "These simple ideas can help you manage your time and work more effectively. Share these tips with your friends, family or co-workers"). Ask students "Who are these instructions for and why are we told to share them? Think. Pair. Share".
3. Write on the board "Time is a social construct: Cultures measure time differently," and explain the difference between linear and cyclical concepts of time. For example, the Western view of time is linear because time passes and you cannot get it back. Indigenous Australians' idea of time is cyclical; it comes back around again. Factors such as location, season, moon-cycles, daylight hours and climate measure Aboriginal time. Also, explain differences between past oriented and future oriented cultures. For example, the United States is future oriented—always looking into the future and cares about what needs to be done, thus this country is seen as fast paced. India might be more past oriented and is more laid back. Conclude that because of different ideas of time, people in different cultures live and think differently, for example, India is not as fast paced as America.
4. Invite students to individually take turns to share with the class their answers for:

- What is your culture and how does your culture measure time?
- Would you need to follow the list of instructions from 'How to manage your time?

5. Team Talk activity: In groups of 4, students sit around in a circle with a stack of cards in the middle facing down. Each card has a question on it such as:

- What does late mean?
- What does early mean?
- What does fashionably late mean?
- How long is a workday?
- What does the metaphor "time is money" mean?
- What does "waste of time" mean?
- How can time be wasted?

Each student in each group takes turns picking out one card, reading the question out to their group and answering the question. Other students in the group can also answer the question and discuss. Then another student picks up another card and repeats the process.

6.   Bring group findings to the class.

As a final thought in this area, we would add that there is one category of textbook in our field that might be particularly easy to adapt, or particularly useful as a basis for moving towards critical discussion of more sensitive or challenging topics. That is the kind of textbook, usually designed as supplementary materials for adults or university students, which is intended to foster discussion. In this kind of book, issues for discussion are typically presented through short texts, usually not authentic but written to a particular level by the materials writer, along with discussion questions. This kind of book falls into the category that some have called "source book" as opposed to course book (Nation & Macalister, 2009b, p. 163). This is a long-standing kind of text; we have copies in our files that go back to the 1970s (Alexander, Vincent, et al., 1978; Alexander, Kingsbury, et al., 1978); a few university texts are in this area (Shulman, 2004), and a recent example is *Impact Topics* (Day et al., 2009).[10]

GOING TEXTBOOK-FREE; STUDENT-PRODUCED CONTENT

The original ideas of critical pedagogy that Freire developed reflect his own specific teaching circumstances and students. He was a teacher of first language literacy to illiterate adults, in conditions of poverty. But his students, who were adults, would have had plenty to say and usually a willingness and capability to talk, so in the classes he discusses (e.g., Freire, 1973) after an initial teacher-fronted presentation, much useful work could be done with topics that were raised by students or jointly negotiated, without any need for pre-written teacher handouts, photocopies, or published material. Thus, in critical pedagogy there is an initial inclination to not base teaching on, nor produce, published textbooks.

In the United States, the first classes that were developed with a critical pedagogy base (cf. Wallerstein, 1983) were adult ESL classes for immigrants, and they probably met a few times a week for a couple of hours in informal circumstances (evening schools and community centers); the teachers probably did have access to copying equipment, and the teachers, though poorly-paid, clearly had preparation time. They did not have set textbooks and did not need to use them. They certainly didn't have exams to prepare the students for and didn't have supervisors breathing down their necks. And in the case of Freire, he had local provincial education

system support for his literacy campaigns (though later, after the government changed, he had the opposite).

Despite the early ideas of critical pedagogy, and the emphasis on each
group of students and course being different, and the effort that must be
made to do something like a critical needs analysis before or during the
negotiation of the syllabus, suggesting today to beginning critical language
pedagogy teachers that they should dispense with the textbook is neither
practical nor encouraging as a first step. Having discussed in this chapter
so far what can be done with existing mainstream textbooks, and also raised
the matter of published material that might be more suitable for critical
language pedagogy, it is only now that we would like to ask, 'What about
content that doesn't depend on a textbook at all?'

For a moment let us return to the early context for the development of
critical language pedagogy, the ESL world of the 1980s. Both then and
now, real-world texts (that is, samples of language in use, not textbooks)
that are relevant and perhaps represent or can be related to problems in
people's lives are a natural part of the critical language pedagogy classroom. The immigrant students Auerbach and Wallerstein worked with,
or even today's urban ESL literacy students, are surrounded by real texts
in English which may have various consequences for them, and which
they need to decode and interpret. In various accounts of critical language pedagogy (e.g., Morgan, 1998), a module or lesson starts with some
problematic or problematized item brought in by students or possibly the
teacher. Also, having students produce classroom content, whether in oral
or written form, has been a standard expectation of the critical pedagogy
tradition since its inception. And in the earliest works bringing critical
pedagogy ideas over into world language teaching (Crawford, 1978, 1981)
that was also an expectation. As we have mentioned before, while teachers
are usually very accustomed to working with a textbook and may find this
principle or advice a bit challenging at first, they appreciate its benefits.
One of our teachers, Mohtaram, said:

> It's so boring for students to read and then talk or discuss about topics they
> aren't keen on. I reckon they can be great facilitators [as] textbook authors.
> Using their ideas, interests and needs for the materials of a textbook has
> a prominent advantage that is their enthusiastic participation in class. I've
> had many sessions when students got really bored with the topic of reading
> or other modules. Very often in [these] situations, students ask teachers to
> skip the task or change it. In my book if teaching materials can be con-
> structed by students' interests, students will get highly motivated.

When Graham and Arman were running a course on critical language
pedagogy with some teachers recently, we used an article that described
how a group of EFL teachers studying for their MA in Hawai'i worked with

immigrant students in an ESL middle school class, to help them develop their own work that then became a booklet of their own writings, and was used as material for the course. Here is part of the report (Chou et al., 2007, p. 19):

> Although near beginners in English obviously could not yet write their own history, they could be helped to produce a fact sheet about themselves and their interests and to personalize it with their own drawings. After collecting a fact sheet from each student, we simply numbered the students' pages, created a cover page, put the students' group picture on the back cover, and photocopied, and stapled. And a booklet was born! Copies were made for all the students and for a few teachers. The following Monday each student was given a copy of the booklet. But what would happen when they went back in the following Monday and gave students the booklets. Co-author Stephanie Yang describes what she observed when the students first received their copies of the booklet:

> Students were slow at first to realize what it was, but when they found their page they were smiling from ear to ear. We asked them to read their pages to each other and to talk about their drawings. They looked proud, and although many were pretending to read, you could see they wanted to read. They asked each other about their drawings, pointing and saying "What's this?" We had a lot of different things we could have done with the booklet, but just not enough time. The students really liked their class picture on the back, which also can be used for more language learning later on. We asked the students to take the booklet home to show their parents...

> Student-produced texts can increase students' motivation in class. Most people are more interested in themselves than in others. And students find it easy to write about themselves because they know the information, so they can focus on using the target language.

> [B]y producing their own reading material, students learn to take control of their own learning. Further, they realize they can use the English language to construct their identity in social situations.

> [S]tudent-produced material greatly increases student-teacher and student-student interaction. Students are highly motivated to learn about their classmates, and reading about them is a good way to learn. When students know each other, group dynamics improve, and students interact with each other more both in and out of the classroom.

While this is an effective way of providing space for students to contribute to classroom materials, a challenge would be the language accuracy of student-produced content. In this regard, Theresa made the following remark in response to Chou, et al.'s experience:

After reading this article, I realise that I have been doing this all along. I often use students' texts to share them with others and get students to make up questions for other students to answer. However, this requires students to be quite capable in producing these texts. It may also be too transparent for some students as they cannot hide and everyone will know their ability levels as their work is published. My question is, is it okay for us as teachers to correct texts first before they are published or should it be very authentic?

One way in which this challenge can be addressed is the teacher's refinement of the content before incorporating it into the classroom materials. Jing answered the question as follows:

I guess it depends on your teaching purpose. If you want to teach your students grammar, sentence structures, or writing rituals etc., you can show the original text to them. However, I think it's better if you can ask for the student author's permission to do so and explain to him you purpose of showing his text to the class, which is not to insult him, but to provide a model for other students. If your teaching purpose is for other use, maybe you can show it after you have corrected.

Another issue in connection with having students produce materials is time. On the positive side, student-produced content may be a time-saving measure, as experienced by the teachers whose work is summarized in Chou et al. (2007):

using students' work cuts down on the time a teacher must spend finding and creating teaching materials, and student work may be more desirable than a commercial textbook because it better approximates what the students can actually do. (p. 19)

However, depending on the context where students are asked to produce content, this may entail added workload on the part of the teacher. Reflecting on the above excerpt, Zahra says:

As one of the advantages, the authors say "using students' work cuts down on the time a teacher must spend finding and creating teaching materials" (p. 19). This indicates that in the context of this study teachers are supposed to (or free to) create their own materials while in many contexts following a lesson plan and covering the commercial textbooks is central to institutes' objectives. In these contexts things won't be easier; rather it takes a lot of teachers' efforts and courage to involve themselves let alone their students.

IN CONCLUSION

Content and materials are always important and of concern to teachers. Critically-oriented materials, or authentic samples of language that stimulate discussion and inquiry, are one major way to get started in critical language pedagogy. These materials are a step towards a focus on the actual concerns and problems that students themselves face. Ideally it is the students who select, explore, inquire into and problem-solve, but we believe that for teachers starting to explore critical language pedagogy, stepping off from the more conventional understanding of materials may be effective. It is a matter of also seeing the limitations of such materials, and adapting them, going beyond them, and perhaps eventually discarding them when circumstances allow.

NOTES

1. For example, Teacher: "Jack and Jill go to the store, did you say? How many people went to the store?" (The teacher is helping a student to correct grammar by emphasizing key content.)
2. But see Crookes and Arakaki (1999).
3. Ayers et al. (2010, p. 72) provide a simple example of a teacher resisting a scripted curriculum.
4. "I consider the fundamental theme of our epoch to be that of domination—which implies its opposite, the theme of liberation, as the objective to be achieved" (Freire, 1972/2000, p. 103).
5. However, the selection of these themes was not negotiated with the students.
6. Though see Nation and Macalister (2009b); Bosompen (2014).
7. This is an idea developed extensively by the critical theater of Augusto Boal (Boal, 1992).
8. Edelsky and Johnson (2004) explain how Johnson's class resisted a mandated textbook; see also Gorlewski et al. (2012).
9. And for critical questions language teachers might ask themselves, see Bartlett (1990).
10. See also: http://iteslj.org/questions/
    http://www.eslconversationquestions.com/english-conversation-questions/topics/
    http://www.esldiscussions.com/

CHAPTER 4

READING THE WORD—
READING THE WORLD

INTRODUCTION

A way to understand reading as including both a focus on individual features and forms and also a critical dimension comes from the work of Luke and Freebody (Freebody & Luke, 1990; Luke & Freebody, 1999). These authors point out that depending on how we choose to read a text, we may engage in as many as four "families of practice." First, we break the code of texts by identifying their fundamental features, such as letters, sounds, sentence structure, and text structure. Second, we participate in understanding the meanings of texts by exploring how they relate to our knowledge and experiences. Third, we reflect on the specific social purposes of texts by asking "what is this text for, here and now?" Fourth, we critically examine texts by analyzing the assumptions underlying them, which are often unstated, and the viewpoints they support, disapprove, or exclude.

Critical reading, which is most evident in the last category, in fact involves all four sets of practices. It is not possible to examine a text critically without recognizing and correctly decoding, or making sense of, its fundamental features, understanding its meanings, and identifying the social purposes

---

Starting Points in Critical Language Pedagogy, pp. 53–89
Copyright © 2022 by Information Age Publishing

behind its creation. In mainstream approaches to teaching reading comprehension, however, there is an exclusive, or major, focus on the first two families of practices, namely breaking the code and understanding meanings. As we've discussed, language learners are rarely encouraged to reflect on the social purposes of a text. To an even lesser degree are they asked to examine what views are favored, challenged, or silenced in the text. In this chapter, while we use any opportunities to highlight the importance of code breaking and basic comprehension as prerequisites for critical reading, our main focus is on the practices which are most closely related to critical analysis of texts.

Before we start to discuss critical reading in depth, a short reflection on how Freire defines reading will be helpful. But first, note that we have emphasized in earlier chapters that these days, language is increasingly viewed as a sociocultural process, that is, a way of developing, shaping, or manifesting an identity that is located in society, since language is not merely a set of structures to be learned. In this regard, Freire presents us with the thought-provoking phrase "reading the word, reading the world." He believes, "it is impossible to read text without reading the contexts of the text, without establishing the relationships between the discourse and the reality which shapes the discourse" (Freire, 1985, pp. 18–19). Freire explains that in the process of reading, we actively use our current understanding of the world to engage with the text. Also, reading the text results in a refined understanding of the world. In other words, "every act of reading words implies a previous reading of the world and a subsequent rereading of the world" (Freire, 1985, p. 18). Therefore, Freire (1985) concludes, reading is an essentially critical process. Keeping this perspective in mind, in the following two sections, we first focus on the principles of critical reading and explain its aims. Then, we describe ways in which we can practice critical reading in a language classroom, starting from the more conventional emphasis on reading to get basic meaning from a text and, with that established, moving on to critical understanding.

PRINCIPLES OF CRITICAL READING

Wallace (2003) discusses a few key principles for teaching critical reading. First, a critical reading classroom or activity focuses more on how the group of learners, rather than individual students, interpret and respond to a text through talk around text. Therefore, a major aspect of the process of critical reading in the classroom is students discussing the text together and sharing their understandings as a group. Second, while it is important to understand what an author tries to communicate through their writing, in critical reading we are more concerned with the possible interpretations of the text and their effects. This does not mean that all interpretations are equally valid. Rather, classroom discussion helps learners identify interpretations which are more credible, and perhaps sophisticated, than others. Third, critical reading is not just about analyzing the logic and arguments in texts. This is usually referred to as critical thinking. Going beyond this, critical reading involves critiquing ideological assumptions which underlie a text and social motivations behind its production. To Wallace, the most important principle of critical reading is that readers remain critical of their own stance to the text and explore the likely reasons behind it. They keep asking themselves "how do our worldviews and previous learnings make us read a text in certain ways?"

Wallace also reminds us that when engaging with authentic, non-pedagogical texts, which are most suitable for a critical classroom, L2 learners have an advantage over native speakers. Wallace explains, "because they are not the primary addressees of texts written for an indigenous readership, second and foreign language learners may be more aware of the way in which texts position readers" and, thus, "are arguably in a stronger position both to perceive and to resist" them (Wallace, 2003, p. 42). This is good news for us as teachers since we are often concerned about the limitations that being non-native puts on our students' ability and, if we ourselves are non-native, our own ability to critique an L2 text.

AIMS OF CRITICAL READING

In addition to understanding the principles of critical reading, we should think about why reading should be critical. This is important since, as teachers, we are expected to know why we teach the way we do, especially when those ways of teaching are less common. Most of the teachers we have worked with have been asked the question "why critical reading?" by their students, colleagues, and managers. If you have taught reading critically, you might be nodding in agreement now! A simple reason why this question is asked is that many teachers tend to have a language-bound view of reading and think of reading as comprehension only and, if anything else, perhaps a little bit of interpretation still within the boundaries of the text. It is easy to trace the origins of this attitude in international tests like IELTS and TOEFL, with Pearson Test of English having recently joined in. Given the undeniably strong share of these tests in reinforcing a comprehension-oriented view of reading, teachers with critical aspirations should be well aware of the aims of critical reading and able to give an adequate answer to "why critical reading?" if asked by others.

Wallace (2003) tells us about three main purposes that teaching critical reading serves, namely linguistic, cultural, and conceptual/critical. First, in a critical classroom we help learners use their linguistic knowledge to think about the effect of language choices made in a passage and understand the ideological meanings embedded within it. For example, we could encourage our students to use their knowledge of the passive voice to reflect on the likely intention of an author to conceal the agent of an action. An advantage that L2 learners have over native speakers who may receive limited grammar instruction at school is that they tend to have a well-developed knowledge of English grammar which they can use as a tool for textual analysis. Second, we should help students explore and understand cultural assumptions and practices underlying texts and identify similarities and differences between texts from different cultural perspectives. Finally, we should help learners develop their critical abilities through enabling them to go beyond the text and understanding events, reflect on and challenge the implications of those events, and make links to their own lives. To help learners develop these abilities, Wallace believes, we should allow them "to change perspective—to shift, that is, from being a cooperative convergent reader of a text to using a text for critique" (Wallace, 2003, p. 45). Using Giroux's (1983) ideas, she goes on to define critique as a form of resistance rather than opposition. While opposition could be "seen as an instinctive, unreflected-upon response to domination," resistance is "a considered, reflected upon, rational stance" (p. 45) which is less affected by ideological pre-judgements.

To achieve these purposes, simple comprehension exercises are far from enough. In fact, these are an essential starting point for a critical reading lesson. But for a reading lesson to be critical, it should involve other types of reading practice. So, now let's look at the ways in which we could engage students in critical reading.

ASPECTS OF CRITICAL READING PRACTICE

In this section, we focus on different aspects of critical reading practice in the L2 classroom, namely helping learners develop the required language and background knowledge to treat passages in depth, selecting materials, and fostering learners' critical engagement with reading passages.

Fostering Students' Comprehension of the Passage

As mentioned at the beginning of the chapter, adequate comprehension of text is a prerequisite for critical reading practice. We should somehow or other make sure our students have a sufficient understanding of the content we want them to approach critically. This is an important preliminary step as our experience shows that the less linguistically prepared and the less familiar with a reading topic, the more difficult learners generally find it to treat a passage in a questioning manner. Comprehension work could range from a focus on the key vocabulary in a text and understanding the key ideas and important details to more sophisticated text analysis, like a focus on comprehending basic events that make up a narrative reading passage. Depending on the topic, we may also need to think of steps to improve our students' background knowledge. If, for example, a classroom text discusses a phenomenon students had not heard about previously, we may need to present them with introductory content about the topic, be it in the form of an extra passage, a video, or an infographic, or encourage students to research the topic. We now share with you two examples which illustrate how teachers have provided their students with the necessary background.

In a university EFL reading classroom in South Korea, Park (2011) included an interesting procedure which engaged students themselves in facilitating the pre-reading stage. In groups of three or four, students chose a classroom reading and, acting as the presenters of the text, they prepared handouts with Park's help that included key terms and discussion questions. Park explains how this procedure was followed with an article on "cosmetic neurology," a trend where students, academics, or business people take drugs (originally intended to treat neurologic diseases) to enhance their brains' function. Park reports:

> The presenters first introduced the class to key terms encountered in the article that they thought would be difficult. The 2-page pre-reading handout contained names of the pills that appeared throughout the article (e.g., Adderall, Provigil) and colloquial and idiomatic expressions (e.g., purple haze, trade-off, levellers).

> Students discussed the meaning of words in the handout in groups of two or three, after which the presenters explained the meaning of each word.... The presenters explained that these pills help people focus on their work and that in South Korea there is a medicine called *chonmyungtang* that serves similar functions.... When presenters encountered trouble in answering or gave an incorrect definition, the teacher stepped in to clarify and help. (p. 33)

This is a good example of how we can foster learners' understanding of a passage and in this way prepare them to engage with it critically. What makes Park's procedure particularly interesting is that she involved students themselves in helping each other understand the article. Giving them a space to have ownership of the learning process helped align the class with critical pedagogy principles.

Another example we would like to share with you comes from Hammond and Macken-Horarik (1999). The authors studied a teacher's classroom practice in a science and literacy program for ESL students in Australia. In a unit of work on human reproduction and egg development in the female, before asking students to engage with texts critically, the teacher included a focus on the genre of explanation, which is an important genre in the study of science. (A simple and broad definition of genre is text type.) Hammond and Macken-Horarik report the teacher's practice as follows:

> The students' earlier efforts in explaining how the sex of a child is de-termined had provided the teacher with information about their starting point in regard to the genre. Because the students had undertaken little prior work on the study of genre, Margaret [the teacher] introduced the class first to key written genres typically encountered in the study of sci-ence. These included explanations, reports, procedures, expositions, and discussions (see Halliday & Martin, 1993). The teacher and students dis-cussed the relationship between genre and social function, and the students worked in groups to analyse the social functions of various genres as well as similarities and differences in their language patterns. The class's focus then narrowed to a more detailed comparison of explanations and reports. All the students participated actively in discussions of differences between these two genres.
>
> Following this, the teacher provided a model explanation. She spent time discussing rhetorical stages of the genre and directed the students' atten-tion to some of the important language patterns, such as the technical verbs that are central to an explanation of the IVF [in vitro fertilization] procedure. She provided a very clear and explicit written framework for the students to follow in their initial work on explanations, which they drafted first in small groups and then independently.

This account clearly shows the serious amount of work the teacher did with the students to help them develop an understanding of explana-tory scientific texts, and other genres in science, as well as the technical vocabulary related to the lesson topic, that is IVF. The students used this knowledge to comprehend the texts they worked on in the classroom and produce their own explanations. Equipped with this linguistic understand-ing which also helped them gain knowledge about scientific topics like IVF, the students were better placed to critically engage with classroom readings and discussions. As with the first example, again, students were directly involved in developing knowledge that is to a large extent a prerequisite for critical reading. Here however the backgrounding goes beyond the still important matter of vocabulary and passage-specific background knowl-edge, and on into the genre of the passage itself.

Equipping Learners With Critical Reading Tools

To prepare learners for critical analysis of texts, it is extremely beneficial to familiarize them with tools of critical reading. We all know that it is not enough to simply ask our students to read a passage critically and let them figure out how to do so by themselves. Many learners approach texts uncritically, and for many, critical reading mostly means opposition (see Aims of Critical Reading section). Therefore, it is best not to assume that our students know how to read critically; instead, we should familiarize them with ways of text analysis. There are numerous reports on how teachers around the world have done so.

At an initial level, in an ESL reading class in Singapore, Macknish (2011), for example, familiarized her students with the terms *nominalization* (forming a noun from a verb for rhetorical effect), *modality*, and *passivization*, as indicating processes that writers use, at a grammatical or structural level, to disclose or hide the actors in sentences or sections of discourse. Going beyond this, a teacher, reported by Alford and Kettle (2017), taught broader, more discoursal or agentive critical reading terms to her ESL students at a high school in Australia. One term she taught was "invited readings"; another was "resistant readings." The point is, if students actually have labels for concepts that have critical analytic force, they will be able to deploy them as tools and thus be better able to analyze or unpack texts. The power of these two terms also depends on a specialized understanding of the phrase "a reading." This can mean something like "an interpretation." And then one can have an interpretation, a reading of a text, that is resistant. Alford and Kettle show us how the teacher taught this fundamental concept, gradually bringing her students to an understanding of this important point, eventually enabling the students to develop a critical meaning of the word "reading" itself. The following conversation extract reflects this observation:

Riva, Lesson 1: What did you think about the Chinese (program called) "China? Pandas' Future?" [Pause]. Was it a positive story?

Nancy: Not really.

Riva: So they are showing that the Chinese people are helping the pandas and it's improving and succeeding. Scientists? Government? Scientists?

Male 5: Scientists.

Riva: Scientists. So it's a very positive picture of the Chinese scientists, successful? Helping? Nancy says not really?

Nancy: Yeah. In that way it is—I don't know really.

Riva: Not really, because? [Riva pauses and waits for a contribution].

Nancy: Because they need—they can't breed and they can't [inaudible].

Ben: Because it is artificial.

Nancy: Yeah, it's artificial.

Riva: Because they can't breed, because the problem is?

Female: Because they won't sort the problem. They are just trying to have...

Riva: Okay, very interesting.

Crystal: Because they can't do it forever. Why would they help them if they try to make a solution [inaudible], you have to make a solution that can help them.

Riva: Very good. What I'm asking you to do is to make meaning from this text and you are making meanings almost in two lines. You are making the meaning that the Chinese Government, the Chinese scientists anyway, are doing a very good job of helping pandas through a very difficult situation and you are also making the meaning that it's artificial, that it's not sustainable. So we can see the same text in different ways, can't we? ... But is any one of those meanings less valid than the other or more valid than the other? Is Ben's meaning more valid than Crystal and Nancy's? [Students shake heads]....They're all valid, aren't they? So why do you make those different readings?

Peter: Because different people have different points of view.

Riva: Exactly. The term we use when we are doing critical analysis is "readings." We say that that meaning that you have made of the text is a reading and it's a noun, -ing, gerund. So it's a reading. It can be plural, readings. It is not the verb reading that you get in the dictionary. It is not reading a book. It's making meaning from a text. The critical meaning of the term "reading" is to make meaning from the text and you can make different meanings. We have names for those different readings (pp. 197–198).

In a higher language level class with a group of international EAP students at a university in Canada, Morgan (2009) introduced video and reading resources on critical literacy—critical reading tools—for the students to get help from in their assignment, which was a critical research essay on media coverage of a current event or social issue. Some of these resources are, effectively, worked examples which show students how skilled critical analysts present examples of how mass media, videos, advertisements, etc., may manipulate the reader. The other resources discuss tools of critical media analysis using familiar and technical concepts. These resources and Morgan's brief descriptions of each are as follows.

Videos

1. *Manufacturing Consent: Noam Chomsky and the Media* (Achbar & Wintonick, 1992). I use a short section describing Chomsky's "propaganda model" of mass media as a way of introducing the course's underlying rationale.
2. *Still Killing Us Softly* (Kilbourne, 1987), or *Killing Us Softly 3* (Jhaly, 2002). These videos analyze depictions of women in advertising and link these images to particular social consequences (e.g., eating disorders, violence against women and trivialization of women's participation in society).
3. *Pack of Lies: The Advertising oOf Tobacco* (Kilbourne & Pollay 1992). This video provides analysis of cigarette ads that target adolescents. It is also strong in its analysis of how particular images act on identity formation, invoking desires for status and peer acceptance and linking these desires to "cool" self-images attained through smoking.

Articles

1. "Selection, Slanting, and Charged Language" (Birk & Birk 1995). This article provides examples (i.e., for first year EAP students) of how word order, choice of connectives and vocabulary can slant for or against our perceptions of an event or person.
2. (2) "With These Words I Can Sell You Anything" (Lutz, 1995). This article is always popular, and Lutz's categories of "weasel words" hollow, meaningless words that appear substantive but promise nothing (e.g., the qualifier help in phrases such as "helps reduce aging," "helps control dandruff") are frequently employed in assignments.
3. "Methods of Misrepresentation" (Parenti, 1986). Parenti's chapter is quite accessible and effective for critical readings of mass media. Analytical concepts such as "framing," "greying of reality" (i.e., the appearance that both sides of a conflict are equally responsible) and 'unbalanced treatment' provide strong links between specific text-internal features (e.g., newspaper headlines, photographs, article placements, vocabulary choices) and their intended functions in respect to power relations in liberal, democratic societies, which makes this article a valuable complement to the video excerpt on Chomsky's propaganda model.
4. "A Critical Approach to the Teaching of Language" (Janks, 1991). Janks' article draws from a Hallidayan, systemic-functional approach to critical discourse analysis (CDA). Some students find the article too formal and abstract. Others find it a revelation of sorts, in that seemingly familiar grammatical categories (e.g., passive voice, nominalizations, article system) are reconceptualized in an ideological framework described in terms of how specific lexico-grammatical choices position readers and frame the reception of content (pp. 314–315).

Reporting on one student's essay, Morgan shows how being exposed to these resources helped the student take up issues marginalized in mainstream media sources and use analytical concepts from the above resources in his analysis. For example, in his essay he used Parenti (1986) to explore the impact of headlines on how a story may initially be received.

What these teachers have in common is a solid understanding of what critical reading involves. What this suggests is that for us to effectively prepare our students to treat a passage critically, we ourselves should be reasonably familiar with text analysis tools. CDA is an approach to the study of language that provides a wide collection of such tools. So it deserves a brief focus here.

The word "discourse" has been defined in several ways, but what all definitions have in common is a view of language that considers it in its social context and focuses on its connections with power and ideology. Van Dijk (1995), who is one of the pioneers in the field of CDA, believes that CDA is a general label for ways of investigating text and talk in a critical and sociopolitical way. To him, CDA focuses on the relations between language and society and pays attention to several aspects of discourse, such as syntax, semantics, phonology, and communication styles, as well as its nonverbal dimensions like pictures and gestures. CDA encourages an analysis of ideologies underlying discourse.

You might be thinking "this is a bit too abstract!" We agree and therefore move towards a more practical treatment of CDA now.

There are numerous resources on CDA which introduce ways in which this toolkit can be used to analyze text. A few which are practitioner-friendly are *How to do Critical Discourse Analysis: A Multimodal Introduction* by Machin and Mayr (2012) and *Analysing Discourse: Textual Analysis for Social Research* by Fairclough (2003).

Some of us may find short readings and guides on the Internet more immediately useful. An example is a short introduction to CDA on a page called "All About Linguistics," in the website of The University of Sheffield which was produced by linguistics students.[1] This link includes a few paragraphs introducing CDA and a short video where Sam Kirkham, a Lecturer in Linguistics at The University of Sheffield, briefly talks about CDA.[2] The link also briefly explains some of the linguistic devices that are commonly studied in CDA and gives helpful examples. We reproduce this section below as it gives us an idea about the things we could focus on in the classroom if we wish to use CDA to facilitate text analysis.

Active or Passive Voice

The use of an active verb gives a clear picture of who performed a particular action, and to whom, for example: "Police attack protestors."

The use of a passive verb states what has been done, and to whom, but does not blame anyone in particular for the action, for example: "Protestors attacked."

Alternatively, nominalization can be used, where the noun form of the verb is used to create even more ambiguity, for example: "Attack on protestors."

Naming

The ways in which people are named can also perpetuate ideologies. For example, the newspaper headline "five Asian youths involved in armed robbery" creates a very different picture than "five young men involved in armed robbery."

Similarly, the way people are described in texts, or after giving quotes can present two different pictures, for example: "Dr Sarah Jones" creates a different picture than "Single mother of two, Sarah Jones."

Pre-modifiers

Pre-modified nouns can present varying views of a topic. For example, "gay marriage" or "same-sex marriage" implies that this is essentially different from heterosexual marriage.

Indirect Quotes

This is particularly common, when the results of a poll are being used, for example "poll shows 70% oppose gay marriage," however there may be no evidence of reported speech saying this.

There are also videos on YouTube which introduce CDA and give examples of critical analysis of text. One which we find to be a useful introduction is called "Fairclough Critical Discourse Analysis." As its name suggests, this video briefly explains a model of CDA proposed by Fairclough.[3] Another video which we recommend is one produced by Dr Florian Schneider, a lecturer of politics at Leiden University, called "Introduction to Discourse Analysis." In this engaging video, Schneider talks about the place of discourse analysis in studying political communication.[4]

These resources can give us a working knowledge of CDA, enabling us to familiarize our students with tools of critical analysis of text. Depending on the age and language level of learners, we may decide to present them with the technical term "CDA," its meaning and principles, and examples of linguistic and non-linguistic devices on which CDA focuses. Alternatively, we may decide that a technical discussion of CDA should be postponed until students have been presented with a few examples of how to critically engage with reading passages and have been given the opportunity to experiment with this approach to reading.

We believe, unless the age and language level do not really allow, it is important to equip students with the kind of language they can use to talk about the linguistic aspects of texts, often called "metalanguage." This is what the teacher reported by Alford and Kettle (2017) did when she familiarized her students with a specialized meaning of the phrase "a reading" and built on that to then present them with other phrases like "invited readings" and "resistant readings." Examples of other words that we could teach to our students to use in critical discussion of texts range from simple and familiar terms like "connotations," that is ideas or feelings suggested by a word, to less familiar and more complex terms like "hedging," which means using linguistic devices to show uncertainty or hesitation, and "over-lexicalization," using many words or phrases for more persuasive power. An effective way to teach the metalanguage of critical reading, or CDA for that matter, is to introduce the terms as the need arises during the process of critically engaging with passages. Presenting students with a short list of such terms, ideally together with simple definitions and examples, could certainly be useful especially after a few sessions of students experimenting with critical reading. As we do not hesitate to give our students grammar terms like *noun*, *clause*, and *sentence* as well as their definitions, to help them learn English more effectively, the same logic, we believe, applies to CDA terms. Finally, if we teach students sharing the same first language (typical of an EFL context), another possibility is to give them a glossary of terms and their definitions in their first language.

"Neutral" Passages on "Safe" Topics

Teachers who have taught reading in a critical way would agree that some passages lend themselves to critical analysis more readily than others. For example, they may deal with a contentious political or cultural topic and present strong views which could be critically examined and perhaps disagreed with, leading to heated classroom discussions and lessons in which students and teacher have plenty of opportunity to engage in critical thinking. Give your class a biased text on gender equality, and before you know it, and without you having to prompt your students, they are deeply engaged in a never-ending vigorous debate, with you concerned about how to bring some order to the class! However, in many textbooks there are passages which focus on so-called neutral topics like tourist destinations, recipes, and cutting-edge technology, are mostly factual, and if they present any opinions, those opinions are usually positive, conveying the over-optimistic idea that "the world is such a nice place and we are all having so much fun in it." Especially early in our trials with critical language pedagogy, some of us may find these passages unsuitable for critical practice. Jing expressed a similar view:

> Most of the texts chosen in our English syllabus cover neutral topics, such as the introduction to a trip to Australia in order to teach students how to describe their experiences, etc.

In response, Arman suggested an alternative understanding though:

> You have made a good point about how the content dictated by the curriculum sometimes limits the space for critical work. Yet, I think, there is space within this very content for us and our students to critically engage with the topics. Building on your example of a trip to Australia, I'd like to argue that, although the content and the tasks designed based on it may not have a critical element, we can incorporate such an element into this apparently mainstream lesson. For instance, we can draw students' attention to issues around how much really people from different socioeconomic classes can afford to take an international (or even local) trip, and engage them in a discussion around whether the passage has focused on this issue and if not why. So, perhaps no topics or texts are neutral in a strict sense of the word. All texts are about topics which are situated within a sociocultural and political context and look at them from a certain perspective. So every topic and passage can be approached critically.

Later in this chapter, we give an example of how another teacher in one of our online courses refined a mainstream reading lesson and gave it critical dimensions. Here is a great place though for us to highlight the usefulness of resistant reading, mentioned earlier in passing, as an approach to adopt towards so-called "neutral" passages on "safe" topics. In the Fostering Students' Comprehension of the Passage section, we emphasized that it is necessary to help our students develop an adequate basic understanding of a passage before asking them to critically engage with it. What that means is for them to comprehend the dominant reading of the passage, that is, the one which is the most common and accepted interpretation of it, the interpretation that the author had in mind when writing it, or simply the author's main idea(s). Reading a text on tourist destinations, for example, we may realize that the dominant reading involves comprehending where each of the described destinations is and why we should visit it. All teachers help their students understand these details and answer comprehension questions. This is where second language teachers who are inspired by critical pedagogy but have had limited prior engagement with it would be wondering, "How do I teach this lesson critically?"

Resistant reading is a good answer. Reading between the lines, we may realize that the dominant reading of this text involves an important key assumption—that those who read the text, that is anyone, can in fact afford to visit the described places and therefore their only concern as a reader is which to visit and what to expect when they go there. Questioning this assumption is a great point of departure for resistant reading following comprehension work. To guide the resistant reading process, we could start with a simple question like "Can everyone afford to visit these places?" and continue with questions like "Who can?" and "Who can't?" Depending on learners' language level, we may choose to present them with more sophisticated versions of these two questions: "Who are the assumed target readers of this passage?" and "Who have been excluded?" Going beyond initial reflections triggered by these questions, we may then ask, "Why do you think the author has assumed that we, its readers, are all rich enough to visit those places?", "Why do you think it has ignored those who cannot afford such trips?", and "What would a more inclusive passage on the same topic read like?" These are only a few out of numerous possible questions that we may ask to prompt our students' resistant reading of the passage and critical reflection about the dominant view underlying it. An alternative way to encourage resistant reading is to invite students themselves to question this and other similar passages as resistant readers.

Comparative Reading of Passages

There are passages which treat the same topic in different ways. For example, they may promote different or opposing perspectives on social issues like abortion, same-sex marriage, animal testing, or the death penalty. Or, they may present different accounts or analyses of the same event like a music festival, a sports competition, an election, a demonstration, a revolution, or a war. Comparative analysis of these passages in the classroom can effectively engage students in critical reading as students may have different understandings of how credible the presented perspectives or analyses are. Also, a guided comparison of passages may help them identify biases, poor reasoning, or even inaccurate information in one text compared to another text.

An excellent example of how a comparative analysis of passages fosters critical reflection in the language classroom comes from Benesch (2006). In a first-year reading class mainly consisting of immigrants in a U.S. college, Benesch asked her students to read two articles which reported on a demonstration in New York against going to war in Iraq. These articles had been published in *The New York Times* four days apart. Benesch asked the students to list similarities and differences between the two articles. The similarities that the students identified were that both were published in *New York Times*, were about anti-war demonstrations, and were written by women. A key difference was that the first published article reported a protest involving a small number of demonstrators leaving the organizers disappointed, while the second one reported a demonstration by a considerably larger number of people which had surprised the organizers. Encouraged by Benesch to reflect on how demonstrators were characterized in the articles, the students found another difference to be the images evoked, namely "noisy" and "crazy" in the article reporting a small number and 'organized' and 'serious' in the other.

The similarities and differences led to a discussion about whether the two articles are about the same demonstration. Concluding that the two accounts reported one event, the students explored their relationship by asking questions like "Why did they change the story?", "Is the *New York Times* for the war?", and "Why did they write the second article?" (Benesch, 2006, p. 57). Here is Benesch's (2006) account of how she responded to the last question:

> I explained to students that Fairness and Accuracy in Reporting (FAIR), a
> media watchdog, issued an "action alert" immediately after the first article
> appeared, urging members to contact the NYT and 'ask them why they did
> not provide more substantive reports about the anti-war demonstration
> in Washington DC on October 26' (www.fair.org/activism/npr-nyt-protests.
> html). This alert was reproduced extensively through emails. I received it
> not only from FAIR, of which I'm a member, but from various other FAIR
> members who reproduced the alert and sent it to everyone in their address
> book. It is likely that the outpouring of protest resulted in the second
> article being published ... though no mention was made of the first report
> when the second one appeared, four days later. (p. 57)

What this account clearly reflects is the great benefits of Benesch's knowledge of common practices in the media that enables her to provide students with an adequate and informed response to their questions and enrich the collective reflection and discussion that the students engage in.

Another type of reading task involving comparative analysis that Benesch reported giving to her students was reading a news or opinion piece and the follow-up letters to the editor that approve of or disagree with the ideas or perspectives expressed in the original article. The classroom process she reported is as follows.

> I distribute an opinion piece, explaining that it expresses the writer's views
> on an issue rather than reporting facts or events. For homework, students
> write a response paper about the reading. This includes summarizing the
> reading, writing questions about it, choosing one quote to respond to (ex-
> plaining why it seems interesting or important), and defining the unfamil-
> iar words. During the following class, after a discussion of their questions,

> I ask students if they have ever read a newspaper article or watched a news report with which they disagreed.

> I ask whether [they] would ever consider calling or emailing the news show to [express their disagreements or concerns] ... I then tell students that I often send emails or make calls about inaccurate or biased coverage as part of my desire to be an active reader or participant in society.

> Next, I distribute the letters to the editor pertaining to the opinion piece read for homework. I ask students to meet in groups, assigning one letter to each group. The members are to ascertain whether the letter supports or contests the viewpoint expressed in the opinion piece and to explain what evidence is offered to bolster the letter writer's opinion. Each group then writes a list of pro, con, or both statements on the board and explains the particular arguments used to support the view expressed. The ensuing discussion focuses on the differences and similarities in the letter writers' opinions, including some that seem to both agree and disagree. (p. 59)

Regarding the importance of this type of critical reading exercise, Benesch (2006) explains that letters serve as examples of how readers can take responsibility for their reading, become active participants in the process of talking back and writing back to publications, and this way change a traditionally receptive reading experience to a space for engaging in dialogue with writers. Obviously this sort of response has become increasingly common and easy to do in digital media. We think it would be worth encouraging students to try their hand at it in digital spaces that are relatively safe and not likely to be immediately responded to by hostile posts (from "trolls").

Another example comes from a middle school in Israel, where Hayik (2015) engaged her female students in a comparative analysis of how women are represented in fairy tales. Hayik presented her students with the Disneyfied version of the traditional Cinderella fairy tale *A Dream for a Princess* (Lagonegro, 2005) and two empowering depictions of women, namely *Cinder Edna* (Jackson, 1994) and *Piggybook* (Browne, 1987). While Cindrella is portrayed as passively waiting for help, Cinder Edna, Cinderella's neighbor, takes steps to actively deal with difficulties she is faced with, and the wife and mother in *Piggybook* stops enduring the heavy burden of doing all household chores and this way resists gender inequality in a family.

Hayik (2015) started the course with a focus on *A Dream for a Princess* and asking the students to write their own fairy tales. Then, they worked on the empowering fairy tales *Cinder Edna* and *Piggybook*. Hayik asked her students to write down their thoughts in response to the stories. Some of the notes in response to Cinder Edna were "strong personality," "independent," and "we should work hard to get what we want." The students also listed Cinder

Edna's and Cinderella's characteristics and identified their similarities and differences which were then put in a compare and contrast table. Following this activity, the students discussed Jackson's possible reasons behind writing *Cinder Edna* and views that underlay this empowering version of Cinderella. Then, Hayik asked them to rewrite the fairy tales they wrote at the beginning of the course. Her account of revisions made by one of the students is worth reading.

> In their traditional fairy tale, [the student] portrayed an ugly girl, Lori, who wished to become pretty. A falling star helped her wish come true and she magically turned into a beautiful girl ... the girls' fairy tale underscored external beauty and ended unrealistically. The quest for ultimate beauty intermingled with magic toward an inevitable happy ending.
>
> In the revised version, [the student] emphasized internal beauty. Through helping a boy find his lost cat and befriending him, Lori started viewing herself as a beautiful, kind girl whom others (the boy) can befriend and praise. The new story still depended on others' approval and ended happily, but nonetheless through a realistic solution. Good deeds uncovered Lori's inner beauty and resulted in changing her self-image and reality. Although Lori's unattractive external appearance remained unchanged, her way of viewing reality did change

This description clearly shows how a comparative analysis of texts can help learners improve their ways of thinking about a given topic and rethink and refine their understandings, especially when a critical reading practice is followed by a writing activity which provides an additional chance for learners to develop and articulate their own thoughts and be exposed to their peers' understandings.

Reading Passages Involving Multiple Perspectives

In the previous section, we discussed the benefits of comparative reading of passages in terms of differences in perspectives each presents on a topic or event. There are also passages within which multiple perspectives are presented together. These passages make similarly useful critical reading materials. A few have been used and reported on by critical language teachers.

An example comes from Kuo (2014), who discusses her use of Browne's (1998) *Voices in the Park*. This short story involves the voices of four different people, a domineering woman, an upset man, a lonely boy, and a kind girl, each telling their own versions of the same walk in the park and thus revealing their varied emotions, perspectives, and personalities. Kuo reported using this story in a General English class in a university in Taiwan. After reading a shortened version of the story, Kuo's students received a discussion handout and a list of common character traits to help them identify the four characters' features. Following a discussion activity, Kuo gave student groups a Character Web poster where they wrote down the name of their assigned character in the middle, and around which they wrote adjectives to describe the character's personality together with examples of the character's behavior to support their perceptions. This was followed by another discussion activity guided by two questions: "Why does the author present the story from four different perspectives?" and "Is it important to recognize multiple perspectives regarding specific events in our lives? Why or why not?" (p. 118). Finally, Kuo assigned his students a perspective journal in which they were asked to report a life experience of their own involving multiple perspectives.

Although the story is recommended for use with young English-speaking pupils (9–11 years old), Kuo (2014) did not observe his first-year university students to have found it and its related activities unchallenging. Perhaps since their proficiency level was between intermediate and high intermediate and the activities were varied and involved their engagement with a reasonably wide range of vocabulary items (in the poster activity), the students found the lesson interesting and beneficial. They thought that the lesson helped them understand how different people see and make sense of the world from different perspectives and encouraged them to re-examine their own lives from a more critical angle. Kuo's paper includes helpful details for those interested in using *Voices in the Park* or stories of a similar nature in their reading lessons. In addition, *The Linking Network* has developed a guide for classroom use of the same story.[5]

Another story similarly engaging different perspectives on the same topic is *Seven Blind Mice* by Young (2002) which retells the Indian parable of a group of blind men who discover different parts of the body of an elephant and describe the elephant based on their limited experience. In Young's version, seven mice engage in the same process of discovery and share their revelations with each other until they come to develop a fuller understanding of what an elephant looks like. In a lesson plan to improve U.S. Grade 4–5 students' critical thinking skills with a focus on multiple perspectives, Shannon Bradford has allocated a section to a set of activities based on this story, which we reproduce here as they can be adapted for use with English language learners of other age ranges:

1. Introduce the book *Seven Blind Mice* by telling students that it shows the perspective of seven different characters. Explain that they will first take apart (deconstruct) the story and sketch it from each character's perspective and then put together all of their images and see if they can get an idea of the entire picture.

2. Distribute a copy of the Sketch to Stretch sheet to each student and explain that each block is to be used to depict the perspective of one of the mice in the story.
3. Activate students' schema by having them briefly discuss how a mouse's perspective is different from a human's. Before reading, have students pretend to take off their shoes and imagine that they are putting on a mouse's shoes.
4. Read aloud *Seven Blind Mice*. Stop after each mouse's description of the object (pillar, snake, spear, cliff, fan, rope) and have students complete a box on their Sketch to Stretch sheet.
5. Before reading the ending of the book, have the students try to put together the images from the different perspectives to infer what the entire picture might be. After this discussion, finish the book.
6. To close the lesson, have the students complete the self-assessment form Can I See Different Perspectives?[6]

The accounts of critical literacy practice reported in this and the previous section highlight the potential that comparative analysis, fostered through reading multiple texts on the same topic or one text involving different perspectives, offers for critical work. Through comparison, students become increasingly aware of the fact that there is no single and universal way to understand an issue and, instead, there are multiple perspectives on a given topic. Therefore, we should be on the lookout for materials that explicitly encourage readers to seek multiple perspectives. Carefully selected materials and well-designed activities based on these materials can create a space for learners' critical thinking development in the language classroom.

Reading Passages Promoting Self-Reflection

Although not common in critical reading practice, and in fact exactly because of this, here we briefly discuss the usefulness of readings, or written prompts in general, which encourage reflection on oneself for a critical lesson. We consider this type of reading useful because reflection on one's own ideas, emotions, beliefs, personality traits, and behaviors can be a major dimension of developing critical thinking and reading skills.

As an example, let's consider Kuo's (2013) report on his critical reading lessons (in Taiwan) involving what he called self-discovery texts. The texts he used were "Who Am I?", from one of the many books in the popular U.S. book series *Chicken Soup for the Teenage Soul*, and three quizzes called "How Happy Are You?", "How's Your Body Image?", and "What's Your Self-Image?" from *Reveal the Real You!: 20 Cool Quizzes All About You* (1999). Following a focus on important words and phrases in each text, the students read it as guided by the teacher, started doing an assignment in the class in response to the text, finished it at home, and discussed their assign-ments in the following session (see Table 4.1). Finally, they were given a vocabulary test.

Table 4.1

Self-Discovery Texts	Assignments
1. "Who Am I?"	A self-introduction poster combining texts and drawings
1. "How Happy Are You?"	A list of 10 things that make me happy or unhappy
2. "How's Your Body Image?'	A picture-of-me assignment
3. "What's Your Self-Image?"	Interviews with 5 classmates/roommates about their perception of you and an evaluation of these perceptions

Source: Kuo (2013, p. 552)

What may encourage us to do similar lessons in our classes is Kuo's (2013) students' positive perceptions of the experience. The students said that the lessons were useful in drawing their attention to issues they had taken for granted, the topics were relevant to their personal lives, the assignments enhanced their understanding of themselves, subsequent classroom discussions helped them evaluate themselves from multiple per-spectives, and they enjoyed the language learning experience they gained along the self-reflection lessons.

This experience reflects the benefits of incorporating texts and prompts, like quizzes and questionnaires, as self-reflection tools and thus their appro-priateness for a critical lesson. Depending on the type of context in which we teach, our students have a combination of multiple roles and identities in their personal, social, and work lives, each deserving careful attention and in-depth reflection. For example, in an adult class, students may be employees, employers, or seeking work, teachers of other subject matters (or even English), students in other settings, mothers, fathers, siblings, or carers. There are reading passages and questionnaires which encourage reflection on these roles and identities, and such reflection, individual and collective, in the classroom would help students rethink and improve how they perceive and fulfill their roles.

This type of reflective practice may not strike some of us as typical of critical pedagogy with its long-standing emphasis on sociopolitical matters and social class. However, as Kuo's (2013) quotes from his students suggest, this sort of personal reflection and student-to-student interaction is often the first time students have had a chance to reflect deeply on their roles in society (important in itself) and, if handled properly, can induce critical (in the non-political sense of the word) reflection that is probably a necessary prerequisite for broader and deeper thought.

Analyzing Rhetorical Features of Passages

In the Equipping Learners With Critical Reading Tools section, we discussed the importance of equipping learners with critical reading tools and mentioned CDA as a toolkit that can be used for this purpose. An area that CDA focuses on for critical analysis of text is its rhetorical features—certain ways of using words which help convey subtleties of meanings, persuade the reader, or evoke emotions or reactions on the part of the reader. Typical examples are the use of metaphors and irony. Depending on the type of text we use as classroom content, a focus on its rhetorical features may enrich the process of critical analysis of the text.

Alford and Kettle (2017) observed such practice in how an English teacher in Australia taught English as an additional language (EAL) students at a high school. In this example, the teacher, Celia, was preparing her students for a speech-writing task. To do so, she asked her students to identify key rhetorical features in the script of Martin Luther King's 1963 March on Washington Speech. After a whole-class guided focus on these features, the teacher summarized the overall effect of these rhetorical features as follows:

> Any other examples now of metaphors, figurative language?... Why are the metaphors used? Can you feel that you become involved when you read those metaphors? So the metaphors create pictures and images of the reality of the situation. They raise the consciousness of the listener(s), the people who are struggling and feeling the oppression, I think after a while, they feel bound by it and they feel that they can't escape from it. When a speechmaker uses a metaphor he takes them to another place through his language use. So he uses these metaphors to first of all show them the reality of their situation and then he wants to take them beyond that point. He's trying to engage his audience, get his people to rise up with him ... [pause] And he puts it together very well. So he says, "It is obvious today that America has defaulted on this promissory note insofar as her citizens of colour are concerned." ... He makes declarative statements as well ... and then he goes into the repetition. There's a mixture of rhetorical questions and we have some more statements of fact, and some more metaphors. A nice combination put together to have a fantastic effect. Does anyone else notice anything different that moves them or persuades them? (Alford & Kettle, 2017, p. 203)

Alford and Kettle's (2017) analysis of the teacher's approach is as follows:

Celia demonstrates a focus on critical aesthetics or the affective potential of language to simultaneously enthrall and sway readers ideologically. As Misson and Morgan (2006) argued, there are "certain obvious formal features of texts that mark it as available for aesthetic reactions and perhaps even requiring an aesthetic reaction from audiences" (p. 35). In making this element present, Celia is making the language awareness work more concrete and less abstract for her learners by connecting it to their affective or emotional responses. She is also engaging them in thinking about the power certain language choices have to enlist hearers and readers ideologically, which, in this case, points to oppression and racism.

Celia's teacher talk includes three main elements that proceed in three distinct phases: from discussion of the formal aesthetic features of the speech, to eliciting an emotional response to the aesthetic, to critiquing the values and ideology of the text and returning to formal features again. In this excerpt, we can observe this progression as she moves from a focus on metaphors and figurative language, to the students' feelings and personal involvement generated by these features, then to consciousness raising about oppression, and then back to the formal features of rhetorical questions and metaphors. If both emotional and rational responses are generated by aesthetic texts ... then Celia seems to be attempting to capture this in her teacher talk about language— being moved is emotional, being persuaded is rational. The two are needed together to have the desired overall effect.

The extract from the teacher's summary reflection on the text and Alford and Kettle's analysis show the great potential that a focus on rhetorical features of text presents for critical reading practice. It is also an example of a focus on emotions in recent practices of CDA, which used to be more oriented towards rational thinking and engaged with ideology.

While most of the previous sections had a major focus on dealing with the content (what was said) of reading passages critically, the kind of reading practice this section presented was mostly to do with the kind of language used to discuss a given topic (how it was said). Yet, neither focus was to the exclusion of the other. What this suggests is that we do best to have a dual focus on the topical content and the language of the text and their interconnections in any critical reading practice. This way, we can help our students develop the analytical skills necessary to engage with both aspects of a text. So it is perhaps safe to say that a critical reading lesson ideally consists of a combination of content analysis and linguistic analysis, and we should keep this in mind when planning our lessons.

Asking Critical Questions

You have probably noticed that in many of the examples of critical reading practice reported above, questioning is a major strategy that teachers use to conduct a lesson or an activity. We all know how important effective questioning is in the language classroom. As teachers, we ask questions throughout a lesson (and in the exams!). What makes questioning particularly important in a critical classroom is that it can foster higher-order thinking including critical and creative thinking. In Chapter 3 (on classroom content, and also elsewhere in the book), we briefly discussed "problem-posing" which is a key principle of critical pedagogy. We said that critical pedagogy does not require us to solve our students' problems. Rather, it encourages us to reflect problems back to the students so they take on the active role of potentially solving their own problems. We also said that critical pedagogy urges us to develop our students' problem-posing skills through engaging them in the very process of identifying problem-situations. A major tool to implement a problem-posing pedagogy is asking effective questions about potential problem-situations from our students. Not only do we ask critical questions of our students, but we also encourage them and help them to develop critical questions of their own about the classroom content and topics, and, this way, question—in their own terms and words—the world, its impacts on them, and their place in it. Borrowing critical pedagogy terminology, effective questioning helps learners 'problematize' contextual issues which are relevant and significant to them.

While a critical lesson, like any more typical language lesson, involves asking different types of questions, in this section we focus on question types that are specifically geared towards fostering critical reflection.

Given the importance attached to making classroom content relevant to learners' lives in critical pedagogy, among the questions that we can ask our students following initial comprehension work should be those which prompt them to reflect on and share their own experiences in connection with the reading topic, or, in other words, to personalize the content.

Let's look at an example from Park (2011). In a critical reading lesson based on an article about neuroenhancement (mentioned earlier—the phenomenon of healthy individuals taking drugs or supplements to improve their cognitive and affective abilities), some of the questions Park posed for the post-reading discussion were intended to establish a connection between the topic and the students' own experiences:

> Do you have any experience taking neuroenhancers? If you did take
> neuroenhancers before, when or why did you take it? If you have not taken
> neuroenhancers, when do you feel the urge to use neuroenhancers the
> most? (p. 35)

Such questions help students explore and understand the relevance of the reading topic to their lives; therefore, these questions increase their engagement with the content, which is a prerequisite for, or rather an initial step in, critical reflection on it.

Another question type which enables students to personalize a reading topic and engage with it more deeply is that which encourages them to think about and share their initial reactions to the topic. The teacher in Hobbs et al.'s (2015) study, for example, asked students for their first reactions to advertisements that they read in the class. The questions he started with were, "What do you think when you see this? How do you feel?" After each response, he asked, "What made you think or feel that?" (p. 457).

These types of questions may not be considered critical and many teachers who do not necessarily subscribe to a critical approach to teaching may ask quite a lot of them in their lessons. Yet, asking such questions prepares students to engage with critical questions about a text. They get them going, if you like. Let's now move on to critical questions.

Many of us might be wondering, "What is a critical question?" In a paper on critical reading practice, Arman suggested that a critical question has the potential to:

1. encourage learners to treat a text in a questioning rather than passive manner,
2. improve their reasoning skills,
3. help them think about issues in abstract terms,
4. enable them to apply knowledge to new situations,
5. develop their ability to propose alternative interpretations, courses of action, etc.,
6. raise their awareness of their own beliefs and biases,
7. develop their consciousness about the current situation and the existing opportunities for and barriers to making positive changes,
8. generate in-depth dialogue among learners,
9. and, as a result, enhance their shared understanding. (slightly modified from Abednia, 2015, pp. 82–83)

We do encourage you to critically examine this list of features and develop your own list. Let's now move on and make the discussion more practical by considering a worthwhile list of critical questions (developed by Australian teachers[7]).

Textual Purpose(s)

What is this text about? How do we know?

Who would be most likely to read and/or view this text and why?

Why are we reading and/or viewing this text?

What does the composer of the text want us to know?

Textual Structures and Features

What are the structures and features of the text?
What sort of genre does the text belong to?
What do the images suggest?
What do the words suggest?
What kind of language is used in the text?

Construction of Characters

How are children, teenagers or young adults constructed in this text?
How are adults constructed in this text?
Why has the composer of the text represented the characters in a particular way?

Gaps and Silences

Are there "gaps" and "silences" in the text?
Who is missing from the text?
What has been left out of the text?
What questions about itself does the text not raise?

Power and Interest

In whose interest is the text?
Who benefits from the text?
Is the text fair?
What knowledge does the reader/viewer need to bring to this text in order to understand it?
Which positions, voices and interests are at play in the text?
How is the reader or viewer positioned in relation to the composer of the text?
How does the text depict age, gender and/or cultural groups?
Whose views are excluded or privileged in the text?
Who is allowed to speak? Who is quoted?
Why is the text written the way it is?
Whose view: whose reality?

What View of the World Is the Text Presenting?

What kinds of social realities does the text portray?

How does the text construct a version of reality?

What is real in the text?

How would the text be different if it were told in another time, place, or culture?

Interrogating the Composer

What kind of person, and with what interests and values, composed the text?

What view of the world and values does the composer of the text assume that the reader/viewer holds? How do we know?

Multiple meanings

What different interpretations of the text are possible?

How do contextual factors influence how the text is interpreted?

How does the text mean?

How else could the text have been written?

How does the text rely on intertextuality to create its meaning?

The question categories focus on several aspects of a text, such as its purpose and structure, its author(s), its focuses and silences, the views it is based on or promotes of its characters, the world, and its potential readers, the context within which it is situated, and possible interpretations of its content. Thus, it is a relatively comprehensive collection of critical questions suitable for critical reading practice. Educators have also developed other sets of questions. One example is the set of questions developed by National Association for Media Literacy Education (NAMLE), a U.S. non-profit organization dedicated to helping with analyzing media and supporting media literacy education.[8]

Regarding how useful these questions are in the context of the classroom, there are a number of issues to keep in mind. To begin with, let's not assume that our students easily understand all critical questions. Some of those listed above, as you must have noticed, are somewhat sophisticated. The teacher in Hobbs et al.'s (2015) study, for example, needed to explain the questions and make sure the students felt comfortable answering them. Also, ready-made questions may not be suitable for all groups of students or different topics. Therefore, we should treat question lists as resources to adapt for different student groups, texts, and contexts.

Furthermore, we often need to develop questions of our own. How a question is worded by us and understood by our students directly affects the process of critical reflection; therefore, in our early experiments with critical pedagogy, it is beneficial to take our time and practice developing questions when preparing our lessons and perhaps ask our colleagues for feedback on our questions. What matters most is for our students to fully understand the questions. Based on our experience, a common risk involved in asking critical questions is that sometimes they can become too complicated to really guide critical thinking. Thus, developing simple questions which facilitate sophisticated thinking is a great skill to have.

Earlier we emphasized helping students to become actively involved in contributing critical questions to the classroom process. A simple way to do so is to give our students a list of critical questions, after comprehension work on a passage, and ask them to choose three or four questions which they find suitable to ask, for critical practice. A more engaged version of this activity would be to encourage the students to tailor the questions to the passage by any slight or substantial rewording of the questions. If we decide to assign this activity in the form of group work, we should be mindful of different levels of preparedness on the part of learners. There are almost always students, not many though, who have had prior engagement with critical thinking, thanks to their parents, other teachers, and so forth. Being more confident in asking critical questions than their classmates, they may unintentionally monopolize the classroom process, including group activities. A solution would be to team up students with similar capabilities so that each would stand a good chance of contributing questions to the team. Another solution would be to put one student from a stronger critical background in each team and give them a supportive mentor role.

Another way to involve students in developing critical questions was reported by Hobbs et al. (2015). In a media literacy activity, the teacher asked his students to match a list of critical questions with different sections of an advertisement analysis (see Table 4.2).

An example of the worksheet used with the question generation activity is reproduced in Table 4.3 from the paper. The worksheet begins with an advertisement for Perrier sparkling water, in which a martial artist with an athletic body is depicted drinking from it using a large straw.

Hobbs et al. (2015) reported that the activity helped the students with their critical analysis skills:

> Students became so active and engaged in these exercises that they remembered most of the key critical questions for subsequent discussions and for a pop quiz at the end of the unit, which the teacher used to gauge students' retention of the key ML [Media Literacy] questions that he wanted them to employ as tools in the analysis of media texts in subsequent units. (p. 462)

Table 4.2

Audience and authors	Authors Purpose	A1. Who made the media text? A2. What is the purpose? Why was this made? A3. Who is the target audience?
Messages and meanings	Content Techniques Interpretations	M1. What is this about? What is the main idea? What are the messages? M2. What techniques are used to attract attention? What techniques communicate the message(s)? M3. How can different people understand the message(s) differently? M4. What is left out of the message(s)?
Representations and reality	Context Representations Credibility	R1. When, where, and how was this shared? R2. What lifestyles, values, and points of view are represented? R3. Is this fact, opinion, or something else? R4. How does the message relate to reality? Are the messages true and correct?

Table 4.3

Instructions. Study the ad and then write the question that fits the answer.

Question:_____

Answer: The company that owns Perrier made this ad for water.

Question:_____

Answer: This ad was in a *Sports Illustrated* magazine in April 2011. It was on a full page next to a story about a basketball player.

Question:_____

Answer: They made this ad because they want people to buy the water. They want to persuade the reader to feel that Perrier water is strong, exciting, and healthy.

Question:_____

Answer: There are a few messages in this ad. Perrier is a healthy drink for strong people. Perrier is exciting, like a kung fu fighter movie star. Perrier is part of attraction between men and women.

Question:_____

Answer: The main idea is that Perrier is an exciting drink for strong people.

Question:_____

(Table continued on next page)

> Answer: The target audience is men and boys who like action movies and want a strong body. Another target audience is women and gay men who like to look at strong men's bodies. This ad was made for middle-class and wealthy people. These people can afford to buy a gym membership.
>
> Question:_____
>
> Answer: The ad uses perspective to attract attention. There is a kung fu fighter on the man's t-shirt. The fighter has no shirt and many muscles. He looks like he is holding the straw in the bottle. The straw is like his weapon for kung fu. It's interesting. (Hobbs et al., 2015, p. 463)

Let's finish this part of the chapter by re-emphasizing the importance of asking good questions in a critical language classroom. Good critical questions foster learners' active engagement in critical literacy practice and increase their share and ownership of the classroom especially when some of the questions are developed by students themselves.

DOING IT WITH KIDS

Regarding using a critical approach to teaching English to children, a question we may be asked is, "Can children think critically and analyze a passage critically?" and another common question is, "Is there any material suitable for critical teaching of (L2) English to children?"

To answer these questions, we share with you a few accounts of how teachers engage children in critical analysis of passages and how capable children prove to be in critical reading. The first example, reported by Roy (2017), is from an elementary class in the United States. Two migrant Somali Bantu fourth graders, Abdullah and Omar, whose reading comprehension is at the first-grade level, and their teacher, Ms. Rios, are reading the picture book *Grandfather's Journey* (Say, 1993), a recommended text in the curriculum which talks about the journey of a Japanese immigrating to the United States and then returning to Japan. One of the examples that Roy gives of how the class engages with this book critically is a classroom discussion which happens during the read-aloud of the story.

Ms. Rios: (reading from Grandfather's Journey) He met many people along the way. He shook hands with black men and white men, with yellow men, and red men.

Omar: (interrupts Ms. Rios) There's the black man right there (points to the black man).

Abdullah: What he means about red men?

Ms. Rios: Good question, Abdullah. Sometimes people describe Native American people as having red skin.

Abdullah: He looks brown.

Ms. Rios: Yeah, those labels can be confusing sometimes. Let's revisit that after I read some more (continues reading). (Roy, 2017, p. 541)

The point to be made about the above quote is that in many circumstances, young children are entirely ready, willing, and eager to ask what adults might think are difficult, even embarrassing questions. Thus, the potential for critical thinking and critical questioning is already there, particularly if the material (or the teacher) facilitates this. Though very short and simple, this conversation shows that the students notice the author's and illustrator's use of color as an identity marker and question the accuracy and purpose of color-based labels. Roy highlights the importance of such conversations, though she also says that, "all too often, opportunities to engage in conversations about race are missed or left to the periphery in classroom discourse, especially in elementary contexts" (p. 541). Thus, short conversations like the reported one are worthwhile as they foster students' critical engagement with social issues relevant to them.

The second example, reported by Lee (2017), is from an elementary school setting in South Korea. Like the previous example, the students were fourth graders whose reading level was lower than their peers'. What made working with these children extra challenging was their tendency to disengage from class activities. Therefore, they had been put in an extra-curricular reading program, where they read a few works of fiction. One story was *The Hundred Dresses* (Estes, 1944) which is about a poor Polish immigrant girl, Wanda, who claims that she has a hundred dresses at home. She is bullied by other girls at school, but her dress designs win a school contest. The following excerpt is a conversation between two students, Duckhoon and Misoo, and their teacher, Youngju, where they reflect on the story.

Youngju: Do you feel pity for Wanda?

Duckhoon: Umm. I don't like it.

Youngju: You mean you didn't like this story?

Duckhoon: I don't know. It's too *bbeonhaeyo* [stereotypical].

Youngju: What do you think is too stereotypical in this story?

Duckhoon: Wanda picked because she is foreigner, and poor. I feel like book telling poor foreigner like Wanda always picked. It's not always true.

Misoo: I was the only Korean in America, second grade. I don't have friends. But some girls were nice. Boys talked to me. We are not friends, but they don't pick me.

Youngju: Then, why do you think Wanda was picked on by other girls?

Duckhoon: Groups have rules. It's not always rich or poor. Strong, weak is rule my school. And some are very special [meaning subtle], but it's not bbeonhajiahna [stereotypical].

Youngju: So, did you feel that the author was telling you the poor foreigner was always picked on by others?

Duckhoon: Yep, but it's not true in my school. (Lee, 2017, pp. 38–39)

This conversation shows the students' ability to do an in-depth critical analysis of the passage. Duckhoon identified stereotypical elements in the story and Misoo joined in critiquing these elements using her personal experience as a counterexample.

Both conversations reported above show the great potential of young learners to examine texts critically and relate their topics and details to their own experiences. The dialogs also show that the students' limited English proficiency does not hinder their critical engagement with the readings. While their utterances are all simple sentences at best and most have grammar and vocabulary mistakes, they do make sense to their teacher and peers and clearly enrich the process of critical discussion. Thus, learners' young age and limited proficiency should not stop us from including critical reflection and discussion in the classroom process. What we need to do, though, is to tailor the level of critical engagement we expect from our students for their age and language level. In the sample conversations, the questions that the teachers ask do not have complex wordings or structures and are easily understood by the students. Therefore, they help the students engage in the reflection and dialogue process. At the same time, materials *are* important. Teaching critical English literacy is more or less difficult depending on the availability of reading materials which, while addressing issues relevant to learners' life situations and suitable for critical literacy practice, are appropriate for low age and language level classes.

As the above conversations mainly show young learners' critical engage-ment with text as guided by teachers' questions, let's now look at an example of students taking the extra step of developing questions of their own about a text. Simpson (1996) looks at an English (Language Arts) class in Aus-tralia with students aged 11 and 12. In this class, a few children's books with sophisticated themes were used and the teacher asked her students to develop, in pairs, questions focusing on what the authors wanted to do in the books and any other things they considered important to discuss. Some of the questions collected from pairs about the *Piggybook* (Browne, 1987) were:

> Why does the mum do all the housework?
> Why don't they know how to cook?
> Why doesn't the mum have a piggy face?
> Why won't they clean up the mess?
> Do the dad and the kids respect the mother? (Simpson, 1996, p. 123)

These questions, though simple, show the children's ability to identify issues relating to how household responsibilities are shared among fam-ily members and problematize the often unexamined assumption that the mother is solely or mostly responsible for household chores. The stu-dents' age range would not allow them to engage in a more sophisticated reflection on problematic patriarchal perceptions of women's roles within a family and their place in the wider society, something which would sound more like what critical pedagogy encourages. Yet, the critical reflection process initiated by this question development activity can be a great starting point, preparing learners for more in-depth treatment of the rel-evant issues in their later stages of thinking, and language, development. Although, unlike the first two examples, the students in this class were native speakers of English, we believe second language learners are able to develop similar questions about a text.

We'd also like to tell you about a study of very young bilingual students (Kim, 2014). The teacher studied in this case "was an experienced teacher who had teaching experience in both Korea and the United States. As an early childhood teacher and educator, her goal in teaching was not only to teach young children language and literacy skills but also to help them grow up as democratic citizens who appreciate differences in a racially, ethnically, and culturally diverse world. Her critical literacy efforts helped the children challenge the author's message, deeply examine the texts, and develop critical attitudes about what they read."

In the report, we find the teacher asking the children to use their own ideas and opinions to resist, question, or provide alternatives to what actually went on in some classic fairy stories that the children were reading. The children definitely have their own ideas. But also the teacher does, on the topic of gender roles, introduce the possibility that Snow White (for example) could do things differently, never mind if she is a woman or a girl.

Of course, you might say that this is an unusual teaching situation (a small class, outside of the more common state education Monday-to-Friday system). That is true, although this teacher too expresses her need and worry to cover all administratively assigned material.

If you are wondering why we included a study of children learning Korean as a heritage language in a course that mostly focuses on English language teaching, it was more a matter of finding something right down at the earliest age range that was also clearly only focused on L2 learning and teaching.

Finally, we'd like to tell you about an interesting program specifically designed to teach children to think critically. "Philosophy for children" is a long-standing award-winning program that Thomas Wartenberg developed to teach philosophy and critical thinking to young children from the first to the fifth grade. Although this program is mainly for children who speak English as a first or main language, the approach and ideas in this program can be adapted to nonnative English-speaking learners. In his book, titled *Big Ideas for Little Kids: Teaching Philosophy Through Children's Literature* (Wartenberg, 2014), he explains his approach in detail and through examples. While we recommend that you read it, if you are too busy to do so, then how about visiting the website created to introduce Philosophy for Children and the links provided there? The URL address of the website is https://www.prindleinstitute.org/teaching-children-philosophy/. The website links to highly useful resources. One of the tabs is a documentary which would be a great starting point for those of us who do not know about the program. It introduces the program through showing samples of classroom practice and kids' participation in critical discussions as well as interviews with Wartenberg, teachers, children, and their parents. Another link takes us to resources Wartenberg has developed. The website also includes a link to a relatively long list of books which can be used to teach philosophical and critical thinking to children. In this last link, short summaries of the books, guidelines for philosophical discussion, and questions for philosophical discussion are given.

A TEACHER'S PRACTICE

In this section we present a lesson developed by a teacher who participated in one of our online courses on critical language pedagogy. The assignment involved modifying a mainstream reading lesson (from *Four*

Corners 3; Richards & Bohlke 2012, p. 70) and making it (at least slightly) critical. The title of the original lesson was "What is your personality?" The passage was a description of the signs of the zodiac. The pre-reading questions were "When were you born? Read the description of your zodiac sign. Does it describe you well?" The reading activity was to match eight descriptions with the correct signs. Finally, the post-reading group activity was: "Think of three people you know. What is each person's zodiac sign? Does it describe their personalities well? Tell your group."

You may agree that this lesson is a predominantly mainstream lesson. Our point is that being aided to question, probe, challenge, and so forth, a piece of largely mainstream thinking, a light-weight piece of text, is still by no means a common practice in classrooms, and can be used to model the practices which we would like our students to be using with more heavily-freighted material (perhaps outside the classroom). Theresa's version of the lesson is as follows:

1. In groups of four students, each group has a stack of flash cards. Each card has the zodiac characteristics on them but not the name of the zodiac sign. Students are to read each card and choose the card that they think suits them.
2. Students are given answers to which sign goes with which definition, by reading the Four Corners passage.
3. Students are to ask themselves:

   - Were the characteristics they chose different to their actual zodiac signs? If different, is the characteristic of their actual zodiac correct as well or not?
   - How much can we trust these zodiac signs?

4. Students are to research about how zodiac signs came about and who were responsible for coming up with them, and discuss findings as a class.
5. Students are to brainstorm in groups of three on one large piece of paper "What are zodiac signs used for?" with two columns "negative uses" and "positive uses."

The lesson begins with flash cards which do not associate personality features with zodiac signs. This enables students' reflection to be informed by their own understanding of themselves rather than categories of personality developed based on zodiac signs. Then, when they are presented with the signs and their descriptions, they are better placed to examine the accuracy of the signs based on the questions in Step 3. The research in Step 4, which can be done in the class if students have access to devices with internet connectivity, takes the lesson a step further in its critical orientation as it engages students in exploring the origins and the creators of the zodiac signs. It is always desirable to put the students in the position of knowers, who find out matters and draw their own conclusions, based on their developing critical abilities. Finally, students are to reflect on the positive and negative uses of these signs. If directed well by the teacher, this part can prompt students to think about positive and negative personal and sociocultural implications of using zodiac signs as valid indicators of individuals' personalities.

CONCLUSION

In this chapter, we discussed various aspects of teaching critical reading. One of the key points that we would like to re-emphasize is that we should make sure our students are equipped with adequate background knowledge about the topic of a reading passage as well as sufficient linguistic knowledge to develop a proper understanding of the text itself which would then form the basis of their critical engagement with the passage. We would also like to highlight the possibility for critical work on texts which are apparently very neutral and therefore considered unsuitable for critical analysis. Through examples, we tried to show the potential for critical reading practice even with these passages. These examples and other examples mentioned throughout the chapter suggest that there are ample opportunities in the classroom for practicing critical reading. Although contextual factors may limit these opportunities, a key determining factor which maximizes them and we are, very fortunately, in control of is our own teaching skills and pedagogical knowledge, improving which always makes sense.

NOTES

1. At the time of writing this book, the URL link to this resource is https://sites.google.com/a/sheffield.ac.uk/all-about-linguistics/branches/discourse-analysis/example-research.
2. The YouTube link to the video is https://youtu.be/RuvankHKk3s.
3. The video can be currently accessed at https://www.youtube.com/watch?v=3w_5riFCMGA. As this video has been produced by a website called flixabout.com, it can also be found at http://flixabout.com/norman-fairclough-critical-discourse-analysis with the slightly different name of "Norman Fairclough Critical Discourse Analysis."
4. The video is in fact an introduction to CDA. The current link to the video is https://www.youtube.com/watch?v=NpJhICZczUQ.

5. The guide is currently available at https://thelinkingnetwork.org.uk/resource/voices-in-the-park-2/.
6. The whole lesson is available at the following link which also includes hyperlinks to the Sketch to Stretch sheet and the self-assessment form: http://www.readwritethink.org/classroom-resources/lesson-plans/multiple-perspectives-building-critical-30629.html?tab=4
7. These were originally made available through the Department of Education, Tasmania, Australia website but the link is no longer active. However, this list has been reproduced in several sources including websites.
8. NAMLE's website http://namle.net/publications/core-principles/ provides a link to the media literacy questions. The link which takes you directly to the questions is https://drive.google.com/file/d/0B8j2T8jHrlgCZ2Zta2hvWkF0dG8/view.

CHAPTER 5

CRITICAL L2 WRITING PEDAGOGY

INTRODUCTION

We'd like to start this chapter by saying that critical writing is an under-developed area. In fact, "critical writing," unlike "critical reading," is not a common and widely used term. Published works on critical literacy education mostly focus on critical reading, with writing often serving as a post-reading activity. While the word "literacy," traditionally and theoretically, encompasses writing as much as reading, writing turns out to be the Cinderella of critical second language education. Thus, in this chapter, we offer only tentative suggestions about what critical writing may mean and how we can teach it, using teaching experiences shared by teachers around the world and extending from this rather limited literature. Yet, we also acknowledge that the primary focus currently placed on reading is not entirely irrational as it is partly to do with the fact that critical writing often follows initial engagement with text, be it a reading passage, an advertisement, our notes, a conversation with a friend or colleague, and so forth.

Before discussing critical (L2) writing, we start with a brief focus on how writing is currently approached in mainstream second language education. Second language teachers teach writing in varied ways, of course; however, many (particularly in EFL settings) are concerned with fostering

Starting Points in Critical Language Pedagogy, pp. 91–114
Copyright © 2022 by Information Age Publishing

their students' language development understood in terms of grammar and vocabulary. So the major focus in many writing lessons is on helping students develop such skills as using correct language, writing with clarity and coherence, and following largely predetermined paragraph and essay structures. What is written (content) and why (purpose) tend to be of secondary importance and sometimes completely ignored.

In critical writing pedagogy, it is almost the opposite. The purpose of writing, personal or social, serves as the point of departure simply because in real life people write for a reason. Content and ideas become important because these are what we want to communicate in order to achieve our purpose. And it is within this overarching focus on the purpose and content of writing that an emphasis on language becomes relevant, significant, and even essential, as the lexical and grammatical choices we make and the structure within which we write have a determining impact on how well we communicate our ideas and accomplish our goals. In the next section, we expand upon these ideas to explore in detail what critical writing may mean and involve.

WHAT IS CRITICAL WRITING?

Writing as Doing

We just mentioned that *why we write* should be the starting point and perhaps the major focus in critical writing practice and pedagogy. As in real life we write to do things, our teaching practice in the language classroom should be similarly informed by a view of writing as doing. Canagarajah's (2002) eloquent explanation of this feature of critical writing is worth quoting here.

> The production of texts is not an end in itself. We don't write simply to produce a text—and leave it at that. We produce texts to achieve certain interests and purposes. Furthermore, after a text is produced, it gets used in unanticipated ways. Launched into the public world, it takes a life of its own and effects results and processes totally unanticipated by the writer. Therefore, texts not only mean but do. Their functionality goes to the extent of reconstructing reality, rather than simply reflecting reality. We need to inquire what the word does to/in the world. (p. 4)

Inspired by Canagarajah's argument that texts do things, including reconstructing reality, and, therefore, we need to explore what words do, we could argue that this view of "writing as doing" is a defining feature of critical teaching of writing. A purpose-sensitive writing lesson or activity starts with, maintains, and concludes with a focus on the purpose of writing. The teacher and students discuss the *why* of the writing practice before a focus on *what* to write and *how*, and the focus on *what* and *how* happens in light of a consideration of *why*.

The discussion of the purpose(s) of writing obviously goes beyond the short-term objective of, say, fulfilling a class assignment and focuses on a real-life purpose beyond the classroom boundaries. This discussion of purpose, be it a teacher communicating the purpose to students, or teacher and students setting the purpose in a collaborative manner, should be conducted in such a way that students come to treat those real-life and genuine purposes as more important than the immediate, classroom-bound, and less authentic purpose of fulfilling a classroom activity and being considered as engaged learners.

Some real-life purposes can be achieved within the process of writing, such as critical reflection on issues related to individual students or society. For example, we may ask our adolescent or older students to write an essay about a recent social trend in their local community or across the world and discuss its benefits and risks. Or we could ask our younger students to write one or more paragraphs about one of their bad habits that their parents do not like, why their parents do not approve of it, and how they think they should change it. Aimed at facilitating critical reflection on a social phenomenon and self-reflection respectively, the writing activities in these instances are personally relevant to students, and their aims are accomplished within the writing process.

Sometimes for a writing activity to achieve its purpose, it needs to go beyond reflection and involve some form of action. Without getting too philosophical, let's pause for a moment here and consider the idea that reflection in and of itself may involve action— that of reflecting on and revisiting an idea, a concept, or a social issue. Furthermore, we have no reason to entirely deny the possible impact of in-depth and genuine reflection on our future conduct and behavior, our *outward* action. Yet, while we, as teachers who are inspired by or are considering using critical approaches to teaching, acknowledge the value and impact of a reflective writing exercise in itself, we may also wish to try to conduct a classroom writing lesson which involves some form of outward and visible action, especially given that combining reflection with action is a major, defining feature of critical pedagogy, which Freire (1972/2000) referred to as "praxis."

In fact, the above activity examples can be expanded to include elements of action. For example, the former can involve students making a post (on Twitter, Facebook, etc.) suggesting, to a real audience, a change in the social trend (previously discussed in their writing) and engaging in dialogue with those who respond. Or in the latter, students could write to their parents apologizing for the bad habit they have described in their paragraphs, promising to try to change it, and asking for their advice and support (and, depending on their parents' knowledge of English, perhaps translating the letter into their mother tongue).

Given the central place of action in critical pedagogy, teachers from around the world have shared interesting and worthwhile experiences of teaching writing which are inclusive of elements of action. As in this introductory section of the chapter, we are only presenting a general picture of what critical writing pedagogy may look like, we will postpone reporting some of these teaching experiences until later in the chapter and instead will now move on to discuss what we believe is another fundamental feature of a critical writing pedagogy, a focus on *what* to write.

Writing as Developing Ideas

In the introduction section of this chapter, we mentioned that in mainstream teaching of writing, a major concern over how we write (e.g., using correct language and following a standard writing format) may push considerations relating to why we write (purpose) and what we write (content) into the background. We subsequently highlighted the importance of viewing "writing as doing" as a key feature of a critical writing pedagogy. "Writing as developing ideas" is another feature of this pedagogy that we discuss in this section.

A dominant understanding of the relationship between ideas and writing is that we think first, then write. Successful writers, however, do not follow this linear thinking-then-writing view. While they do start with thinking about the topic of their writing and developing initial ideas and then engage in writing, they in fact continue to think and (re)develop ideas while writing. In fact, writing itself is *"a way of getting and developing ideas"* (Barnet & Bedau, 2013, p. 229; emphasis original). This view of thinking-writing as a cyclical and iterative process underlies critical writing pedagogy. We now turn to a more specific discussion of how we can put this view in action in the classroom.

Let's start with a statement of the obvious: to do the issue of content and ideas in writing justice, we should encourage writing truthfully! The reason we think it is important to emphasize genuine writing in a critical writing lesson is that just the opposite may sometimes be promoted. In language test preparation classes, such as IELTS or PTE classes, teachers encourage students to decide on what to write based on how well they can present content linguistically rather than how important or true that content is. The genuineness of the content simply does not matter in those classes, while in a critical writing lesson, we obviously want our students to be genuine in their writing. Given how popular test preparation classes are and how strongly tests influence learners' understanding of language and language learning, we, as critically inspired teachers, need to take account of the dominant culture of an exclusive focus on linguistic performance that these classes promote at the expense of genuineness. This issue takes us back to the focus of the previous section. How well we communicate to students the relevance and significance of the purpose of a writing activity to their lives outside the classroom has a direct impact on how genuine they will be in the ideas they express in writing.

What further helps cultivate a classroom culture of writing as developing ideas rather than as getting the grammar and structure right is when teachers actively express an interest in students' ideas and experiences and in *hearing their voice* in their writing, even if this means them making more grammar and vocabulary mistakes. Teachers can show their interest in what students have to say in different ways, some of which we briefly discuss in the following.

First of all, it is important to design writing activities the purpose and topic of which students consider to be relevant and significant to them. We are sure you noticed us saying that students should think of a writing activity as relevant and important. Regardless of our intentions when developing activities, what really matters is our students' perceptions of those activities. In the chapter on content, we discussed at length how we can make the classroom content relevant to students' lives.

It would also be helpful to take a process, rather than a product, approach to writing. For example, instead of merely assigning topics to students and asking them to write full essays and hand them in, we can ask them to first outline the ideas they would like to present in the form of notes, without worrying about grammar and sentence structure. This step would give the teacher and students an opportunity to discuss the content of the students' writings and how this aspect can be improved. Only then would students present their ideas in full sentences and paragraphs. And when they hand in their writings in full, depending on our time constraints, we could continue to engage with the content of their writing through making comments, or rather sharing our thoughts, on the ideas and issues that they raise.

Speaking of teacher comments, the way we give feedback on writing can help immensely with maximizing students' engagement with the content of their writing. We believe that for teacher feedback to lend itself well to critical writing practice, it should be similar to how we respond to an utterance in a real-life dialogue. In a conversation, we show agreement, disagreement, uncertainty, sympathy, enthusiasm, confusion, and so on. We also ask questions, want the speaker to elaborate, or present an alternative view and ask the speaker what they think of that. Ideally, we should use these speech acts in the way we comment on the ideas, experiences, and issues our students share in writing. Expanding from the examples we just gave of how we converse, we list possible types of feedback on students' writing here:

- Expressing agreement with ideas or analyses, perhaps accompanied with further supportive ideas or examples
- Appreciating anything new that we learn from what our students have written
- Asking (critical) questions to encourage further analysis and reflection (see "critical questions" in Chapter 4 Asking Critical Questions section)
- Asking for clarification and elaboration of underdeveloped or vague ideas or arguments
- Presenting counterarguments and counterexamples that we would like our students to take account of and encouraging them to share their thoughts about them in their revisions
- Showing disagreement, gently worded and supplemented with reasoning
- Engaging emotionally with the writing through expressing emotions such as enthusiasm, sympathy, surprise, confusion, sadness, and when the occasion arises, disgust, shock, anger, or fear, especially if the student feels the same way!

Second language teachers practicing critical writing pedagogy have reported using some of these feedback types when commenting on their students' writings (e.g., Abednia & Izadinia, 2013; Ghahremani-Ghajar & Mirhosseini, 2005). Yet, in line with the general lack of literature on critical writing, which we mentioned in the introduction section, regrettably very little has been written on how to give feedback for the purpose of critical writing practice. The studies we just cited as examples do not go beyond a brief explanation of teacher feedback either. This said, an in-depth understanding of critical pedagogy, in general, and critical writing pedagogy, in particular, would enable us to devise and deploy feedback strategies which foster our students' critical writing and thinking development.

Engaging with the content of our students' writing through ways we just discussed puts us in the position of our students' audience who are interested in what they think rather than teachers who only help with language. In fact, as a social skill, writing, just like speaking, essentially involves an audience. We always write to communicate something to someone, even if that someone is ourselves, like in keeping a diary. Considering the audience is indeed another key feature of critical writing pedagogy, and thus the focus of the next section.

Writing as Communicating

Writing as communicating is closely linked to writing as doing, as one of the purposes, or perhaps the most important purpose we have when writing is to communicate. Yet, writing as doing and writing as communicating reflect two major features of writing as a social-critical skill. While writing as doing highlights the transformative nature of writing, its potential to bring about changes (which is why we foregrounded "action" in our discussion above), writing as communicating draws our attention to the dialogical nature of writing—we usually write to be read. Again we cannot help quoting Canagarajah (2002) on the dialogical nature of writing.

> For many of us, the stock image of writing is that of the lonely writer locked away in his small apartment (in crowded New York City) or a cabin (in the quiet woods of New England] pouring his thoughts on paper under mysteriously received inspiration. But writing is not a monologue; it is dialogical. One has to take account of the audience (implicitly or explicitly) while writing. This may involve a set of intended audiences, but it also involves an ever-expanding unintended audience (stretching limitlessly across time and space). In constructing a text, a writer is conducting a conversation with all this diversity of readers. (p. 4)

Teacher feedback on content, discussed in the previous section, reinforces the view of writing as authentic communication, here with the teacher. Those of us who have done extensive writing and received feedback regularly and especially on multiple drafts of the same writing gradually develop an ability to predict the types of feedback we would receive. When writing in an academic context, for example, guesses like "my lecturer would like me to include a counterargument paragraph in my persuasive essay" or "my thesis supervisor will probably ask me what I mean by this term" often prove to be quite educated especially after a few rounds of feedback. The reason is that we get to know our audience better, and the outcome is more effective communication with them. These examples well reflect the dialogical nature of writing, that we as writers are not the only ones who decide what to write; rather, our intended audiences do have an impact on those decisions. Or, as stated by Voloshinov (1973), "word is a two sided act. It is determined equally by whose word it is and for whom it is meant" (p. 86).

An active focus on and engagement with the content of our students' writing helps cultivate the view of writing as communicating. What gives this approach a critical flavor, making it suitable for critical writing pedagogy, is when we serve as our students' questioning and reflective audience by posing critical questions or comments on their ideas and arguments, of the types we listed in the previous section, and thus creating a space for critical dialogue.

Such critical dialogue, however, should not be limited to one between student and teacher. Peer dialogue can provide another rich learning space for students in a writing lesson. We agree that learners themselves may be going through early stages of developing critical literacy skills, and, therefore, their contributions to their peers' thinking and writing development might be limited. Yet, unlike teacher-student dialogue where the student is often on the receiving end of comments and questions, in peer dialogue students share the equal position of being each other's "critical friends." As a result, they can be expected to closely engage with the ideas and arguments their peers express in their writing and try to have an impact on their ways of thinking or at least acknowledge the ideas they find interesting in their peers' writing. Also, compared to peer language feedback which students may resist giving or receiving given their perceived inadequacies in their, and their peers', language knowledge, students would probably be more ready to engage in peer dialogue on the content, although this dialogue may sometimes necessitate a focus on the language of writing. A further benefit of such dialogue is the very opportunity it creates for students to talk to each other about matters of importance in their personal lives as students and young people. As the mainstream classroom rarely provides this type of opportunity, once given the chance, students probably welcome it readily. All these reasons lead us to believe that peer dialogue on writing is a suitable candidate for critical writing practice. We, as teachers, should scaffold this process by providing prompts or protocols to guide peer dialogue.

Engaging with the teacher and peers in a writing lesson or task can, under favorable conditions, create rich opportunities for learning and critical thinking development. To reflect and incorporate more of society in the classroom, which is a major commitment of critical pedagogy, we should foster our students' engagement with a wider spectrum of audiences in writing, ranging from those in the immediate educational setting, like the school principal/college manager, to those in the wider society, like the city council, the department of immigration, or higher authorities! The classroom examples that we will discuss later in the chapter reflect the potential of critical writing tasks to engage students with different types of audience.

Engaging learners with varied audiences would mean creating opportunities in the classroom for the students to take account of the experiences, views, beliefs, sensitivities, and biases that the audience of a particular type of writing may have and to decide how to communicate ideas so as to achieve the intended purpose(s) of the writing task at hand. The *how* of writing, then, becomes a significant focus of critical writing practice. In the introduction section of this chapter, we said that quite often the only focus of conventional writing pedagogies is on how to write, and such focus is mostly concerned with grammatical and lexical accuracy and following "standard" paragraph or essay structures. Then, we argued that critical writing pedagogies similarly include an emphasis on the form of writing. Yet the linguistic dimension of these writing pedagogies becomes most meaningful and justified within an overarching focus on the purpose and content of writing, as the vocabulary, grammar, and writing structure choices we make have a direct impact on how well we communicate our ideas and accomplish our goals. It is with this understanding of the interconnections between the *why*, *what*, and *how* of writing that, having discussed the first two dimensions, we now turn our focus to the last one.

Writing as Thoughtful and Informed Choice of Language Forms and Writing Conventions

In real-life communication, depending on how developed our language is—be it our mother tongue or an additional language—we often try to use the most suitable words and structures to express ourselves. In other words, we choose our words (and structures) carefully, especially in sensitive situations. For instance, if we (dare to!) write a letter or email of complaint to our manager, we make sure we use a soft tone, avoid words which are remotely offensive, and voice the complaint in a positive context (e.g., as an area of improvement) so that the letter will be interpreted as one of suggestion rather than complaint. We also make sure that we express uncertainty about our understanding of the situation, yet we explain the situation as clearly as possible, and perhaps end on a positive note. Fulfilling these functions involves numerous linguistic choices in terms of vocabulary, grammar, writing structure, and perhaps genres.

You are probably thinking "These are just too obvious! Then why are Graham and Arman stating them?!" Well, we believe the process of making context-informed and purpose-driven language choices in writing is worth highlighting here since despite this process being part and parcel of writing for real-life purposes, it is too often ignored in the language classroom, with the main focus put on grammatical and lexical accuracy which, while important, is far from enough. In Chapter 6, we discuss at length how teaching grammar can go beyond a mainstream concern with grammatical accuracy and complexity and focus on the important role of these language components in critical language work, including critical analysis of texts we are exposed to or effecting a change in society through producing text, like the letter we mentioned above. Thus, in the rest of this section, we briefly focus on genres.

A genre is a type of writing which is defined by its style, content, purpose, and intended audience. There are several classifications of genres. For example, some of the major literary genres are tragedy, comedy, satire, drama, poems, and songs. Or in academic writing, some of the major genres are reflection paper, response paper, and persuasive essay. A range of genres can also be found in media such as letters to editors, press releases, posters, flyers, and webpages.

All genres have a place in critical writing pedagogy, as each can be used to serve multiple purposes and present multiple types of content. Yet, some may lend themselves more readily to critical writing practice. "Diary/ journal writing" is one example as it involves in-depth and honest self-reflection in the safe space of a personal journal. This genre can take a shared form to involve written dialogue with others, in which case it is often referred to as a "dialogue journal." If students write a paragraph or essay in reaction to a text they have read critically, then the genre they engage with is termed "reaction paper" or "response paper." This and many other types of writing may involve "argumentation," which leads us to the genre "argumentative essay" as another popular candidate for critical writing practice.

While students can take relatively varied approaches to writing in these genres, there are conventions that each genre may require or encourage. In argumentative writing, for example, one such set of conventions is the widely used method developed by philosopher Stephen Toulmin, often referred to as the Toulmin model. This model of argumentation breaks an argument down into six components:

- **Claim** is the main argument that the author wants to support.
- **Grounds** are the evidence that support the claim.
- **Warrant** links the grounds to the claim and explains how the grounds support the claim.
- **Backing** is additional support for the warrant, like an example.
- The **qualifier**, or modality, shows the degree of certainty about the claim (e.g., all, some, utterly, somewhat, etc.).
- **Rebuttal** is an acknowledgement of exceptions or alternatives to the claim.

While critical writing pedagogy should provide a space for learners to pursue and practice their personal styles of writing, following a framework, such as above, would facilitate their critical thinking and writing process. You may agree that the Toulmin model offers a perhaps commonsensical and helpful, rather than limiting, structure to guide a writer through the process of thinking, developing arguments, presenting them, and, this way, pursuing a real-life aim, which could be attempting to convince the reader of a certain viewpoint. Therefore, presenting this model to students would help develop their argumentative writing skills.

Now let us put this discussion in the overall picture that this chapter is presenting of what critical writing pedagogy may look like in the reality of the classroom. In a mainstream lesson on the argumentative essay, the teacher would most probably make this genre the overall focus of a lesson, teach its structure, present models to the students, and then get the students to write an argumentative essay on a given or negotiated topic.

There is no reason to doubt the effectiveness of this lesson as far as writing instruction is concerned. However, as we have mentioned a few times in this chapter so far, a writing lesson aligned with critical pedagogy, which prioritizes authentic engagement with language and situates language practice within the students' real life, would make the purpose of writing, rather than the genre, the point of departure and the overarching focus.

At the same time, the critical writing teacher who is engaging with genres needs to explain to their students that genres are (merely) social constructions that change (albeit slowly) over time and are themselves in a sense manifestations of power. Thus on the one hand, it is necessary, in order to have the right effect, to master the conventions that a genre embodies. On the other hand, it may be possible under some circumstances, to challenge them. Certainly they are not God-given nor cast in stone.

But what would a critical writing lesson which incorporates a focus on genres look like in practice? One possible way in which such a lesson can be conducted is as follows:

The teacher starts with an introduction like this:

> As human beings, we think differently about things. This is fine, but some opinions might be more reasonable than others. Also, in some situations we may need to reach an agreement. While we can't, nor should, force people to agree with us, we can encourage them to consider our ideas by supporting them through giving reasons and evidence.

The teacher gives an example of a situation where they convinced someone of a different viewpoint or were persuaded by someone to think differently about a topic. Then the teacher goes on to say:

> Now, think of a current situation where you and someone else, like your friend, sibling, parent, teacher, coach, etc. don't share the same opinion about something, and you think that maybe you have a better perspective. In your notebooks, describe the situation and write your own and the other person's opinions.

After the students make initial notes about their situation of choice, the teacher asks them to list the reasons which support their opinion. Then, the teacher invites them to put themselves in the place of the other person and list reasons which may support the opposing view. The next step would be for the students to reflect on how valid the other person's reasons are and, if possible, to question them. The teacher may then ask the students to share their reflections in pairs or groups and see what their peers think.

At this stage, the class may be well placed to start to engage with the Toulmin model of argumentation and use it to enrich their reflections on their selected situations.

Having learned about an argumentation model, each student now writes a letter to the person they have in mind and persuades them to agree with their opinion.

This hypothetical example shows how learning a writing structure can become an important aspect of a critical writing lesson which yet maintains a real-life purpose of writing as its overarching theme. This contextualized focus on the form of writing can be expanded beyond the structure of an argument and take other forms, such as a focus on the grammar and vocabulary choices. Earlier in this section we mentioned that as these aspects are discussed in Chapter 6, we do not focus on them here. Yet, it is worth further developing the above imaginary lesson by adding a vocabulary topic as an example of how a critical writing lesson can be enriched with focused language work.

A linguistic focus we thought would lend itself well to a lesson on argumentation is hedging. Hedging is the use of linguistic devices to express the appropriate level of certainty and show caution when necessary. In the above example, the teacher may encourage the students to hedge their language especially when they express opinions rather than solid facts. In fact, the teacher can incorporate an explicit focus on hedging in the lesson probably after the students have drafted their letters and now want to revise them. The lesson may proceed, in that session or the following session, as follows:

Maintaining the focus on the real-life purpose of writing, the teacher says:

Try to remember a situation where someone close to you made a critical comment about an idea of yours and suggested a different perspective. Although they meant well and what they said was more or less logical, you didn't like the way they delivered it and wished they had said it differently. What do you think was wrong with the way they commented? How else could they have made their comments so you would listen to them willingly and perhaps accept their ideas?

The students reflect on these questions individually and then share their experiences and reflections.

Following this discussion, the teacher tells the students that what they just discussed is sometimes called hedging or vague language and goes on to explain it.

The teacher distributes a list of words and phrases used for hedging, asks the students to study the list, makes sure they understand the examples, and encourages them to add to the list.

The teacher says:

> We just discussed the impact of the way others comment on or question our ideas or behavior on whether we welcome their comments or resist them. Well, others react in similar ways to how we word our comments! So please go back to your letters and try to improve the tone using the hedging words or phrases from the list.

Alternatively, if the students are comfortable swapping their letters, they can read each other's letters as if they are the intended recipients. Then, they explain how the letter made them feel and give each other feedback on where the letter may need improvement.

The students revise their letters for more effective argumentation.

The lesson can end with the teacher giving feedback on the aspects of grammar and vocabulary.

This hypothetical lesson shows how a writing lesson can start with a focus on a real-life purpose of writing (why), establish the relevance of the content of writing (what) to learners' life situations, and facilitate learning about the form of writing (how) within the context of authentic language use. The end of the lesson indicates further space for form-focused work. A major question which remains to be tackled though is "how much of a focus on the form of writing is necessary or beneficial in critical writing pedagogy?"

The idea that we would like to promote is that for writing to do its job, or in critical pedagogical terms, to have a transformative impact, the form, while important, does not have to be perfect or even almost perfect. This statement would probably strike many as outrageous a few decades ago, as public writing for the purpose of making changes used to be limited to letters to editors usually written by linguistically adept writers. Such space, therefore, would not be available to ordinary people. However, thanks to technological changes, more people are writing for authentic, social, purposes. The varied types of space for dialogue which the Internet and social networking platforms have created have enabled people of different walks of life to interact and have an impact, limited or significant, through writing. They post comments which are read and replied to as tens, hundreds, or more, read and reply to each other's posts. These posts display different levels of writing ability and language proficiency which may affect but by no means entirely determine the impact of the posts. Aware of this reality of writing in the social space, a critically-minded writing teacher can say that a little amount of writing which is superficially imperfect might help the writer accomplish a real-life goal no less effectively than a linguistically sophisticated and properly structured piece of writing. Based on this understanding and the educational goals set for a language class, the teacher can decide on how much of the instruction should be form-focused.

The sample writing lesson that we presented in this section is, as we mentioned earlier, hypothetical. In the rest of this chapter, however, we present real examples of language teachers implementing critical writing pedagogy in the classroom. These examples show a variety of ways in which critical writing can be taught and practiced. Although they may vary in how they are implemented, they all prioritize the purpose and content of writing over its form, yet they emphasize form as an important tool for the writer to accomplish the purpose and deliver the content effectively.

EXAMPLES OF CRITICAL WRITING PEDAGOGY

As the literature on critical language pedagogy does not offer many accounts of engaging young children in critical reflection and action, let's start with two examples from the context of Kindergarten, both reported by Vasquez (2004). Although these examples are situated in the English-speaking context of Canada, we believe that the language skills that Vasquez's 3- to 4-year old students are equipped with make these two examples suitable for the purpose of developing an idea about how critical writing pedagogy could be practiced with young bilingual children whose cognitive and linguistic skills are yet to develop considerably. In addition, this is a good point at which to repeat that critical writing does not always have to be syntactically or lexically demanding; there are genres in which the message can be effective even though the language may be brief, note-like, and functional, like in the case of haikus, advertisements, posters, or even graffiti.

The first example comes from a session where Vasquez (2004) facilitated a classroom discussion which included a focus on saving the rainforests. Conversations about the benefits of the timber industry for people who produce, sell, or buy wood led to a critical writing activity where students engaged in writing a letter to their parents or guardians asking them not to buy wood harvested from rainforests and developing a poster asking lumber yards not to sell such wood. An example of a letter that Vasquez presents reads, "No I No I No MOM R DAD" over a drawing of a person using an ax to cut down a tree (p. 54). This very simple child's piece of writing is the kind of literacy we would expect from a 3-year old, but, despite its simplicity and relative vagueness of the phrase, it orients critically to a problem in the world, with the visual elements enhancing the clarity and effectiveness of the message.

This example shows the student's use of their understandably limited English vocabulary and writing ability together with relevant visuals to convey an important message. Taking this activity beyond the boundaries of the classroom, the letter to the parents/guardians was included in the class newsletter, and the poster was mailed to the lumber yards in the city where they were living.

Another example reported by Vasquez (2004) was a petition that her students wrote after they noticed that some of the older children who were taking French had set up a French Café in the school and would go there with their parents. The petition was an outcome of a class discussion that the children initiated, and Vasquez facilitated, about the fairness of the situation and how they could change it. A group of the students formed a petition committee and wrote a petition letter to which they attached a sheet of paper for signatures and delivered it to the kindergarten classrooms. The petition reads, "ROOm 115. TEACHER'S V.VASQuEZ. THE [junior and senior kindergarten classes] WANT TO Go To THE French CAFE NEXT YEAR" (p. 96). While this letter is more linguistically sophisticated than the poster mentioned above, probably because it was an outcome of a collective attempt, it is still a good example of where students' limited language resources do not necessarily prevent them from engaging in transformative action. In fact, in response to this petition, the principal said that the Kindergarten students would be included in future French Cafés.

Vasquez reflects on her role in enabling students to take the above potentially transformative actions as follows:

> My role was not to tell the children what to think or how to act, but based on their inquiries, to offer alternate ways of taking action and a way of naming their world within the stance they chose to take. (p. 101)

These examples speak to the possibility of implementing critical writing tasks with second language learners who are similarly in the early stages of developing their cognitive and linguistic skills. The first example also shows that even when learners have little or no print literacy in English, they can still express their thoughts and emotions through drawings. The significance of this experience for critical language practice is that intellectual engagement with topics through visual means will prepare learners to use language as a critical tool more readily than when they have not experienced this critical engagement. Now, let's look at examples of critical writing practice with L2 learners.

Within the EFL context of Iran, Ghahremani-Ghajar and Mirhosseini (2005) present an account of Mirhosseini practicing dialogue journal writing with thirty 16-year-old male high school students in a private high school in Tehran. The students' English background was explained as follows: "Three of the students had lived in English speaking countries for one, three, and five years, and 25 of them had attended private language institutes for at least one and at most eight years" (p. 288). The students wrote journal entries on topics of their choosing on a weekly basis. Mirhosseini encouraged them to focus more on expressing their ideas and emotions than on vocabulary or grammar although he would sometimes highlight the role of language forms in effective communication of ideas. Students were allowed to use Farsi words when their English vocabulary knowledge did not enable them to express themselves well. Mirhosseini read and responded to the journal entries every week, focusing mostly on the content and less often on language forms. He engaged with the content of his students' writing by commenting on the ideas expressed, answering the questions raised, and asking questions to encourage critical thinking. His feedback on their language use was mostly indirect and sometimes direct and explicit.

The students wrote about various topics ranging from what they were doing in the class to social issues. They often wrote about more than one topic in each entry and wrote from less than half a page to several pages. Mirhosseini consistently highlighted the importance of going beyond descriptive writing and moving towards writing critically and creatively.

The authors' analysis of the students' journals showed a shift in their writing from mostly descriptive and personal to more critical and creative. The journals also yielded several examples of the different ways in which the students expressed their ideas and emotions in writing, which the authors considered to reflect their empowerment. Some of these examples together with the categories into which the authors classified the identified ways of self-expression are as follows:

I hate that
By the way your classes have become so boring

I think it's good
My Idea about two class of last week. For me It's good I like this teach and I think It's good for student.

I think
I believe that the best way for learning is seeing, looking, wathing [watching], and observe something.

I asked myself why
You'd told us we can write everything we like …. so why did you tell me I
was impolite in my previous journal? (pp. 290–291)

As the examples show, these students' English is still quite limited, yet they
are able to express their opinions and make critical comments.

Now, let's look at another example, this time of advanced EFL students'
experience with creative writing at a Japanese two-year college with a foreign language curricular emphasis. Stillar (2013) had his students write
journal entries and letters as if they were individuals or communities marginalized or ignored in the students' culture in order for them to develop
a more empathetic understanding and critical awareness of those individuals' or groups' experiences. He encouraged the students to research
and read about the topic for a better understanding of their new identity.
Stillar assigned the writing exercises to the students as homework, which
they had one week to complete. After completing each writing assignment,
the students read their journal entry in the class and shared how they felt
about the writing.

One of the topics that the students wrote about was "a day in the life of a
North Korean." Stillar (2013) explains that this topic was selected because
the tensions between North Korea and Japan had led to feelings of fear
and hatred among many Japanese citizens. Such feelings were reinforced
by the Japanese media which, on a regular basis, would expose people to
news on North Korean threats, and limited attempts to distinguish between
the North Korean people and their leaders.

The discussion following the reading of their journal entries showed that
writing from the North Korean people's perspective enabled the students
to show sympathy for them, express awareness that North Koreans cannot
be blamed for the problems in North Korea, and that the media and state
propaganda have a significant impact on people's understanding, including North Koreans'.

Another journal entry that Stillar's (2013) students wrote was from the
perspective of a member of the Sea Shepherd Conservation Society. This
environmental activist group protests Japanese whaling operations, and
its multiple criticisms of and confrontations with Japanese whaling vessels
have been covered in a negative light in the Japanese media which present this group as a terrorist organization whose activities stem from racial
discrimination. The Western media, however, portrays a positive picture
of this group as heroic saviors of the marine ecosystem. The students'
journals reflected the students' critical view on whaling and its impact on
the balance of the marine ecosystem, their awareness of the government's
intention to justify this activity, and their emphasis on the necessity of a
collective attempt to prohibit it. The ensuing class discussion, however,

showed other interesting aspects of the students' reflections on whaling as reported by Stillar:

> The majority of the students were upset with the anti-whaling groups only because the group appeared to be anti-Japanese and not because the students wanted to eat whale. In fact, all the students admitted to not being particularly fond of whale meat. However, when I directed the topic to tuna conservation, many students claimed that tuna was an integral part of their culture and that they would rather see the marine ecosystem harmed than be deprived of delicious tuna. The discussion finished on the topic of the price individuals must bear in order to protect the environment. (p. 170)

The excerpts that Stillar reports from the students' journals clearly show their highly developed English skills, which he builds on for including a focus on complex topics, such as those mentioned above, and a sophisticated treatment of these topics in journals and classroom discussions. However, unlike Ghahramani-Ghajar and Mirhosseini (2005), Stillar does not mention how, if at all, language forms were focused on in the writing activities and the ensuing classroom discussions.

Another example of critical writing practice that we believe is worth reporting here comes from Hong Kong, where English, while an official language, is not spoken (well) by everyone. In an advanced undergraduate English for Business Communications class, Chun (2016) presented his students with a fictional workplace scenario focused on racial discrimination and tasked them with writing a business memo, taking on the role of the Director of Human Resources, to their staff members. Below is the scenario:

> As the Asia-based Director of Human Resources of Global Translation Services (GTS), you have become increasingly concerned by the national media attention over the last few days. It was recently revealed by the media that GTS has been reported to the Equal Opportunities Commission (EOC) on the grounds of racial discrimination. A Malaysian woman had applied for a position in the Hong Kong office and she was informed in the first-round of interviews that 'she'd never be hired if she wore her headdress to work'. The candidate, who is a permanent resident of Hong Kong, has lodged a complaint with the EOC office, citing the claim in the EOC's website (http://www.eoc.org.hk) that "It's against the law to discriminate against any potential or current employee because s/he wears clothing that is required by her/his religion." (p. 190)

Based on this scenario, Chun asked his students to write a memo of up to 250 words, as the Director of Human Resources, explaining the case reported in the scenario as well as two other cases of discrimination, related to gender, race, disability, and so forth, that they have had to address in the company. They had to emphasize the company's policies against discrimination and also ask the staff not to respond to any media contact regarding the reported case.

After presenting the scenario and the task, Chun added a linguistic focus to the activity by outlining the specific moves his students could use in the genre of a memo. A move is a particular linguistic or rhetorical pattern or structure which performs a communicative function in writing or speaking. Chun summarized the moves that he encouraged the students to use in a three-paragraph memo as follows:

1. What is the main topic or issue and why is this important?
2. What do you want from me?
3. What are the advice, recommendation, solution and/or directives offered? (p. 191)

Chun (2016) proceeds to describe, in detail, possible ways to develop students' understanding of the move structure of this particular business memo so they can write a compelling one. His account, below, is a great example of what we discussed earlier in this chapter. A really important feature of critical writing practice is incorporating the more conventional focus on the lexical and grammatical choices with the higher-level structure of the genre (moves) within a critical writing task which is itself meaningful to students and potentially relevant to their lives.

This can be done by demonstrating to the students several ways in which a story can be presented. For example, are the sentences written in an active voice, foregrounding agency, as in "The staff behaviour in this incident is intolerable and I will seek appropriate measures to reprimand those responsible", or the passive voice, "This recent incident reported by the news media is a reminder that such practices are not to be tolerated in this company"? Students can write several versions of the opening paragraph by using both the active and passive and comparing what effects these might have on the intended reader—the staff members reading this memo.

This leads to the second move of 'what do you want from me?' in which teachers outline with students what recipients of this email would expect from the Human Resources Director.... This necessarily entails constructing the subject position of the reader (staff members) of the email in certain ways, such as in "You are hereby instructed not to talk to the media regarding this latest incident", and the subject position of the writer of the email as well, for example, "I am greatly alarmed at these egregious violations by my staff". These lexical and grammatical choices not only reflect a certain power dynamic in the relationship between the writer (Human Resource Director) and the reader (general staff), which is already in place of course, but it also serves to reproduce and reinforce it. Perhaps these power relationships can be somewhat mitigated through the third move of the closing paragraph featuring advice, recommendations, solutions and/ or directives. For example, it might be illustrative to highlight with students the use of the first-person pronoun "I" with the plural "We" in constructing possible adversarial or solidary relations in a business email between writer and reader. Having students consider the implications of a sentence beginning with "I am deeply disappointed in the recent violations committed by your fellow staff members" versus "We should strive together to create and maintain a work environment in which all are accorded respect and recognition" can prompt discussions around particular discourses of oppositional stances and communal well-being in professional and institutional contexts. (pp. 191–192)

In addition to incorporating a focus on formal features of writing, Chun (2016) suggests encouraging students, now equipped with an understanding of the specific demands of writing in the genre "business memo," to develop a critical understanding of the structure of this genre and take informed control of it. Earlier in the chapter, we briefly highlighted the importance of raising students' awareness of the fact that genres are themselves social constructions and a manifestation of power, and, therefore, ideally they should be revisited and challenged. In Chun's critical literacy practice, this awareness-raising involved encouraging students to reflect on why and how business documents are written in such a formidable language and may reinforce power imbalances and to seek alternative ways of narrating and formulating ideas and concepts in such genres.

Chun (2016) ends this rich account of critical writing practice by suggesting additional activities which we believe are worth including here.

1. Have the students bring in some examples of work-related emails from their countries and compare the move structure—the specific steps a writer takes in trying to accomplish the communicative purpose of the message—with the structure of a business and/or work-related email featured in curriculum materials.
2. With the students, discuss possible ways in which the dominant form and structure of a business email prevalent in predominantly English-speaking countries can be redesigned to incorporate elements of local cultural and linguistic practices.
3. Have students write a company policy in which the company's hiring practices are stated in support of acknowledgement and recognition of applicants' diversities (p. 194).

The examples of critical writing practice we have looked at so far represent most of the critical literacy literature in terms of the types of writing activities used, namely reflective journals and writing letters. There are a few published accounts, however, which present other genres of writing that lend themselves as well to critical literacy practice.

One example comes from Habulembe (2007) who engaged his students in project proposal writing. Habulembe took his 45 high school senior students to the District Resource Center in Monze, Zambia, where they engaged in a one-week workshop to develop a project proposal in response to a major health concern in their country, namely HIV/AIDS. The workshop started with brainstorming led by the District Resource Center Coordinator who asked the students to independently generate five questions about the topic. The questions were then collected, read, and categorized, and five representative questions were selected for further brainstorming:

1. What do the letters HIV/AIDS stand for?
2. What is HIV/AIDS?
3. How or when is HIV/AIDS transmitted?
4. Are students "affected" or "infected" by HIV/AIDS?
5. What should students do to address HIV/AIDS? (p. 38)

The students responded to the questions in writing. Their responses were evaluated, and better responses were developed into one answer to each question. Using these responses and a project proposal sample obtained from the UNICEF office in Zambia, the students generated their own formal HIV/AIDS project proposal through a drafting and revision process which took four days. Identifying themselves as the "Anti-AIDS Association (AAA)—Monze Boarding High School, Monze, Zambia," the students included the following sections in their relatively detailed proposal:

- Mission statement
- Problem statement
- Objectives
- Target group
- Project sustainability
- Organization
- Description of Anti-AIDS Association
- Budget Estimates

Habulembe concludes by highlighting the impact of the project on the students' English writing skills, although he does not discuss any supportive evidence, and them developing the ability to apply these skills as the next generation to combat HIV/AIDS.

Grigoryan and King (2008) focused on another less-commonly used genre in critical writing practice, the "advertisement." In this case, Grigoryan and King put attention on "adbusters," which they define as "a form of media that looks like an advertisement but actually opposes the values and assumptions presented by a corporation through its advertising campaigns" (p. 3).[1] Unlike the examples of critical writing instruction mentioned so far which all report on real classroom practice, Grigoryan and King do not go beyond proposing a lesson plan. The aim of the lesson plan they describe is to enhance learners' critical media literacy through an academic writing lesson to use with college or university students. An example of an adbuster is an advertisement which shows the negative side-effects of taking weight loss pills like organ damage or depression, in response to advertisements which promote such pills through images of, mostly, women who have taken them and are therefore healthy and happy.

Grigoryan and King (2008) propose a few steps to follow in this type of lesson. The lesson starts with students' free-writing in reaction to what they see in an advertisement. Then, they share and discuss their writing in groups. Following this initial engagement with the advertisement, they further analyze it by reflecting on the elements of the advertisement and identifying its purpose(s), underlying assumptions, and likely consequences. Based on this analysis, they engage in writing about and critiquing the core, explicit message of the advertisement and its hidden assumptions. This critical engagement with the advertisement prepares the students to then decide on the theme to focus on in the adbuster they will develop in response to the advertisement. This stage will involve another phase of writing where students reflect, in a few paragraphs, on the theme they have selected for their adbuster and the messages they identified in the examined advertisement that they want to challenge. Following this reflective writing, students decide on the images they will use in their adbuster and again present their thoughts and reasons in writing. Through a process of peer review, they read and comment on each other's choices and written reflections. So does their teacher. Based on the feedback, students improve their writing and design their adbusters which they present to the class. Their presentations and written reflections can be subjected to self-, peer-, and teacher-assessment.

A few variations of the lesson proposed by Grigoryan and King (2008) could be implemented. For example, especially with students whose English is limited, the writing component could be reduced to one or two paragraphs, a few sentences, or even only notes, each a legitimate type of writing worth practicing. Focused writing work could be done in which students choose words, phrases, or sentences to include in their adbusters. Another way to design and conduct this lesson, if learners' proficiency allows, would be to focus on the analysis of an advertisement and writing a compelling analysis, for example in the form of an argumentative essay, without requiring students to develop an adbuster. Such practice does not have to be limited to high proficiency learners only. The teacher in Hobbs et al. (2015), also discussed in the reading chapter, conducted advertising analysis activities with U.S. high-school immigrant ESL learners whose English proficiency was low. Using critical reading questions provided by the teacher, the students analyzed advertisements they chose from a website provided by the teacher in groups and wrote their analyses in paragraphs. After receiving the teacher's feedback on their grammar, they revised their group analysis and posted them online. Then, they presented their analysis to the class and received teacher feedback on their pronunciation and the ideas they expressed. What makes this activity a rich learning experience is the combined focus on critical literacy and language skills, a combination which we have emphasized a few times in this chapter.

Our last example comes from Lau (2012) who reported on her collaboration with a teacher in conducting a poster activity, among other critical literacy activities, to improve the students' critical literacy skills. We mentioned earlier that Vasquez's (2004) students also developed a poster in a critical writing activity. However, this focus was inevitably brief as Vasquez herself did not report on this experience in detail. Therefore, we believe that the idea of developing a poster as critical writing practice is worth a more in-depth consideration here, at least partly because for L2 writing, posters are an excellent target genre, as it is a genre that does not demand highly developed language skills and yet can still be action-oriented and provide a chance for learners to express themselves on topics important to them and their contexts.

Lau (2012) reports on a Grade 7–8 class in Canada, where 15 students experimented with poster writing. Most of these students were from China, had a beginner to lower intermediate English proficiency and had been living in Canada for less than one year. The students were taught basic comprehension skills followed by critical literacy strategies. They began to complain about being bullied at school because of their limited English, which led the teacher of the class, Ms. Li, and Lau to change their original plan and include a focus on bullying so that the students explore the issue in depth and develop anti-bullying strategies.

The lesson on bullying started with reading *Marianthe's Story* (Brandenberg, 1998), which is about a new ESL immigrant's challenges. The first writing activity involved students writing about a bullying incident they experienced or witnessed, followed by a group analysis of the incident. In their analysis, the students were to identify the bully, the target, and/or the bystander and the reason or motivation behind their behavior. In groups, students then rewrote the incident describing a more active and transformative way of dealing with the situation. "By rewriting the incidents, they began to see a possibility of change, that they could actually assert themselves and use the appropriate language to insist on a more respectful and fair treatment from their peers" (Lau, 2012, p. 326). This was followed by students designing posters where they encouraged a target audience of their choosing (i.e., the bully, the target, or the bystander) to take appropriate action to tackle school bullying. To prepare students to design effective posters, the class studied how different textual and visual design features help convey the message in advertisements. The students made attempts to use these design features in their posters. One of the posters that Lau presented in the article has the headline "Don't Be Scared. There's always HELP!" in a large font size. Under the headline, there is an image of a closed office door with a notice on it which reads, "Bullied Other People." and a big cross on the door. Four lines of advice are at the bottom of the image. One, as an example, reads, "You can choose go to tell your teacher someone has bullied you" (Lau, 2012, p. 326).

CONCLUSION

The literature on critical (L2) writing practice, as we previously mentioned, is far from extensive. Yet, the published accounts, with some reported in this chapter, contribute valuable insight into how we can teach writing critically despite the dominance of a mainstream view of second language education which encourages teaching writing in a way that rather exclusively aims at language skills development or, if treating language in its context of use, then often maintains an uncritical and safe approach.

While some of the examples did not report including an explicit focus on language forms, a few showed what an effective integration of focused language work into a critical writing lesson may look like in practice and, therefore, reinforce the perspective that critical language pedagogy does not exclude language practice; rather, it can arguably do a better job of fostering language development because it establishes the personal and social relevance and significance of such practice and, therefore, engages students in the learning process more effectively. Some of the examples also showed that it is possible to practice critical language pedagogy with young learners and those with limited English proficiency.

NOTE

1. The word "adbuster" comes from the name of a Canadian-based not-for-profit organization, called The Adbusters Media Foundation, which implements design and media strategies aimed at resisting and transforming the consumerist culture that this foundation believes advertisements in general cultivate.

CHAPTER 6

GRAMMAR

INTRODUCTION

Direct instruction in grammar (sometimes called "focus on forms," supported and organized by a "structural syllabus") is the starting point of many second language teachers' practices and drives their most common classroom procedures. Thus, if critical language pedagogy is to start where many language teachers are, we (your authors) must tackle this area. A teacher might be interested in, or indeed dissatisfied with, their teaching of grammar for a number of reasons. Here we assume you might be dissatisfied with it because it does not involve a critical dimension. So the question we all may share an interest in addressing is, "How do we teach grammar critically?"

When teachers say they are teaching grammar, they may mean that they are teaching a foreign (or second) language in more or less a grammar-translation style, in which case they are working with a structural syllabus, using the L1 extensively to explain grammar points, and indeed probably doing a fair bit of translation, and there is not much actual use of the L2 by students for anything even approaching communication. This kind of teaching will typically also include vocabulary along with grammar as the main aspects of language taught.

Starting Points in Critical Language Pedagogy, pp. 115–138
Copyright © 2022 by Information Age Publishing

Having established this sort of language teaching as the focus of our initial discussion here, we can go on to say that the traditional or conventional view of second language vocabulary and grammar instruction has a number of features that are significantly different from what a critical view of language and of teaching would suggest. First, language is being treated as made up of static entities, as if it merely consisted of a number of grammatical and lexical facts. And second, as in most traditional teaching, these facts must be transferred to students. This is done by way of teaching "grammar rules" (and providing opportunities to practice using them with language items, such as sentences, not to mention vocabulary). And overall in this perspective, grammar is taught out of context, and as a result, students do not go much beyond a context-reduced grasp of the basic structural and semantic understanding and use of grammatical items. This is, then, what critical pedagogy calls a "banking" approach to teaching. It focuses on the transmission of knowledge, not the fostering of development, unlike even conventional mainstream views of learning L2 forms, in terms of skill development (e.g., what Larsen-Freeman (2001) calls "grammaring" in the case of grammar instruction).

WHAT DOES THE CRITICAL LANGUAGE PEDAGOGY LITERATURE SAY ABOUT TEACHING GRAMMAR?

To answer this question, we begin by turning once again to Auerbach and Wallerstein's (1986) classic critical ESL pedagogy textbook, which was developed at least partly to be an example of what could be done in critical language pedagogy. Its emphasis is primarily communication but the authors often include a section, usually secondary in a given unit, in which sentence structures are focused upon. Another one of our senior figures in this area, Hilary Janks, in her materials and explanations of how to teach language critically, often focuses on certain grammatical structures as implicated in deceptive language use and needing to be exposed by a critical perspective on texts (e.g., Janks, 1991). Critical language pedagogy specialist Brian Morgan (2004) shares a useful quote from Janks on this topic: he noticed that she says "The critical approach provides students with a reason for mastering the forms" (p. 196). That is to say, if classroom tasks are chosen to correspond to problems and issues that are meaningful to students, they (or at least many of the tasks the students do) will call for accurate command of a range of grammatical structures and vocabulary items. At the very least, students and the teacher will inquire into the real-world language needs that these real-world tasks involve, including a reasonably high need for appropriate and accurate grammar.

Terry Osborn, a specialist in critical language pedagogy for world languages, has provided us with a broad sketch of the role of a grammatically-organized syllabus for critical language teaching purposes (Osborn, 2006). As a world languages specialist, he has a perspective in which substantial cultural content (about the cultures associated, for example, with languages such as Japanese, French, Chinese, or Spanish) is particularly appropriate; a thematic strand involving culture is a major element of many world languages courses in U.S. high schools and universities. Thus, even while grammar and vocabulary are being focused on, he believes (and explains) that this can be done while focusing also on themes that critical language pedagogy would also favor. He therefore approaches the matter with 15 themes in mind, grouped in four major areas: identity, "social architecture" (that is, the structures of society), language choices, and activism. The 15, grouped under those four areas, are:

- Identity, which includes Affiliation; Conflict, struggle, and discrimination; and Socioeconomic class
- Social architecture, which includes What we believe: Ideology; Historical perspectives: To the victors; Schools and languages: Hidden curricula; and Media: Entertainment
- Language choices, which includes Beyond manners: Register and political or power relations; Whose culture is whose? Hybridity; Media: Journalism and politicians; Who is in control? Hegemony
- Activism, which includes Law, rights, resistance, and marginalization.

In addressing these, he is quite clear that specific grammatical forms will need to be worked on, and that some forms are more likely to be found in connection with some of these rather than others.

In another case, critical ESL exponent Morgan and his students drew on pre-existing communicative grammar materials (Jones, 1992). Morgan (2004) comments that, as the teacher, he felt he should

> focus on providing students with accessible descriptions, clear examples of target structures, and useful practice activities. Yet I also wanted to organize this lesson in ways that reflected the complex social and political contexts influencing my students. I didn't want to present these grammar forms as closed meanings within a graded hierarchy of structures, functions, or tasks. Instead, I wanted to conceptualize this lesson ... as a social practice. (p. 162)

Specifically, Morgan links the lesson content to issues of identity and investment, concerning his students' relationship to their original homes in

Hong Kong and their new homes in Canada. And throughout, he refers to this grammar lesson as having a grammar consciousness-raising intention. So, Morgan is reporting a case where students' identity-related and other real world issues drive their interest in, and need to understand, modality. An active role for the student, established critical inquiry-based classroom procedures, existing conventional reference materials and easily accessible authentic materials meaningful to the students and their community, as well as a skillful teacher, all combine to enable a critical pedagogy grammar lesson or unit to be jointly created by teacher and students.

At one level, the answer, then, to "how do you teach grammar critically?" is simple. There always has to be content in a language lesson. The critical teacher will try hard to make that content relevant and to put the students in an active role with respect to it. One can also recognize that most pre-scriptive syllabuses these days are not "single-strand" syllabuses in any case: grammar is typically coupled with notions and functions, vocabulary, or at least themes and topics. Simple present tense can indeed be coupled with inanimate objects of little particular personal relevance ("this is a pen"), but, as Osborn (2006, p. 62) implies, this can just as easily be coupled with the initial steps in articulating basic identity "(Who am I, who are we?); affiliation (Who are we? Who are they?); conflict, struggle, and discrimination; and socioeconomic class." Once socioeconomic class is included in the content of the course (something notable for its absence in mainstream textbooks ("we are poor; they are rich"), we are already on the way to a critical pedagogy ("Why are we poor?").

Kourosh shared a significant moment in a grammar lesson where he invited his students to share their perceptions of whether the idea presented in a sentence they read in a grammar activity applied to their local context:

> One of replacement drills in the class yesterday ... was the sentence "We acknowledge the boys just like the girls". Here instead of giving my direct thought on the subject I ask the class in a nonchalant way: "Do you believe women are acknowledged the same as men in Iran?" and I got a loud "NO!" It was surprising since my adult students are all male. Didn't push it much afterwards and continued with the drill but I think that loud "No" was also surprising to many of them as it was to me.

In addition, grammar itself, as a form of explicit knowledge of the language, can and should be taught critically. In that sense, we are referring more to the processes of instruction, that should be interactive, participatory, and dialogic. Later in the chapter, we will look at an example of teaching grammar dialogically reported by Jones and Chen (2016).

FOCUS ON FORM OVER MEANING AND USE

The vast literature on form-focused instruction clearly shows how effective an explicit focus on language forms, including grammar, is in language learning. This strand of literature encourages situating such a focus within the communicative context of language use. Perhaps a good example of this view is a series of four textbooks called *Grammar Dimensions* (series editor: Diane Larsen-Freeman), which teach grammar through the three dimensions of form, meaning, and use. Even where form-focused instruction acknowledges the usefulness, or sometimes the necessity, of a pre-planned focus on linguistic forms and developing students' explicit knowledge, it does not deny the benefit of a combined focus on the meaning and use of the forms to learn them.

In the chapter on writing, we discussed form, meaning, and use in terms of *how* we write, *what* we write, and *why* we write, and argued that in a critical language classroom, a focus on *why* and *what* should be a prerequisite to a consideration of *how*. But what do we mean by "prerequisite?" We understand that teachers often need to incorporate a pre-planned focus on linguistic forms, and in some contexts, like in a class entirely focused on grammar, they should do so more than often. But this need does not contradict a focus on *why* and *what* being a prerequisite to a consideration of *how*, because by "prerequisite" we do not necessarily mean "prior." We simply mean that a focus on use and meaning should "inform" engagement with form. In its strongest manifestation, this focus may indeed serve as an explicit driver of a lesson, starting it and maintained throughout, but, alternatively, it could form a less explicit background to engagement with form, or simply *be* in the background of such engagement and brought to the foreground when necessary or helpful. We believe that no matter how a focus on use and meaning takes place, an English lesson cannot afford to lack this focus. But, how is this discussion relevant at all to critical grammar pedagogy?

The agreed key argument in favor of a combined focus on form, meaning, and use is that it enhances learners' ability to use language in context. There can be some criticality to this argument, where the use to which we put language may have a significant impact on individuals or society. An example we discussed in the chapter on writing was teaching how to write an argumentative essay. In this example, we explained that a teacher can establish the relevance of this genre to real life by drawing students' attention to situations where, after some evaluation, they regard their own opinions to be, in some respects, more valid than their friends', classmates', and so forth, and therefore would like to encourage them to consider their opinions. Learning how to present an argument in an essay in the classroom will translate into effective reasoning as a life skill.

Let us take this discussion beyond a focus on the benefits of a combined focus on form, meaning, and use, and shed some light on the risks involved in teaching grammar where form receives an exclusive focus or takes priority *over* meaning and use. We all agree that even though grammatical accuracy and complexity generally increase communicative power, it should still be informed by a consideration of the communicative and social functions of the forms in question. When decontextualized, a focus on form can cultivate a harmful culture of encouraging students to produce complex structures regardless of the communicative intent and attaching value to students' writing which showcases grammatical complexity. Worse, this may lead to looking down on students' works if they involve the use of simple language forms, failing to appreciate their success in effective communication which is in part because of that very simplicity.

Encouraging students to produce complex language for the sake of linguistic complexity is not in line with a critical understanding of language and language pedagogy. In fact, it is common knowledge that simplicity and clarity of language facilitate communication. An emphasis on using complex language which is not grounded in a concern for effective meaning making is indicative of a narrow understanding of language which does not take account of the social context in which it is situated and the real-life functions it is originally meant to serve. Teaching in such a form-obsessed manner involves a more serious risk, namely that students exposed to this approach are likely to adopt a similarly harmful and myopic approach in how they judge their own and their peers' language use.

Arman still vividly remembers a few conversations he had with his students who had been led to attach value to the use of complex language regardless of its intended function. In a graduate Academic English class, Arman tasked his students with giving feedback on paragraphs written by their peers. While circulating among the groups, Arman noticed one student asking his peer why she had only used simple present tense in a paragraph instead of a variety of tenses and why her sentences were not complex. To help him understand that a focus on meaning and ideas should be the basis of a focus on grammar and structure, Arman asked him whether using other tenses or complex sentences would have helped her express the content more effectively. In response, the student emphasized the importance of using complex language and a variety of tenses regardless of the specific purpose or context in which complex language would be conducive to communication. Arman tried to explain to him about the importance of taking the content and the context of language use into account when making grammatical choices. Another experience Arman thinks is worth mentioning here is that in an undergraduate general English course, in response to Arman's emphasis on the importance of clarity of expression and simplicity of language when more complex structures are not necessary, a student recalled another lecturer telling them that he would be "offended" if a student submitted an essay with simple language. Arman could not help explicitly expressing his disapproval of his colleague's view as illegitimate and indefensible.

A CRITICAL APPROACH TO GRAMMAR THAT FOCUSES ON STUDENT AGENCY AS OPPOSED TO MEANINGFUL TASKS

In this book, we are continually looking for the first steps, the baby steps. In that case, the above accounts are not quite elementary enough, perhaps. They involve learners who are sufficiently competent with the language to have a perspective on the use of structures like the passive (or direct and indirect speech, which is the example covered in Wilkinson and Janks (1998) and reported later in the chapter). Perhaps there is an earlier phase that is possible, in which the emphasis is less on the content that the grammar structure might transmit, and is more concerned with the class itself.

Shifting the perception and practice of the class from the teacher-driven, potentially authoritarian form that is conventional to one closer to Freire's idea of teacher-students and student-teachers engaged in a shared learning and investigating practice would also be the goal in a developing critical pedagogy. It is not a goal that is easy to achieve when starting from fully conventional (student) expectations. So, one could ask, "What might the initial phase look like when placed in the context of a conventional grammar class or part of an ELT lesson which focused on grammar?"

One useful if non-critical response to the question is, "Just put the students in a more active role." Grammar teaching specialist Thornbury (1999, p. 42) describes using a "jigsaw" technique. In completing a fill-in-the-blanks worksheet on use of the English article (a/an/the), students are provided with grammar rules for the article. (There are very many, as you know!). But the rules are divided into three, and allocated to each of the members of groups of three. Students then have to work together, and explain, dispute with, and teach each other, to complete the grammar activity. Relatedly, though at a very advanced level, Wright (1994) is a rare example which provides learners with examples of language, including forms, and guides learners in investigating them. It could perhaps be mined for critical grammar activities, though it does not itself have an inherently critical edge.

This would be a start, heightening student agency. Building on it, our next answer would be similar to the brief account provided by Edelsky and Johnson (2009) of a U.S. elementary ESL class. In it, a teacher (Johnson) worked with her class using obligatory, required textbook and curricula materials. They were state-mandated but she had professional reservations concerning them. As she was not closely supervised, she was able to share her concerns with the class, and after discussion of what students and teacher felt about the material, they proceeded to use *some* of it, unchallenged, and other parts in a more distanced manner, and they even spent some time investigating why it was required.

This is broadly consistent also with the advice Shor (1992, Ch. 3) gives about the legitimate need to teach conventional academic material in a class in which the teacher has a critical pedagogy philosophy. The point is to make the subject matter itself the subject of investigation, rather than take it for granted or use it as if it is inherently legitimate and legitimated by the administrative structures that deliver it to us in the form of a textbook or syllabus. Once the material has been placed in the status of "under inspection," it has less power and the students and teacher have more power over it; at least intellectual power, even if the material has administrative power, in a sense.

In addition, one can consider the interactive and negotiated aspects of working with conventional grammar exercises. If the class *as a whole* decides and agrees to perform certain possibly tedious but administratively-mandated translation exercises, say, or verb-transforming exercises, or sentence-constructing exercises, then (Arman and I think) that the class is already one step further towards a critical grammar class than it was when the teacher *did not* provide the students with that much choice and exercise of at least a minimal amount of authority over the material. The importance of learner choice is very important (and also comes up in recent discussions of grammar teaching: Cullen, 2008).

Finally, as we may have said before, a language class has to be "about" something. Even if isolated sentences are to be constructed, the sentences still refer to something and can carry implicit assumptions (*the boy kicked the girl*) or can be a site of resistance (*the revolutionary kicked the dictator/ the language teacher kicked the textbook out of the window*). Masoud, who had to cover a lot of structural material in his course, commented as follows:

> Sometimes we really don't have a choice. Just take a look at the syllabus of this grammar course I teach:
>
> Grammar PRE-TOEFL
> Session Lessons
> 1 PRESENT TENSE
> 2 PAST TENSE
> 3 FUTURE TENSE
> 4 Nouns and Pronouns
> 5 Parts of a Sentence

6 Prepositions

7 Articles

8 Comparatives and Superlatives

9 Word Order and Word Form

10 Final Test

Just in the very first session, they expect me to teach the present tense, including simple present, present progressive, present perfect, and present perfect progressive. I have to teach them all in 90 minutes! The students are pre-intermediate or at best intermediate and many parts of the lessons are totally new for them. It HAS to be a teacher-fronted class.

But I think even this class of mine has a little bit of a critical attitude. I use power point presentations for teaching grammar and, in addition to the funny pictures that I add to my slides to make the lessons less boring, I try to add local and sometimes politically-charged sentences and pictures and encourage my students to produce similar examples. It is interesting how the sentences that students produce are infused with their values or concerns even in a grammar lesson.

This is consistent with what grammar-oriented SLA expert Ellis (1994) says: "It is the need to get meanings across and the pleasure experienced when this is achieved that provides the motivation to learn an L2" (p. 516). But this assumes that the meanings the student is expressing are important enough to want to get right. This is seldom the case in traditional (teacher-determined) grammar practice activities. Learners have very little, if any, personal investment…. Personalizing lesson content so that it is relevant to the learner could be a major factor in regaining motivation, as our teacher quoted above is suggesting. The adjustment is slight but the spin-off in terms of learner investment is likely to be significant.

But let's not neglect the difficulties too; Mitra commented in response:

The grammar points which we as teachers are supposed to teach in lower levels are simpler and this simple grammar does not leave room for us to bring up complicated discussions with regard to such complex topics as referendums for example; I mean the content (grammar points) also sometimes limits teachers who are willing to practice CP in their classes.

Managerial surveillance must also be regarded here; we are absolutely forbidden to talk about issues which are so-called sensitive.

Usually in teacher-centered systems such as what we have here, usually teachers' viewpoints dominate the discussions.

I also believe that in our context (where students and teachers come from the same community and share the same L1), issues to pick up for discussion in such Critical Pedagogy circumstances are less in number, though, not non-existent.

However, Arman, who is quite familiar with the social and institutional contexts in question, remained optimistic (when he replied, as part of that discussion):

> While I agree that managerial control is a real problem, I don't think we are totally forbidden from conducting critical tasks since even at the managerial level, some of those in charge are the reflective and critical type and therefore would allow or even encourage, though often implicitly, a critical approach to be adopted in teaching.

PEDAGOGIC GRAMMAR TERMINOLOGY

One thing the specialists we have mentioned so far say little about is their pedagogic grammar terminology and the extent to which they would make use of terms from any particular theory of grammar. In this area, our initial suggestion is to actually teach some descriptive grammar terms in the *second* language, which is probably not a common practice in EFL or LOTE classes. This may seem like introducing unnecessary vocabulary. But if students are going to inquire into the forms (and content) of language, they do need some terms of art. Practically speaking, keeping this register only in the L1 also will encourage unnecessary code-switching back to the L1. On the other hand, we recognize that in many cases substantial discussion of choice of material and issues arising would have to take place in the L1. When we are teaching knowledge about language (which at one level is what teaching grammar is), we must also be teaching knowledge about language function: critical language awareness implies critical grammar consciousness as well as critical pragmatics consciousness.

FORM BEYOND GRAMMAR:
VARIATION, DISCOURSE AND LEXICO-GRAMMAR

Although a critical pedagogy for "teaching grammar" certainly does not dismiss the idea of grammar, or the need to focus on forms when appropriate, a critical perspective on language structures does depart from one of the most characteristic, if implicit, features of standard instruction concerning language forms. It will be very important, both in terms of truth and equity as well as in regard to the active, inquiring, and critical role of the student, that the role of variation in language be introduced in a course, as soon as possible. Far from insisting on one right way and one right form, critical language teachers must alert students to the coexistence of forms, both forms with power and those without. With the increased availability of samples of authentic language, it is possible for teachers to help students find out about non-standard variants and help them inquire into the continuing and immediate nature of language change. Thus a critical perspective on teaching about the structures of a language must be embedded in critical language awareness that both students and teacher have or develop.

Another shift that a critical teacher will need to aim for, even with simple language, is to present language, even that as brief as a sentence or an utterance, as discourse. If this can be done, in the long run, it will be easier to present discourse and genres as social creations and social practices. What passes for sentence structure is also at least partly a social creation as well, but perhaps it is too big a step to present grammar itself as an outcome of social practices in the early phases of a lesson on grammar.

Going on from this, what about terminology for dealing with language as social process? Gebhard et al. (2007) have provided examples from classroom practice with ELLs, though still this is at the level of dealing with academic language. Nevertheless, we should be starting out by orienting students to the fact that language is different depending on the relationships between participants (interpersonal), whether it is being used to convey meaning or ideas (ideational), and whether it is written or spoken (textual).

EXTENDED EXAMPLES

In this section, we will look at four examples of how critical grammar pedagogy can be approached and implemented in the language classroom. The first three examples show how a selected grammar topic can be taught in a critical manner where the focus of the lesson is relevant to students' lives. The last example focuses on how the style of teaching grammar, not necessarily the grammar topic itself, can have critical features.

It is possible that the way in which we have structured this section may suggest that we consider the content and method of teaching as two separate concepts. Far from it! In fact, we would like to emphasize the usefulness of paying conscious attention to both the content and the style of teaching when developing critical grammar lessons. The reason we believe this is important is that the most typical approach to critical grammar pedagogy appears to be one which advocates using explicitly critical content. Perhaps the most well-known example of this approach is the passive voice which texts on critical discourse analysis actively use to show how grammatical choices can be politically motivated. While such content in and of itself makes a grammar lesson critical, it is still up to the teacher to decide *how* to design the lesson.

For argument's sake, it is possible for such a lesson to start with a teacher-fronted lecture on the politics of passivization followed by an activity which asks students to categorize a few sentences taken from two pieces of news on a protest into "published in a radical left outlet" and "published in a radical right outlet," where the answers are fixed and non-negotiable. You may agree that while dealing with a critical feature of language use, the design of this lesson is more didactic and traditional than dialogical and collaborative. We do not wish to present such lessons as inadequate. We simply want to show that it is possible for a lesson to have critical content but not (much of) a critically-inspired method of instruction, and, therefore, emphasize the value of developing grammar lessons which are both topically critical and methodologically critical. We also want to argue that in cases where it is less possible to approach the content of a grammar lesson from a critical perspective, it may still be possible to teach it with a critically inspired style of teaching, such as teaching in a dialogical way.

We will see that the first three examples have, in different ways and to varying degrees, both elements of critical content and critical methodology. The last example, however, highlights a case in which the content has not been, and perhaps could not be, treated critically but was taught in a critical, here dialogical, manner.

Schneider (2005) has provided a helpful, practical, discussion of grammar from a critical point of view that connects with our earlier point about critical content. In a report on his U.S. university classroom (where he was working with international students), he emphasizes the potential and necessity to link grammar with local issues. He illustrates this with a discussion of a specific grammar point that has often been identified by critical discourse analysts and critical language awareness specialists as particularly important for the development of critical reading skills: the passive. In his report, he also illustrates the importance of bringing in what is happening right now that might be relevant to students' and teacher's immediate lives. At the time he was teaching his course, there was a teaching assistant strike going on at the American university where the class was offered. Schneider reports that when his students heard about the matter, they were curious about details, so he developed a lesson on it. In the lesson, he taught some relevant vocabulary, for example, "'contract negotiations,' 'to file unfair labour practices,' and 'bargaining.'" He put together a handout based on some real extracts from "quotations from the local and campus newspapers, and from some official statements made by both the TA [Teachers Assistant] union and the university" (p. 300). Then he made a worksheet that asked students to make simple judgments about the extracts and quotations. He says that he "asked students to determine the source of each statement: the university (U), a student (S), a member of the TA union (TA), or a newspaper (N)" (p. 300).

So the worksheet was made of elements like the following:

After months of unsuccessful contract negotiations, the union representing teaching assistants, readers and tutors has decided to strike. The union [...] represents 11,000 employees on all [university] campuses ... **(N)**

The planned strike comes after a one-day walk-out by [union] members in October. At [our campus], where more than 1,400 academic student employees are union members, TAs didn't show up for 36 out of 311 classes scheduled to meet that day. Eleven of the classes were taught by a substitute and 25 were cancelled. **(N)**

I'm disappointed that they believe this is something they need to do. **(U)** (p. 300)

Returning now to our discussion of how to teach grammar from a critical standpoint, we can see that here, in the first phase of the lesson, the teacher asks the students to identify some examples of the grammar point that is the focus of the lesson, with the examples taken from real contexts concerning the immediate situation of the students and their teacher. After recognition of grammar examples, the next teaching point concerns the communicative function of the grammar point. The students are treated as having some knowledge; their views on the matter are sought and considered by the teacher, and held up for consideration by the class as a whole.

Then in the next exercise, the teacher (Schneider) provided another short worksheet, in which he had altered some of the original sentences. The task was to compare the altered sentences with the originals, and say what the differences are. They then went on to some more controlled exercises. Schneider comments,

This meant moving out of our community context for a time, but I did not want the students to leave class with a critical awareness of why speakers and writers might use passive voice without an understanding of the structure's sentence-level mechanics—because throughout the academic quarter I had observed many instances of incorrectly formed passive constructions in student writing, and I felt that some controlled practice would help those students who were still struggling (like when and where to use "been" and "being"). (p. 303)

The penultimate phase of the lesson was what is often called "controlled practice" and is thus quite conventional. The final phase of Schneider's (2005) lesson was to return to what he describes as the "community context," from which the grammar focus was originally taken, and discuss the topic some more. (A somewhat similar pattern can be found in at least one other item in the small literature on critical teaching of grammar: Wilkinson &

Janks, 1998, and see Huh (2016) for a model for combining conventional formal L2 instruction with critical L2 instruction in an EFL context.)

It is worth noting that "community," which is the key word here, sounds like more than the context many talk about in ELT. To us, "community" conveys a sense of the context being immediate to the learners, its being part of their immediate life situations and concerns. The topics which are used as the springboard in the grammar lessons reported both by Morgan and by Schneider are immediately relevant and significant to these authors' students. And we think it is a big advantage of a critical lesson for learners to be dealing with those issues where and while they are taking the lesson.

Following on from the matter of context, Mowla, one of our teachers, provided an extended example of his use of context to situate grammar-focused instruction. This example arises directly from the oppressed conditions of the students and the teacher's awareness. Our teacher said that his lesson followed one of the discussions provided by our online class and the article by Schneider (2005) that we included in it.

> Teaching grammar through community issues is an interesting work which has inspired me to take what is relevant to my students as a point of departure and then move beyond the immediate context to relate the issues to the broader context. I mean we can begin from [the] local community and then situate the problem within the context of the whole city, country, the world.

> As you [Arman] noted, sometimes it is difficult for us to take our materials to class. However, teacher talk, whether in written or oral form, can make up for that. That is, we can situate teaching grammar within our community context by producing proper examples. To pave the way for our students to reflect upon the issues, we can write them on the board.

> For instance, [in] my context, a large number of people are having difficulty putting ... bread on the table due to the economic sanctions imposed on the country. When the President ... came to power, he firmly promised to improve the economic conditions; however, he has not fulfilled his promise yet. Even [worse], the price of some vital goods such as bread soared up.

> I couldn't prepare enough materials to take to class owing to some restrictions. Anyway, the other day I was teaching "although, though, even though". I started the class by posing some questions about the economic situations of their families. Then, I drew their attention to the promises which the President made. (Of course, it would have been great if I could have displayed the President's talk, but we are deprived of the facilities.) We reached the point that he strongly promised to make the condition better, [but] he has not managed to do so.

Afterwards, I wrote on the board:
.... *the president firmly promised to improve the economic conditions, he has not done so.*

I asked them about the word we need to complete the blank. Their answer was "agarche" (means although). Next, I wrote the first clause on the board and let them complete the rest.

Although the president promised to improve the economic conditions,

.......Some of the sentences were

Everything is getting worse and worse.

We have a difficult life.

My parents are working hard.

The most tragic part was when I realized that a large number of them were working in unsafe workshops.

I work at night in a furniture workshop.

We inferred that "although, though, and even though" are used to talk about what runs counter to our expectations. Finally, I asked my students to think about the reasons behind why the president has not succeeded to fulfill his promise and make the situation better. [Students] were asked to make sentences like:

Although the president firmly promised to make the economic conditions better, he has not fulfilled his promise yet because ....

However, a problem which I have faced while using serious topics to teach grammar is that students place a higher value on the message they are going to get across and consequently pay less attention to the form. I mean this is the meaning which most probably wins the competition for attention. [Accordingly] I have tried [to] be lenient with the linguistic problems while in the grammar stage and offer gradual feedback in the post-grammar phase.

We think this is a good example of a class mostly focusing on specific forms of the target language which at the same time derives its content from (as the teacher says) serious topics. We would describe it as having a critical perspective and yet one by no means imposed by the teacher, but actually arising from the class's real life context, concerns, and issues.

Wilkinson and Janks (1998)[1] reported their experience of teaching reported speech in a critical manner. In this example, unlike the previous two, the choice of grammar focus was not reported to have arisen directly from an immediate concern of the class. Yet, as explained in more detail later, the content of the grammar lesson was socially relevant. Although Wilkinson and Janks's students were South African high school students who spoke English "as a main language" (p. 183), we believe that a similar approach can be adopted with intermediate or higher-level ESL/EFL learners. The authors stated that, despite the social and ideological effects of speech reporting, this grammatical topic is often taught with little relevance to its real-life use in South African schools they examined. This is probably generally the case. Wilkinson and Janks highlighted an additional gap in the way we teach speech reporting, namely that we tend to teach direct speech (DS) and indirect speech (IS) only, leaving free indirect speech (FIS), which sits somewhere between direct and indirect speech, out of the picture. FIS creates a space for reporters to determine how closely they wish to stay to the speech they want to report by the decisions they make about grammatical transformations which create distance in person, place, and time. Therefore, Wilkinson and Janks believe that a critical approach to teaching speech reporting should involve a serious focus on FIS as this speech reporting style enables reporters to blur the boundaries between their own voice and the voices of those reported. The researchers developed a critical language awareness program which Wilkinson implemented with Grade 11 students. A shortened version of the program is reproduced below (Wilkinson & Janks,1998, pp. 185–187).

Activity 1

Students were asked to analyze the ways in which different textbooks dealt with DS and IS…. This activity had the added advantage of constructing students as critics of textbooks and not as passive receivers of them.

Activity 2

Students were given a list of the different rules for converting DS to IS, which they then evaluated with reference to the textbook they had studied.

Activity 3

Students were then given text-based exercises in which it was not possible to obey the rules for converting DS to IS without distorting the meaning. The aim of this activity was to destabilize the rules and to help students understand that language rules are generalizations based on common patterns but that they are not fixed and in the case of speech reporting have to change in relation to the context.

Activity 5

Students were asked to identify DS, IS and FIS in a number of extracts about the ousting of Francois Pienaar[2] from the South African rugby team. As in previous activities, texts pertaining to topical issues were selected so that students could see the relevance of the representation of speech to daily discursive practices. In addition, students were asked to consider the effects of the choice of DS, IS and FIS.

The selection of what to actually quote out of everything that was said was also illustrated. Here is what Mordt (one of the selectors) is said to have said, according to two different newspapers.

> "You will have to speak to the coach, Andre Markgraaff," was all he would say when asked whether the decision to drop Pienaar was unanimous among the three selectors. (Star, October, 16, 1996)

> In the wake of the Pienaar axing Mordt summed it up better than anyone else. "The coach gets what he wants," was his cryptic comment. And while it would be criminal to put words into Mordt's mouth, it must be added that the coach will probably get what he deserves. (Weekly Mail and Guardian, October 18, 1996)

Activity 6

The students were asked to analyze the use of DS, IS and FIS in the text below, taken from the *Saturday Star*, August 24, 1996.

Nicotine is a drug, asserts Bill Clinton

Washington—In a dramatic crackdown on teenage smoking, President Bill Clinton has decided to declare nicotine an addictive drug and bring it under the control of the Food and Drug administration, the White House said yesterday.

The action hands the President a potent election-year weapon against presidential rival Bob Dole who has expressed reservation about regulating tobacco.

"Devices"

"With this action the president in essence has accepted the FDA's determination that cigarettes and smokeless tobacco are delivery devices for the drug nicotine", White House press secretary Mike McCurry said.

The regulations, as expected, closely resemble Clinton's 1995 proposal to strictly regulate tobacco advertising, sales and access aimed at minors, McCurry said.

Activity 7

Having worked together with Wilkinson on this text, students were invited to find their own texts to analyze. All the students were able to find texts which illustrated a variety of speech reporting. They were also able to distinguish between DS, IS and FIS. Many, but not all, of the students were able to provide some analytic interpretation.

Activity 8

Wilkinson recorded and transcribed a talk show program on the topic of Rave culture. Students were then divided into six groups, with four students per group in order to write a report of the show. In three groups students were asked to background the issues of drugs, parental involvement, and commercialism. In the other three groups students were asked to foreground these. Both groups had to rely on the same transcript, and the exercise demonstrated clearly how the position different students were developing led them to use quotes from the transcript in different ways.

Wilkinson and Janks (1998) reported an improvement in students' ability to identify and critically interpret the use of DS, IS, and FIS. Table 6.1 (p. 189) was included by the authors to present insights they expected their students to be able to offer of the text in Activity 6. We take the liberty of reproducing it here since it serves as a very helpful example of a critical analysis of speech reporting.

The examples presented so far all focus on teaching a selected grammar topic from a critical perspective through establishing the social relevance of the topic to students' lives. Another way in which we can conceptualize critical grammar pedagogy is for the style of teaching itself to have critical features, such as adopting a dialogical, rather than didactic, approach to teaching grammar, selecting content in a negotiated manner, allowing

Table 6.1

Text	Analysis
Nicotine is a drug, asserts Bill Clinton	FIS, which is close to DS, is used. The strong reporting verb, "asserts," suggests power. Does Clinton actually say this? It is not clear.
Washington – In a dramatic crackdown on teenage smoking	The reporter frames this with the word "dramatic." This suggests that the announcement is unexpected and sensational.
President Bill Clinton has decided to declare nicotine an addictive drug and bring it under the control of the Food and Drug administration, the White House said yesterday.	The speaker is framed by his title of rank. Has he actually made this declaration or just decided to do so? "Declare" is a strong reporting verb. This whole sentence is in FIS and is attributed to the White House not to the President.
The action hands the President a potent election-year weapon against	These are the reporter's words which frame the declaration as both "potent" and a "weapon."
Presidential rival Bob Dole	Dole is named in terms of his relation to Clinton, not as the leader of the Republican party
who has expressed reservation about regulating tobacco.	FIS is used to report the gist of Dole's position. No actual words are reported. It is not in fact clear whether or not he said anything at all. The use of "expressed" is used to suggest that speech is being reported. It is a neutral reporting word like "said." The opposition is not quoted directly. The boundary between what Dole actually set and his generally assumed position is unclear.
"Devices"	Scare quotes are used to signal that this is not the reporter's words.
"With this action the president in essence has accepted the FDA's determination that cigarettes and smokeless tobacco are delivery devices for the drug nicotine," White House press secretary Mike McCurry said.	This is the DS of a spokesperson for Clinton. This puts the quote at one remove from the President, in case there is a negative reaction.
The regulations, as expected, closely resemble Clinton's 1995 proposal to strictly regulate tobacco advertising, sales and access aimed at minors, McCurry said.	this is FIS as it is difficult to separate the reporter's voice from Battle Macquarie Clinton's representative speaks first, last, and most. His voice is given the floor by the reporter. The pro-tobacco voice is silenced in the report.

students to question the effectiveness of the classroom materials, and so forth. We are not suggesting that the styles of teaching in the above examples did not have critical features. In fact, we find it difficult to imagine a grammar lesson which teaches critical and socially relevant content in a largely teacher-centered or didactic manner. Yet, we believe it is important to pay conscious attention to both the content and the style of teaching when developing critical grammar activities, lessons, or programs. The last example we present here is of a lesson whose content does not have any explicit critical focus, but it showcases an example of teaching grammar using dialogic pedagogy.

Across seven classes in a primary school in Sydney, Australia, Jones and Chen (2016) explored "the potential of a dialogic approach for engaging learners in learning about language and for promoting metalinguistic understanding through opportunities to talk about language and meaning" (p. 45). Although the article does not provide any demographic details about the students, we assume the students were either native speakers of English or, if from an immigrant family, were most probably highly fluent English users, hence the focus on developing students' metalinguistic knowledge. Again, we argue that a similar approach, though with some variations, can be adopted to teaching ESL/EFL learners, but we will leave a more detailed focus on why we think so until after a brief look at Jones and Chen's study.

The literacy session comprised three stages, namely orientation, collaborative activities, and a teacher-led review, as shown in Figure 6.1 (Jones & Chen, 2016, p. 53).

A short version of the authors' description of the stages of the lesson is as follows.

> The literacy sessions began with a teacher-led orientation of 10–15 min in duration and comprising two phases: a brief review of previous work and explicit instruction in the grammar focus for the session…. This initial stage was followed by a number of collaborative activities, usually 15 min in duration and related to the grammar concept under focus. These activities were designed to provide further practice in identifying and applying grammatical concepts and included activities such as games, small group reading with the teacher, individual bookwork and writing on the class blog…. Student talk was more evident as they took more turns in dialogue; initiating moves, responding to the contributions of others, seeking clarification from one another, affirming the responses of others and not infrequently disagreeing and correcting responses. The collaborative activities included a set of games … to support … learners' understanding of the grammatical concept … [such as] dice and spinner games, "fishing" games and jumbled sentences. The final stage was a teacher-led review of the work completed during the collaborative activities (pp. 53–54).

Figure 6.1

Literary Sessions

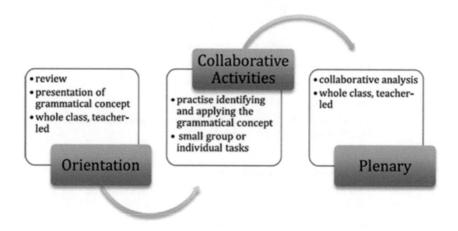

In the article, the authors present three excerpts of classroom talk to show how dialogic pedagogy was used to teach grammar. We reproduce one from an orientation phase to show that, although this stage of a literacy session mainly involves a teacher-led presentation of a grammatical concept, it can involve significant student contribution to the conversation and engagement in learning.

The focus of the lesson is simple clauses, and the teacher is using an image of a busy summer day at the beach where people and their pets are walking, running, swimming, or sunbathing. The clause that the teacher and students collaboratively devise and analyze in the following conversation is "The kids are splashing in the waves." The aim of the lesson is to help the students identify the Process or verbal element (are splashing), the Participants (the kids), and the Circumstances (in the waves). The teacher uses the semantic prompts together with color coding, namely "What's happening?" (green), "Who or what is involved?" (red), and "Is there any extra information?" (blue). The focus on the Process also involves the students physically acting it out. The reported classroom conversation extract is as follows (Jones & Chen, 2016, pp. 54-55; IWB stands for Interactive WhiteBoard) (see Table 6.2):

Obviously, students' level of English proficiency has a major impact on the teacher's ability to teach grammar dialogically and involve learners in a collaborative process of making sense of grammatical concepts. As we briefly suggested earlier, varied forms of the above example lend themselves to teaching ESL/EFL learners. Using a less complex grammar

Table 6.2

1	Tch:	Now here's the picture we've been looking at on our blog (image from picture book is on IWB)
2		Have a look very carefully
3		Have a look for something happening in the picture
4		You might want to choose one person
5		You might choose the one preferred to you
6		Put your hand up
7		If you'd like to tell me a sentence about what's happening in the picture (nearly all students put their hands up)
8		Matilda?
9	M:	The kids are splashing in the waves
10	Tch:	THE KIDS ARE SPLASHING IN THE WAVES (types and text appears under image on IWB)
11		Excellent …
12		Okay now which part of the sentence tells us what's happening, the process?
13		Tommy?
14	T:	Are splashing
15	Tch:	Excellent, can you show me are splashing?
16		Stand up
17		And show me splashing? (Tommy shakes her head)
18		Or someone else? (many hands go up)
19		Astrid … Sam, show me splashing (Sam acts out splashing, other children giggle)
20		Alright, fabulous
21		Go and sit down. (Sam sits down again)
22		So I'm going to make that green (Sam sits down again)
23		Okay who or what? (many hands are raised)
24		Frankie?
25	F:	The kids
26	Tch:	Excellent
		So I'm going to make that red for the participant (teacher selects red font for "the kids" on IWB)
27		And is there any other information?
28		Where, when or how? (many hands go up)
29		Alex

30	A:	In the waves
31	Tch:	IN THE WAVES
32		So what colour are we going to make that /one/? Sorry?
33	A:	/blue/blue
34	Tch:	Fantastic. (teacher selects blue font for "in the waves" on IWB)

terminology is one option. For example, we can use "what" and "who" instead of abstract words like "process" and "participant." Even the teacher in the above example did not use "circumstances." Body language can be of great help, especially when teaching grammatical concepts that can be represented through physical activities. In typical EFL contexts, where students and the teacher share the same mother tongue or official language, the teacher can give some of the essential explanations or the students can ask some of their questions in that language.

CONCLUSION

In coming to the end of this sequence of substantial, even quite long extracts of materials and accounts of practice, we hope we have shown you, as realistically as text will allow, actual images, or snapshots, of critically-minded teachers taking their students through grammar-focused lessons or activities that at the same time have critical or participatory dimensions. Our reason for doing so, as we, the authors of this book, have discussed together, is back to the repeated problem that we, as critical language teachers, have never (or rarely) experienced an apprenticeship of observation, where, back when we were students in school or student teachers at university, we were not exposed to critical pedagogy practice. It is much easier to teach if one has seen a teacher in action. But it is rare to see grammar taught critically.

Earlier in the chapter we worked up to these extracts by building on an initial recognition that grammar or structurally-oriented teaching is still the default setting. Without dismissing this, we noted also that conventional studies of second language acquisition have provided plenty of evidence in favor of "focus on form" though, coming at this from a communicative viewpoint, they are less enthused about building all lessons and each part of a lesson as having a focus on forms. The critical language pedagogy view of this is, we are fairly task-focused, in the sense of getting the meaning across and achieving our goals to influence, persuade, inform, and derive underlying meaning, and so on. To what end will the ability to control language at grammatical or syntactic levels be put? How will the critically-minded student be supported in their ability to see through, also, the sometimes deceptive functions to which grammar is put? To address these questions, we as critical grammar teachers need to work hard on both content (how grammar is used, from a critical point of view) and process (how can we make grammar lessons dialogical and participatory, ones in which students can find their own interests and agency respected and supported). That is the task we have been engaged upon in this chapter.

NOTES

1. At the time of writing this book, a downloadable version of this paper is available at https://hilaryjanks.files.wordpress.com/2015/01/dsisfis-97.pdf.
2. For anti-apartheid political activities.

CHAPTER 7

CRITICAL L2 SPEAKING AND LISTENING

INTRODUCTION

At the beginning of this chapter, the question we can ask ourselves as a way to begin our discussion is, 'What are typical, conventional, mainstream practices in teaching speaking and listening in second languages, from which a teacher developing a critical orientation would be starting?' That is, as our discussion of critical L2 speaking begins, it should start where an inquiring language teacher, considering critical possibilities, might start.

Whether we are thinking about ESL or EFL classrooms that involve oral work, common speaking practices in the ELT classroom involve developing fluency and accuracy. In more traditional classrooms, typical classroom activities in this area may include reading aloud, memorizing or at least correctly repeating textbook dialogues, and possibly doing short presentations, in which students may read from their own writing, or (better) speak from notes.[1]

In these activities, teachers and students are quite likely to be concerned primarily with language learning goals defined in terms of the forms of language, that is, correctness, and students' ability to use them with confidence, that is, fluency. By implication, though, this kind of focus means we may be neglecting the content of learners' talk. We might not

Starting Points in Critical Language Pedagogy, pp. 139–160

be sufficiently asking students to express themselves in their speaking—to share their own views and opinions. And certainly in most conventional EFL and ESL circumstances, the idea of helping students become participatory international citizens—a strong implication of a critical ELT perspective—is nowhere in sight! The increasing focus on teaching EFL/ESL using communicative approaches has meant more student talking time, but not necessarily more space for students' (and the teacher's) ideas and experiences to become part of the classroom content. Nor has it promoted students' critical thinking as a major aim of classroom interactions.

Jing reflected on past practice:

> I think of my own classes. I have been proud of myself of having some pair work and discussions in my class, while most teachers in this school don't provide such form of activities. However, this ... just reminds me of how useless and meaningless sometimes the pair work activities and discussions I designed for them. They are only for ways of giving them a chance for them to practice the new words and phrases they have just learned. Even in reading class, the questions they discussed were not to strengthen their critical thinking. Seldom did I give my opinion, cause I think it would save me some work. Or when I did give some, it would be the answers I want my students to have or the direction in which I want them to think. It would take some time for me first to internalise the way of using dialogue to promote students' critical thinking and then design relative activities.

Conventional approaches to L2 listening practice are also far from critical (see section 7.5 below). In listening classes, or phases of a class that focus on listening, learners are mainly encouraged to improve their ability to make sense of short extracts of speech and do some comprehension-based tasks, such as True/False and multiple choice questions. They are rarely encouraged to analyze the content of what they listen to critically and make sense of it in their own ways. Speaking from experience, Fereshteh said:

> Some teachers come to the class and play the video or audio just as listen and repeat. Three years ago, I would participate in Listening class, my teachers just drew our attention to vocabulary and grammar points in listening, and less attention was paid regarding improvement of critical thinking of content.

We have already briefly referred to dialogue (Chapter 2) and problem-posing (Chapter 3). In this chapter we suggest ways in which dialogue and problem-posing can occur in oral activities focusing on speaking (followed by some attention to listening). First we will look at things that can be done without having to make major changes in regular practice. Then we will look at slightly more challenging activities. (For a helpful taxonomy of speaking activities, see Kayi, 2006.) Theresa made the following encouraging initial comment:

> I think that speaking is an easy opportunity to integrate critical pedagogy. Students need to practice their speaking skills anyway, so instead of the typical and usually boring topics like describing family and friends, this is a great opportunity to engage students in critical dialogue and at the same time practice their English speaking skills.

TOWARDS PAIR-WORK AS A FIRST STEP

Traditional or conventional second language classrooms are teacher-centered. That means the teacher does most of the talking, and if students are called upon, they speak individually, addressing the teacher rather than the class. We suppose that more oral work could occur even within this set-up, if students were given opportunities by the teacher to speak at greater length—that is, if the teacher did not talk so much. But in general, a teacher-fronted language class does not constitute an efficient use of class time. (In big classes, one student might only speak once, in a period, or less!) And if we want students to express themselves, a teacher-fronted class may be too exposed or challenging an arrangement. So, we have to think about expanding our use of pairwork and groupwork.[2] Then consider that (as has often been commented on in the professional literature), *all* classroom activities have to be about *something*.

A common practice in many ELT classrooms is to use a reading passage as a core element in a lesson. After reading the passage, students are faced with "comprehension questions". While some of this is to help students work on grammar and vocabulary knowledge, or even practice reading strategies, also in many classrooms, teachers will ask students to review their answers orally, possibly allowing some discussion with another student. So, this is a common practice that can be used and provides a first step towards more student-student interaction.

So, here we need pairwork or groupwork tasks whose content is at least based on students' real-life experiences (if not, as yet, critical). With guidance or challenge from the teacher or other students, and with adequate preparation and "scaffolding" (from the teacher, or by way of a written worksheet), this may support the development of critical ideas, allow students to articulate more critical positions, or provide material to help them think (and speak) about critical issues. Given the importance of adequate scaffolding for students' critical thinking, we focus on this aspect in the next section.

FURTHER GUIDELINES

A recent discussion of the prerequisites for classroom practice by Salas et al. (2013) for "participatory and exploratory civil dialogue" in EFL classrooms provides more useful guidelines that fit well with our needs here. Salas et al. take off from the position that "exploratory and participatory civil dialogue" is both good for learning and also needed for democracy. They first identify, as unsatisfactory classroom practice, the all-too-common "IRE" form (Initiation-Response-Evaluation), where it is the teacher who initiates and evaluates. (They also dismiss the use of debate with teams to engage with social issues.)

Their proposal assumes a course can accommodate themes (or topics), for example, "friendship." Their model has six facets.

1. Engage students in lived experiences. This means the themes should come from the students' concerns.
2. Provide multiple opportunities to prepare. This is common sense, but it also is consistent with what we have repeated several times here so far: Critical language pedagogy is sufficiently different from what most EFL students have experienced that it has to be worked up to gradually. Allow for "various ways of expressing agreement."
3. Keep the conversation horizontal. This doesn't mean the teacher hides his/her opinions but at the same time, the teacher must not just "teach" or this won't work! Also, the teacher may comment about "individual's frequency of participation" and comment positively on cases of student-student interaction (e.g., "I appreciate that Spencer invited Leo into the conversation by asking him what he thought").
4. Focus on meaning and value active listening. The authors include allowing the discussion to focus on meaning and also that falling back on the L1 is not to be completely disallowed. (How much is ok could itself be the subject of discussion, preferably before first attempts, and revisited later.)
5. Align progressively more demanding dialogue with student goals.... It's nice to think of this building and getting better through say a year's work; and to have it tied in to other curricular goals or objectives, Student Learning Outcomes, and Program Level Outcomes.
6. Honor difference.... And the teacher should try to bring closure ... and let's consider non-oral means of language work. Here the authors are using writing as a way for those who didn't get enough chance to speak to conclude and get out what they wanted to say. Alternatively, particularly if you have access to Course Management

Software, or a blogging space or online class discussion board, those who don't have such loud voices can make themselves understood and communicate their views as well; and this can even be before any oral component.

STIMULUS MATERIALS

Given what we have suggested thus far, it is probably clear that students will have to think, reflect, and in some way articulate their own ideas. In conventional classrooms they are not used to doing this. So, to help them, we should provide them with time to think and time to make a few notes. And they may need "stimulus materials" which we and/or they can bring in to generate discussion. This is the basic position taken in a recent explanation of how to teach L2 students to engage in discussion (Salas et al., 2013). The authors comment that in talking to learn, "far too often, in our classrooms and communities, discussion is adversarial, polemic, and insular" (p. 24). They note that *spontaneous* discussion about certain topics may not be easy or desirable, but rather, pre-discussion preparation would be necessary for some topics at least: teachers should "make sure that students are given access to multiple information sources and ample content preparation in order to discuss the topic in an informed manner" (p. 19). Having read this article, and referring to the need for "thoughtful preparation," Shiva commented:

> Giving students some time to think and write has dual benefits. Firstly, all students will start to think about the issue more deeply. Secondly, this activity helps learners who are not interested in spontaneous speaking (or even speaking at all), like shy, introverted or reflective students prepare themselves for share something with class. I personally believe that most of the time, these students have great ideas (or potentially can develop some), but they cannot express themselves without having some time to think.

Theresa said:

> In the reading "Talking to Learn across classrooms" one of the most important [ideas] and the one I often neglect is to "Create multiple opportunities for participants to prepare" (p. 20). It is often so easy to put students on the spot and get them to turn to the peers next to them and start talking. However, students need to prepare and take the time to think first especially to create a deep and meaningful discussion for them. This should also eliminate students trying to outtalk "each other and competing for the teacher's attention." (p. 18)

> I think the simplest activity for this is "think-pair-share", when students think and write down their thoughts first, then in a pair, they discuss their thoughts, and finally, share with more peers. This activity is good because it gives them the confidence to engage in meaningful dialogue because they have the opportunity to think about it first and to share with one other person before actually talking in a large group

Many regular second language textbooks do not provide stimulating content for discussion at all. On the other hand, for a quick historical perspective, we'd like to point out that EFL-oriented textbooks that provide *some* relevant content have been in print for decades (issues-discussion texts, such as Alexander & Vincent, 1975; Alexander, Kingsbury & Chapman, 1978; Alexander, Vincent & Chapman, 1978; Coelho et al., 1989; Numrich, 2003; Shulman, 2004; and for a more recent example: Day et al., 2009). But we recognize that a problem for many teachers is obtaining and paying for this internationally-published material, even assuming that they have the relative freedom to use it in the classroom. If it is not free and on the web, for us to point out this material, whether old or new, is not so helpful. Noting that it exists, though, is one step towards getting it, or using these ideas as the basis for our own in-house materials, perhaps.

At this point, we have initially been presenting these ideas as if the burden and responsibility for finding and bringing in material is on the teacher. However, if a more critical pedagogical mode of operating is moved to, then students will play an increasing role in finding and bringing in topics and material that will stimulate discussion (as we mentioned in Chapter 3). But for the time being, let us continue to think about what the teacher can do in preparing for such a shift, or beginning it. Two things need to be done, almost simultaneously. One is to find appropriate content, and the other is to develop students' abilities to engage in discussion of it, in what Freire broadly calls "dialogue," or in what Salas et al. (p. 18) call, more specifically, "participatory and exploratory civil dialogue." Now maybe if the teacher has shown, or has explicitly stated, an openness to students' considering topics or discussion on matters of importance to them, we do not have to worry too much about the specificity of the materials chosen. That is what is indicated by this comment from Zahra:

> Reviewing and reflecting on [some] speaking tasks reminds me of one of my first attempts to take content for discussion to the class. It was a few years ago when I had this advanced class covering some units of *Summit* textbook (Saslow & Ascher, 2006). They were some 15-year-old high school first graders and the textbook's content and topics were too serious to be of their interest. So I decided to take to the class some entertaining materials also good for talking about. I selected some short animations and, as I was expected to, checked with the department to see if the administrations are

ok with them. They were some 3/4-minute long animations with little dialogue and language content, and we watched them in the last 15 to 20 minutes every other session and used the topic for a short discussion. In fact, I
didn't focus much on the language content of animations, rather I wanted
entertainment for last minutes of class + topics for discussion appropriate
for that level of proficiency; sort of "edutainment," so to speak.

The first animation was titled "One Minute Fly". Maybe you have
watched it; the story of the fly who lived only one minute while it hecti-
cally tried to fulfill as much as it could; addressing the concept of bucket
list, you know. I can't recall details, but I remember that after explaining a
bit about the idea of bucket list, I asked if they had such list in their mind.
And then I asked their ideas about the fly's hard work to fulfill a lot within
a short time without enjoying the outcomes. The students started sharing
their ideas about the virtue of working hard as the secret to success. Then,
I changed the subject to our achievements without getting joy out of results
of our success, and asked if they had had any experience in this regard. To
my surprise, they burst in expressing a lot of serious comments about the
school's demands on them and the way they were directed towards memo-
rization and covering some subjects they didn't find interesting. Some of
them noted they don't know why they should study all those physics and
math subjects, and why they were repeatedly told that "these subjects would
be useful for them in the future but students can't understand it now."
Another point they raised was that school and parents wanted them to
get good grades, and this wouldn't leave any time for spending with their
friends and have fun.

The things that I hadn't expected were: First, I didn't expect they would
relate the topic directly to their schooling issues. Second, the session after
that, a few of them asked to read their reflection journals on this animation
to the class, and then they continued the discussion with new outlooks. I
missed some time of this session but it was amazing how they came up with
new views in this regard. I wish I'd copied the journals and audio-taped the
conversations.

Whereas Zahra used animations for her 15-year-olds, Arman used documentary clips found on YouTube for his class of adults. In the following
excerpt, he explains how one clip fostered the participants' critical engagement with a relevant topic, as reflected in a period of silence before an
in-depth discussion.

One of the most thought provoking clips was an interview with an old lady
who had been left in a nursing home by her children and would not get
visited by them. She asked the interviewer to ask her children on TV to pay
her a visit; after, I guess, a few months the interviewer went back there and
realized that she had developed amnesia and consequently had totally for-
gotten that she had children; extremely moving, one of the big guys cried
towards the end of the video and the rest were sitting there brooding for a

while after the video was over. I guess all of us were revisiting how we were treating our parents (or grandparents). I actually liked that silence because obviously we were all seriously thinking about important things.

As a final example of possible source material, we note a couple of richly-illustrated books, or to be more accurate, photographic essays: Menzel (1995, 2007). These works document, through photographs taken in many countries in the world, what an ordinary family owns and what their houses and possessions look like. Although we may think we are aware of the differences between rich and poor, so-called developed and so-called underdeveloped (and who did the developing?), the vividness of the differences is sure to spark discussion. Once again, our point is not to suggest to readers that they must somehow amass an expensive and difficult-to-obtain library of realia, but rather, knowing that particular kinds of source or stimulus materials exist, and given the access that the internet provides to such content, the point is to encourage teachers to structure lesson and out of class time so that similar material could be tracked down including by one's students, not just oneself.

Earlier in this section, we briefly mentioned that the assumption underlying our focus on alternative materials is that teachers have the relative freedom to use them in the classroom. Of course, this assumption is not always valid. In many contexts, teachers are required to cover pre-determined mainstream materials only. Yet, this at least leaves us with the possibility of making these very materials (more) critical. Regarding speaking practice, the focus of this chapter, we stand a great chance of introducing a bit of critical pedagogy into speaking post-tasks following reading or listening activities.

One such task was developed by one of our teachers. The original lesson was a reading lesson in *Four Corners 3* (Richards & Bohlke, 2012, p. 80). The topic of the lesson was "Finding solutions" and the title of the reading passage was "One-of-a-Kind Homes," describing three houses which had been built so that they were environment-friendly. While the lesson could be considered somehow or other critical because of its focus on the environment, in an attempt to give it a different and perhaps more tangible touch of criticality, Masoud modified its speaking post-task. The original task was a pairwork activity with the prompt: "Have you heard or seen any unique homes or buildings? Were they environmentally friendly? Tell your partner." Masoud modified it as follows.

I'd ask the first pair work question from the whole class. I'd listen to students' answers. I think it is likely that they would refer to houses in slums and shanty districts around Tehran. If they didn't, I would raise the subject myself. I would then ask students to work in pairs on these questions instead of the one in the book:

What are the differences between the houses of these districts and the ones in the book?

What do you know about these houses and the people living in them? What can we do to help them or alleviate their situation?

I would then ask for their feedback and we would listen and reflect on different suggestions and experiences.

Masoud also provided links to photos of actual shanty towns, slums, and/or homeless encampments in the nearby city, familiar to students and teachers, as potential prompts to facilitate classroom discussion.

TEACHERS' OPINIONS

Now that we are getting into more detail about actual topics and content related to discussion, perhaps we can return to a point made initially in Chapter 1, about how or to what extent teachers can express their own opinions. Let us start, though, with the assumption underlying this discussion—that teachers should have their own ideas and express them in the class. Reflecting on a reading in one of our teacher education courses (and citing it), Masoud said:

> Teachers should be able to present their opinions—but always as just one more opinion. "Peterson (1994, p. 40) maintains that when teachers 'pretend to have no opinions on controversial topics', they send a message that it is 'OK to be opinion-less and apathetic about important issues.'" (Edelsky & Johnson, 2004, p. 132)

How far teachers should go in presenting their opinions has been a regular concern expressed by teachers we have worked with. Jing shared her own experience as a participant in a seminar where the lecturer apparently had the intention of engaging the students in dialogue but ended up imposing his own opinions.

> I like the point about teacher's opinion as one more instead of being the standard on or the one all students should agree with and obey. This reminds me of a seminar I took this Tuesday. The host or the lecturer did very well at the beginning by involving all the participants to take part in the critical thinking process and then asking us to share our opinions. What he didn't do well or the part I disliked about his lecture is that he didn't create a free and safe environment for us to talk. After hearing our opinion, he would judge what we say, and say that your thinking is still very traditional and it seems hard for you to change your mind etc., which made

us very embarrassed. After all the talk, he would present his opinion as the one we should follow and as the correct one he expected us to say.

While Jing's observation focused on how teachers may fail to create a dialogical space, Hoda highlighted a student-related challenge:

> I like [Masoud's] idea that: "Teachers should be able to present their opinions—but always as just one more opinion." By doing this, the teacher shows that all opinions are valued the same way, no matter whose opinions they are.

> But the problem is that in some cultures, the students have learnt to respect teacher's opinion to a great extent which might result in ignoring others' ideas. I mean when the teachers express their idea, the students may not feel free to express opposite ideas because they might think it is rude to disagree with the teacher. What do you think the teachers can do to share their ideas with the class but not impose them on the students?

Jing, drawing upon her above-mentioned negative experience, responded to Hoda's question as follows:

> I guess we do that by asking them to share their opinions first and then sharing ours, by at the same time stressing that our opinion is just one of the possible solutions instead of being the standard one.

Picking up on the issue of when for teachers to share their views, Masoud presented the following critical reflection:

> What is not discussed in the readings we have had so far is the time teachers should voice their own opinions in dialogs, that is, is it OK for teachers to present their own idea on the matter of discussion right at the beginning, should they hold it back and express their personal ideas sometime after the start of the discussion, or should they do it at the end? It is an important question to me since doing each of these alternatives can have different effects on the whole dialog. For example, if a teacher supports one side at first, no matter how hard he tries to say that it is just his personal opinion, it is likely that most students agree with him and decide to take the same side in the discussion, and if he waits and does it after the discussion is finished, students may think that he is declaring the winners and losers of the argument, that is, the ones that he agrees with and the ones that he thinks are wrong.

While the suggestions made by our teachers in the above set of excerpts are very helpful and valuable, we would like to conclude this section by presenting some additional tips on preventing teachers' opinions dominating classroom discussions and acknowledging students' ideas as equally legitimate. Whenever possible, the teacher should:

- explicitly mention that they are going to rethink about their own ideas based on the student's opinions. Example: "Batsa, you just gave me hundreds of thoughts to think about on my way back home."
- incorporate the students' ideas into the rest of the discussion Example: "As Ali said, we should also pay attention to ..."
- support students' opinions. Example: "Juana, another reason I think what you said makes a lot of sense is..."
- acknowledge the stronger rationale behind a student's opinion than their own. Example: "Thank you Akachi. What you just said sounds like a more convincing explanation of the situation."
- acknowledge limitations of their own perspectives. Example: "I am not sure this is the best way to look at the topic, but at the moment I think ..."
- be explicit about the possibility of changing their perspective later. Example: "... Having said this, I think there are still things I am not focusing on at the moment. This discussion and your interesting ideas will help me go beyond my current understanding."
- encourage students and give them space to elaborate on their ideas. Example: "Chen, could you please explain your position through any examples or relevant experiences which you have had?"

CRITICAL DIALOGUE

Many oral activity types exist; considering them in terms of size and complexity, we could place those which call for just a couple of students, as with pair work, discussion, dialogue at one end of a continuum, and forms which tend to larger numbers or whole-class involvement, such as role-plays, simulations, debate and beyond, at the other. The largest and, because of its potentially public nature, most challenging of these is drama.

There is a lot of basic guidance available to L2 teachers about doing all of these. But from the point of view of critical pedagogy, whichever of these oral activity types the teacher is using, it is important that it have a critical dimension. As Brookfield and Preshkin (1999, p. 21) write: "In our experience, generating the conditions for critical and democratic conversation takes considerable time." We agree—because it requires a serious, sustained modeling of the dispositions outlined in Chapter 1 and the setting of ground rules that prevent the power dynamics of the wider society from reproducing themselves inside the classroom. Unless we understand the complexities of a critical approach, it's easy to conclude prematurely that it isn't working and that we should give up hope of ever galvanizing a class through its use.

As we mentioned in Chapter 2, a core idea in the perspective we are advocating here is "dialogue," a term that Freire used very often and made stand for both theoretical concepts and actual practices. In more recent literature, there is the slightly more specified term "critical dialogue," which we find useful. One definition of this is "collective inquiry into the processes, assumptions, and certainties that comprise everyday life" (Schein, 1993, as cited in Marchel, 2007, p. 2). This may have at least two somewhat distinct aspects. First, we could consider critical dialogue as occurring in a conversation between individuals with significantly varied or opposing views, who try to arrive at a conclusion through juxtaposing these views. While this is an accurate understanding of some instances of critical dialogue, we'd like to emphasize that (secondly) critical dialogue can also happen when discussants explore a joint perspective together. In response to one of her peers who appeared to have the former as her definition of critical dialogue, Jaleh said:

> Do you ... think in order to have a hot debate or fruitful discussion people/ learners should have different and opposite ideas?! Yesterday we had a discussion in one of my [upper-intermediate] classes ... about "poverty"! I have an attorney in law in the class and he was in the middle of helping a very needy family whose breadwinner has been in jail for about a year just for [300 US dollars]. And this was the reason this topic was chosen and discussed.... You cannot even imagine, all my 11 learners were on the same planet, they had the same idea and they talked and discussed for about 95 minutes. So, personally I think in order to run a CP-based discussion, there's no need to be against each other.

Given ordinary understandings of dialogue as something spoken, it seems that critical language teachers should be making an effort to get this into speaking and listening classes (at least). Marchel expands Schein's definition, helpfully pointing out a couple of key aspects that are independent of modality (i.e., whether spoken or written):

> [First], it pays particular attention to the role of personal bias, especially with regard to patterns of power and privilege. Second, critical dialogue is a collaborative act in which peers assist each other in mutual examination of biases. This collaboration is necessary because assumptions and biases are too easily overlooked in solitary reflection, especially when applied to

situations where race, ethnicity, or economic status privilege one group over another. (Marchel, 2007, p. 2)

In a review of critical dialogue, Laman et al. (2012) identify three key aspects of the matter. (1) Time. "Critical dialogue is complex and rarely accomplished within a single exchange" (p. 203). (2) "The role of the facilitator" (p. 207). Trying to set things up or encourage learners to articulate their views on the topic within "patterns of power and privilege" (ibid.) is necessary. It might happen without much encouragement if students are already fired-up about a topic (as Zahra's quote indicates). On the other hand, students may feel deeply about a matter but be so unaccustomed to expressing either feelings or analysis that they are hesitant to do so in a classroom (so this would need our pedagogical attention). Overarching critical questions may need to be provided by the teacher, or a modeling of what are critical questions and what is a critical disposition may be needed. (3) "Textual, visual, and quotidian tools" (p. 207). These are what the older critical pedagogy literature calls "codes," and language teachers sometimes refer to as *realia*—concrete material objects, which could be linguistic, but don't have to be. Laman et al. 2012 (looking across five studies in particular within critical pedagogy and critical literacy literature) mention "picture books…. Young adult literature, photo-essays, printed bills and paychecks…. Texts reflecting living expenses" (p. 210).

So, there are a number of key requirements to get the possibility of critical dialogue going in a second language classroom. Let us emphasize the third of these for a moment. We have mentioned the limitations of conventional textbook materials and we have alluded to, on the one hand, the comparative absence and indeed limited applicability of pre-made critical materials for language teaching. And while we have recognized the limitations that teachers in less well-resourced schools or poorer parts of societies work under, we have also on the other hand pointed optimistically to what can be obtained more easily (under most circumstances) from the internet or web. So, let us here show a few examples of partial lesson plans that our teachers shared with us, as having the potential to produce some critical dialogue.

The first case, as Jaleh says, concerns gender equality. Perhaps it is obvious, but video (even though we are exposed to so much) is potentially highly motivating. Its immersive qualities, its potential immediacy and apparent authenticity (though perhaps dangerous, since they are also products of production techniques) give it, as "realia" or stimulus material, a power that most conventional language textbook writers can't attain. Also because of the diversity of material available on the web, the critical teacher can select culturally appropriate treatment of even challenging topics.

The Courage to Tell the Hidden Story

Topic: Women have voice in the society
Level of Proficiency: Upper Intermediate
Age: Adult (18 upward)
Number of Learners: 7 males and females
Time: 20 minutes
Objective of the Task:

The reason or better to say the objective of this task is providing my learners with the fact that men and women should be treated equally in society. As this class is a mixed one, I found this topic argumentative enough along with letting them know any individual has its own right in the society that should be seen and respected.

Engagement: 3–4 minutes

Learners were asked to think about the subject matter and if they have any particular idea about the way people, esp. women should act to be seen and heard in the society. This part was done in pairs.

Video Watching: 4–5 minutes

The video was taken from Ted.com.

[https://www.ted.com/talks/eman_mohammed_the_courage_to_tell_a_hidden_story]

Learners were asked to watch it once for about 4 minutes.

After Watching: 8–10 minutes

Learners were asked to share their ideas about what they had watched and also they were requested to see if they do face such issues in their own country. Then all learners were supposed to provide the class with some sentences using "unreal conditional—2nd type" structure, the grammar point they had been taught in previous sessions. They were asked to give answer to the following questions:

"What would you do if you wanted your voice is heard in the society?

If you wanted to be in the limelight, what kind(s) of action you'd take?"

Homework: 1 minute

Learners were asked to write a 3—paragraph essay about … [the] topic.

To increase the potential of Jaleh's task for generating critical discussion, we suggest a few possible alterations or additions:

A. Discussion questions: General questions for discussion are very useful but perhaps as the starting point. Therefore, we would ask the two questions Jaleh has used toward the end of her lesson at the engagement stage. In the post-listening/watching part of the lesson, we would ask more specific questions based on the content of the video. Two examples would be:

1. The speaker says: "At times of such doubled war, including both social restrictions on women and the Israeli-Palestinian conflict, women's dark and bright stories were fading away."
   Why do you think she considers social restrictions that women are faced with to be a war?
2. The speaker goes on to say "Because of my gender, I had access to worlds where my colleagues were forbidden."
   What worlds did she have access to?

   Being a woman provided her access to these worlds despite all hardships she had been going through as a woman. What resources and opportunities do you think women in our country have access to?

B. Grammar: Type 2 conditional is a relevant grammatical point to focus on. However, since the content is about our ability to make changes (our transformative potential), the lesson could benefit from going beyond the unreal (unlikely or hypothetical) conditional and encouraging learners to use Type 1 conditional in their discussion. By doing so, we would help them think about possibilities which are there and can be drawn upon for real transformations. This approach is sometimes called "pedagogy of hope" (Freire, 1994) or "pedagogy of possibility" (Kumaravadivelu, 2003).

C. Pronunciation: To add another critical dimension to the task, we could also incorporate a reflective activity on the issue of accent. Drawing students' attention to the speaker's Palestinian accent, we could ask them to address the following questions in a whole class or group discussion:

1. How does her accent sound to you?
2. How does it make you feel about her abilities as a language user and a person/citizen?
3. The speaker is presenting at an official TED conference probably attended by people from around the world including native speakers of English. It has also received more than a million views on the Internet. What does this suggest about her?

The second example, from Theresa, likewise uses a video from a similar source. It was not difficult for the teacher to specify a short (8-minute) segment from this inspiring talk about feminism by an African activist. A number of points seem worth making. First, obviously again this is challenging and critical material, though possibly the video nature of the material and the polished nature of the speaker's delivery (and the fact that she is a role model of a woman of color speaking in a position of some authority) make this not a problem. Second, in this task, the teacher is indeed focusing on forms: vocabulary is taught explicitly. Third, students' initial response to the material is not a demand to speak or construct an answer to teachers' questions to the whole class or in front of a large group, but mere movement, though based on comprehension. However, there is a call made by the teacher (perhaps to more competent or confident students) to explain their views. And then there is an increasingly commonly used "Think/Pair/Share" phase in which there's a safer opportunity to use language in response to this video. Note that Theresa's students are in the upper secondary years.

> Listening Task for year 11/12 students (16–17 years old)
> Listening video/audio of Adichie's speech at TEDx talk 7.45mins duration attached in an email to you all.
> Full speech 30mins available here https://www.youtube.com/watch?v=hg3umXU_qWc
> Pre listening:
> 1. Purpose: to discuss and define the necessary vocabulary:
> Match the word to the definition exercise. Allow for discussions as they arise with students while working—not to be completed in silence
> – gender
> – expectations
> – feminism
> – masculinity
> – femininity
> – emasculation
> – ego
> – physical attributes
> – intellect
> – shame
> – breadwinner
>
> 2. Purpose: to acknowledge own attitudes, perspectives, knowledge, and emotions about the topic so that when listening, can follow the speaker with an open mind, without making judgements and

without allowing emotions to get in the way:

Values line: Students to move to one side of the class if they disagree and move to the other side of the class if they agree (or in the middle). After teacher calls out each statement and the students have decided where to stand, teacher to choose a few students who are standing at different places to explain/justify their position. Also, teachers to point out the number of girls and boys in each position after each statement.

– To be a leader you have to be more physically fit than be smart and creative

– Men are stronger than women

– Women and men are the same

– There is no such thing as gender expectations

– You have never experienced discrimination based on your gender

– Your parents have taught you how to cook and clean

– You really want to marry someday

– You don't mind staying home and looking after the children when you have your own family

– Only females are victims in this society because men rule the world

– Males are victims in this society as well

During the viewing/listening of the speech:

3. Make notes about the main points to assist with attention and for review later

After:

4. ThinkPairShare

What is the main purpose of Adichie's speech?

What are some of the solutions she poses for these gender issues?

Do you agree or disagree with her main argument?

How has this speech made you change or reinforce your views of the statements from the values line activity completed before?

5. Feminism is often criticized as being "Man hater." How has Adichie argued that males are also victims of gender expectations and that it is not the man's fault for women's oppression?

L2 LISTENING

If we accept for a while the conventional idea of "four skills," then in the area of oral skills, we can give somewhat separate attention to listening, as nominally distinct from speaking. Consistent with what we've just written about needing to move towards pair-work and interaction as an early step towards critical language pedagogical practice in this area, what are common L2 listening practices and can they be made more interactive? And after we've answered that question, we will ask two more: "What will be the role of listening in critical oral skills?" and "Is there such a thing as critical listening, or a critical language pedagogy for L2 listening?"

A general sense of typical listening teaching practice is provided by Vandergrift and Goh (2012, pp. 4–5):

> Listening activities in many language classrooms tend to focus on the outcome of listening; listeners are asked to record or repeat the details they have heard, or to explain the meaning of a passage they have heard. In short, many of the listening activities do little more than test how well they can listen.

Regarding negative aspects of the continual focus on accuracy in listening, Vandergrift and Goh suggest that L2 learners dealing with listening can experience stress and anxiety (and from our own experience, we agree):

> Because learners are often put in situations where they have to show how much they have understood or, more often, reveal what they have not understood, they feel anxious about listening. In addition, when they not only have to understand what the person is saying but must also respond in an appropriate way, learners' stress and anxiety levels increase even further.

Vandergrift and Goh in addition point to the regular absence of the teaching of listening strategies:

> Learners also face the challenge of not knowing how to listen when they encounter listening input. Although pre-listening activities are a common feature in some classrooms, these activities mainly provide learners with the background knowledge they need to make listening easier. Learners are "primed" to listen to a specific piece of text through a pre-listening activity, but they are seldom taught how to listen once the audio or video begins....
>
> Once learners begin listening, they are often expected to complete the listening task without any help along the way. The nature of spoken text, experienced in real time, does not normally allow the listener to slow it down or break it down into manageable chunks. Many teachers also feel that they should ask learners to listen to the input without any interruption

or repetition because this mirrors real-life communication. The downside of this practice is that learners are constantly trying to understand what they hear but never get a chance to step back and learn how to deal with the listening input.

Now certainly, Vandergrift and Goh, as specialists in L2 listening, would encourage us to go beyond this passive or unstrategic version of L2 listening. Their perspective emphasizes helping learners develop the tools needed to exercise autonomy in judging their L2 learning needs. They recommend that teachers provide learners with the metacognitive skills they need to gain control of their development in L2 listening abilities. (If learners don't have this, then teaching L2 listening becomes just testing L2 listening.) What this means is that learners should be aided to plan their deliberate use of listening strategies (such as choosing which parts of a piece of audio to concentrate on, activation of schemas for such material, possible use of note-taking strategies, and so on). And they should be helped to evaluate their success (or lack of it) in the use of these strategies. This is important and puts the learner in a more active role or one with some degree of control. Perhaps, it is not particularly critical but enhancing learner agency within the learning situation is surely part of the critical agenda.

ACTIVE AND CRITICAL LISTENING

The idea of going beyond "passive listening" suggests we should look out for any discussions of "active listening." The term is in general use and goes back at least to the very influential work of Carl Rogers and the humanistic psychology of the 1950s (in the United States: Rogers & Farson, 1957). Reference to Rogers' work, and to this idea, can be found both in general discussions of interpersonal communication (e.g., Goddu, 2011) and as applied to L2 learning material (Rost & Wilson, 2013). In active listening, the listener consciously directs attention, develops, and holds an appropriate attitude, and adjusts to the speaker and the content of what is being said. This is valuable and an improvement on passive listening. But as we are working towards critical language pedagogy, it would be natural to attach the word "critical" to "listening" and ask, or imagine, what might be involved in "critical listening."

Some attention has been paid to critical listening in the educational literature of the past. Actually, we can take advice (from a scholar of the history of ideas) to go all the way back to the first century (C.E.) literature of imperial Rome: "To learn the art of listening, we have to read Plutarch's treatise on the art of listening to lectures.... The art of listening is crucial so you can tell what is true and what is dissimulation, what is rhetorical truth and what is falsehood in the discourse of the rhetoricians" (Foucault, 1988, p. 32).[3] We agree with Foucault. It is striking to think that this kind of advice (e.g., from Plutarch [75/1969]) has been around for two thousand years! In modern times, we find the term "critical" applied to this kind of listening (or equally, to reading) —careful listening that seeks out the underlying assumptions of what is being listened to, or of the speaker's intent. And in this form, it was advocated for (L1) teaching at least as far back as the early 1960s (e.g., Duker 1962; Lundsteen, 1966). So, it is actually not difficult to introduce into our classes, as the following teacher comments suggest:

Mahsa: I always ask my students this question: What is the difference between hearing and listening? [cf witnessing vs. spectating, in quote below from Taylor (2015)]

Zahra: [asks her students:] "Do you think the speaker knows the subject? Is he qualified to talk about accident prevention?"

Or in case of [an ad students were listening to]:

"As you listen, ask yourself if the man is trying to sell a particular product to you."

"Ask yourself if he is trying to make you think in particular way."

"What do you suppose his message to his viewers really was?"

We can go on from here, following a case study by Taylor (2015).[4] This teacher, drawing on the important work of Boler (1999, on the role of emotions in education), discusses the choice of challenging or disturbing material for video viewing and listening. She calls this the "pedagogy of discomfort," and part of it relates to listening, in a particular way, to material that would probably produce engagement with the more difficult topics that are naturally part of a critical pedagogy, though which are, indeed, challenging or uncomfortable to attend to. Among many important points in this exceptional, perhaps unique report, is reference to the need to attend to the emotions brought up by listening to difficult or challenging material. Here is a relevant if lengthy extract (Boler, 1999, p. 120):

The pedagogy of discomfort proposes a view of listening that challenges students to learn how their emotional investments inform their listening responses; how, for example, one's fear of talking about race complicates one's ability to see students' experiences of racism as reasonable, or how one's discomfort with disabled bodies colors one's response to disabled people's testimony about their lived experience, perhaps even in spite of one's best efforts at practicing the virtues of good listening. Boler (1999) distinguishes between empathetic listening or "spectating" that sustains cultural practices of exclusion and critically engaged listening or "witnessing" that interrogates power relations and disrupts these practices. An examination of emotional responses supports the development of this latter form of listening because it offers students an opportunity to explore how social practices, symbols and discourses define our interior realms and how our emotional responses enact and sustain social and cultural meanings (Boler, 1999, p. 142). It is this understanding that responsiveness to emotions can be at once compassionate understanding and critical analysis—that emotions can be analyzed and critiqued—that lays the groundwork for the ultimate view of listening as a political act. By critically analyzing their place within social structures and the way these appear to them, students can come to recognize how listening—in both its emotional and cognitive aspects-has political and ethical implications.

Taylor (and the other contributors in Waks, 2015) emphasize the role of *teacher* listening (to students), as much as students listening to the teacher or to textbook-provided materials. And there is also a clear role for active listening, which we as teachers need to both do ourselves and enable students to do with and for each other. We should help students to listen carefully, sympathetically, and in what Taylor calls a "witnessing" way to each other. Perhaps it is also worth saying that sometimes critical pedagogy is not about solving problems, or even addressing problems. Sometimes it is more a matter of providing a space for something to be said, something to be listened to, that otherwise won't get any "air time." In this regard, Hoda's comment is worth noting:

> While watching the video,[5] I remember the times I was sad about something and wanted to talk to a friend. Sometimes I was not really looking for a solution, because there was no solution or I didn't like to find any at that time.

> It is the same in the class. When during a discussion students express their opinions, they might not really be looking for opposing ideas or pieces of advice; they want to tell how they feel about a particular issue because they have found a chance to express themselves, or they might be simply just practicing their language without meaning anything special behind every word they say. So, we as teachers should not "judge" them based on what they say, because any judgment will affect how we approach that class (or that student) from then on.

IN CONCLUSION

What do we do in critical listening, once we or our students have found interesting or challenging material to listen to? Basically, there are (we think) two options. One is to investigate how the language has its effect. This is an extension of the critical listening position, that using a degree of skepticism and investigation, helps us understand, from a critical discourse analysis point of view, how language is working.

And the other is that the understandings or the challenges produced or emanating from students in response to this material then forms the basis of critical dialogue. So within listening we then return to speaking, re-entering dialogue (and potentially, of course, go on to reading and writing, and perhaps action).

NOTES

1. Of course it is dangerous to generalize. Less traditional (more communicative) classrooms offer a wider variety of speaking activities such as debate, group discussion, interview, and information gap activities, not to mention out-of-class activities that can be different again. See Sundqvist and Silvén (2016) for a quick review across a number of countries.
2. For those of us who favor broadly communicative or interactive perspectives on language learning and teaching, pairwork and groupwork are still not sufficiently common in many ELT settings, despite being sought by specialists since before the beginnings of communicative approaches (e.g., Barnes, 1971), and despite the availability of advice tailored to large classes in EFL contexts (e.g., Allwright et al., 1989; Nolasco & Arthur, 1994).
3. For further discussion of this classical source, see Harrison (2013).
4. In Waks (2015), a rare book-length collection of approaches to listening based in Freirean perspectives, though without a language learning orientation.
5. https://www.youtube.com/watch?v=FwEltOeW9aY (A case for active listening: Jason Chare at TEDxTokyoTeachers).

CHAPTER 8

HANDLING PRONUNCIATION CRITICALLY

Issues and Techniques, Standards, and Varieties

INTRODUCTION

In introducing this topic, we will first focus on some challenging changes that are not necessarily associated with a critical perspective, and come to the critical aspects next.

The field of ELT used to think that learners should basically end up like "native speakers," in pronunciation (as well as in the other skill-areas of their second language). In taking this as the goal, it did not recognize the multilingual nature of almost all societies (that is, it ignored the fact that in the majority of countries around the world,[1] second language speakers are highly prevalent), it did not recognize the value of the full range of varieties of English, and it made the mistake of taking the so-called native speaker as the target. Things began to change as English as an international language (EIL) became World English*es* (note the plural) and more recently English as a Lingua Franca (ELF) has become an important idea

Starting Points in Critical Language Pedagogy, pp. 161–171
Copyright © 2022 by Information Age Publishing
All rights of reproduction in any form reserved.

(Crystal, 2003; Jenkins, 2003; Phillipson, 1992; Seidlhofer, 2001); all this at the same time as the multilingual turn (e.g., Conteh & Meier, 2014) also puts the native-speaker concept in question.

If English is indeed the most widely used language for communication across language and national barriers, it is indeed a *lingua franca*. And as such, it does not belong to any one group. Furthermore, in practice, when we consider what actually happens in various regions of the world where it is widely used but not the main national language, local patterns of use do not converge on one of the main standards. That is (according to specialists such as Jenkins, 2000), neither Standard American English nor Standard British English are really operating as more than a nominal target in many parts of the world, nor are they more intelligible to L2 users than more local varieties of English.

In the area of pronunciation, the ELF perspective may be resulting in a noticeable shift of perspective among specialists. Researchers such as Jenkins (2000) particularly focus on pronunciation in their studies of ELF. Given the existence of ELF, in L2 pronunciation instruction, there should be less emphasis on developing a native-like accent even while there is still awareness of the importance of intelligibility (Goodwin, 2001). When reflecting on pronunciation instruction, we should think in terms of oral interactions with people from around the globe *most of whom are non-native speakers of English*. In L2 listening, this has led to giving less importance to focusing on (and teaching) the major accents of English (such as American and British), as opposed to attaching more importance to understanding speakers, whether they have native or non-native accents. This reflects the increasingly globalized nature of a world in which English is still the dominant global language, but one in which "non-native speakers" outnumber the rest, and in which native speakers no longer own or fully control the English language. However, if the matter of teaching pronunciation is left at this level of analysis, it simply takes the new situation for granted and responds instrumentally.

Now let's address a *critical* understanding of pronunciation. This involves recognizing power in pronunciation. This can be in reference to the older native-speaker and standard English model, as well as in pushing back against it. This is at one level a matter of description (we need an up-to-date and accurate answer to the question 'How is the world of Englishes really operating these days?') and at another level a matter of defending the legitimate identities and practices of "L2 users"[2] of English, who have been disempowered by dominant modes of ELT teaching. And it can also be at the level of looking to see how power is manifested by an individual L2 user (or learner) in even a single utterance (as we will see through one study summarized below). Overall, the full implication of the changes we have just mentioned as happening in this area have by no means fully worked themselves into all classrooms and teaching (not to mention testing) contexts, so the critical ELT practitioner has plenty to do.

In the next sections, we will address a range of issues arising from the alternative views briefly mentioned above. We will review a few relevant articles (though there is very little published directly in this area) on "critical L2 pronunciation instruction." We'll also draw (perhaps more extensively than usual) on the contributions of our teacher course-members, who had a lot to say on this topic and as EFL specialists (and non-native speakers) espoused fairly conservative positions! At the end of the chapter, we will suggest general guidelines and list a few practical examples to help teachers translate critically-oriented ideas about teaching pronunciation into practice and developing pronunciation tasks for their own classrooms.

WHAT IS, OR ARE, RELEVANT CURRENT PERSPECTIVES?

A useful relatively recent overview of (L2 English) pronunciation teaching, though not one very explicitly critical in nature, is that of Levis (2005). The title of his article is significant and goes along with what we've just been writing: his title is *Changing contexts and shifting paradigms in pronunciation teaching*. One of Levis's main points is that this area hasn't been well-based in research, and instead has been driven by teacher intuition (which is not sufficient) and unfortunately, by what he calls "competing ideologies." One of these is the ideology (or principle, he also calls it) of "nativeness." We agree with Levis when he says "very few adult learners actually achieve native-like pronunciation in a foreign language" (p. 370). In our view, it is then dangerous when teachers take this as nevertheless "an achievable ideal" (p. 370). The other principle that Levis identifies, which is in some sense at the opposite pole from a concern for native-likeness, is a primary concern with intelligibility. The implication of focusing on this is that pronunciation teaching becomes instrumentally focused on whatever pronunciation features are claimed to aid "intelligibility." (It is probable, however, that intelligibility is not a general matter, but depends upon which speakers are involved, under what conditions of power equality or difference.)

Levis's (2005) next point is that context is particularly important. An easy point he makes about the importance of context concerns the limited nature of pronunciation textbooks. Most of them are still focused on mainstream varieties of the language "although most native speakers of English speak neither General American nor Received Pronunciation" (p. 371). This explains the common experience of learners of L2 English, upon newly arriving in an English-speaking country and being unable to understand the bus or taxi driver who picks them up or takes them to their final destination, and so on.[3] He then extends this to think about major categories of English user (native speaker, inner circle English speaker, outer circle English speaker) and the various challenges that might be faced by diverse pairs of interlocutors taken from these three groups, when having a conversation. Accent familiarity or unfamiliarity can have major effects on intelligibility, and empirical evidence (e.g., Jenkins, 2000) shows that it is not the case that the so-called standard accent is most comprehensible across different kinds of English user.

VARIETIES AND THE CHALLENGES FACED
BY NON-NATIVE ELT SPECIALISTS

In beginning this subsection, let us put the voices of our teachers first, as they are mostly non-native teachers who have had to deal with the problems faced by any teacher of an additional language who is not a native speaker, in a world that tends to mostly see the native accent and variety as naturally dominant or most prestigious ignoring the considerable diversity within it.

> **Arman:** More than two billion people on this planet are Chinese and Indians. Their English accents tend to carry the phonetic features of their native languages. The same is true about many others from many other countries. This is a fact and we cannot simply say they have got to adopt a native-like accent. They are already the majority! And many of them are business owners and decision makers in other countries like Australia, New Zealand, etc. So, if we ask them to follow a native accent, they have every right to respond "you fix your ears buddy!" They just need to be understandable.

> **Elahe:** I do agree that we should incorporate different varieties in teaching grammar. And our classes should convey this point that the time for one main standard version of English is over. I have always found this most challenging. Mostly I avoid explanation and I do my own job.

> **Jing:** When I was in Australia, I once had an assignment to write which was called "English as the world language". In this essay, I discussed several questions concerning what is a world language and who and why English is the global language now. However, as we all know, English nowadays has more varieties than ever before because of its global

influence. In many countries, there may be a problem as to which variety to choose to teach the students. However, in China, schools, especially government schools all follow the British English standard, in terms of the pronunciation, grammar, words spelling, etc. therefore, there is no need to argue which variety is the most appropriate to teach in China. Students may also choose American accent if they like, as long as it's right and good. These two kinds of accent are the most popular and widely accepted in the world. Using them won't cause any confusions when students speak with foreigners.

However, I do agree that students need to be exposed to as many varieties of Englishes as possible, so that when they are talking with English speakers who are from non-English speaking countries, such as European countries, they can still have fluent communication. This balanced approach needs teachers to give as many opportunities as possible in class to remind students of the existence of many Englishes spoken in the world. I used to mention to my students that Japanese English is different from Chinese English. When I mention this, there is no harm meant here, just talking of a fact. When Japanese people speak English, they try to make it Japanese English, like Indian English, with their own features and accents and they are proud of it. While when Chinese people speak English, they try to sound as authentic as possible. Chinese people prioritise mimicking, imitating the accent—British accent or American accent, the more authentic the better.

Hoda: It is a good idea to expose students to different varieties of English including American and British English, though being exposed to these two native varieties does not necessarily result in less confusion in the students' future interaction. Students' needs and target situation should be always considered while teaching. Sometimes talking like a native speaker impedes communication, because the person you are talking to might not be a native speaker.

I remember a student who was a business woman and had learnt American English for 2 years. Actually she was running her own business in Dubai. After her first trip

> to U.A.E. she told us that she had a lot of problems with
> Arabic or Indian accent. She really didn't need to learn
> American English; and talking with an American accent
> made it difficult for Arabs or Indians to understand her.

The latest perspectives in this area (e.g., Tupas, 2015) draw explicitly on a critical view of language varieties, which emphasizes the linguistic equality of varieties as well as recognizing the way power plays out to suggest still that one or another is best (as well as disempowering non-native teachers of languages). But these perspectives have not penetrated the field as a whole nor have they been fully accepted in countries where some aspects of them (e.g., ELF) are visible, such as Singapore. In addition, such is the power and desire for a prestige accent among some English learners, that teachers who do not have one may find themselves under pressure. From contacts with Korean high school English teachers, Graham reports that some of them have received complaints from their students' parents if they are perceived not to have an accent that sufficiently approximates to what the parents believe to be a standard American accent. (South Korean parents and school principals even appear to look down on British and Australian accents!) On the other hand, the situation (like language itself) continues to change in most L2-using contexts. In the Korean context, the fact that the Secretary-General of the United Nations in recent years has been the Korean diplomat Ban Ki-Moon may have affected attitudes somewhat. Koreans have been faced with the example of (from their point of view) an extremely high status Korean making regular speeches in English, in an English that they see as fairly strongly Korean-accented, and no one (apart from a few Koreans) is criticizing his English. Some Korean English teachers I (Graham) have had contact with, who used to be self-conscious about their English, are moving to a position of "if it's good enough for the number one international (Korean) diplomat, it's good enough for me."

A related aspect of this phenomenon is as follows. Arman comments that Iranian EFL teachers whose local accents are perceived as "strong" and influenced by L1s other than Persian in that country are apparently not so valued by students (as indicated in these cases our teachers reported).

> **Mowla:** Almost all my colleagues at a private language institute
> highlighted that they tend to adopt a British accent since
> (they say) it is "prestigious and impressive". At a public
> high school where I have been teaching for three years,
> the students showed strong resistance against one of my
> colleagues who speaks English with a Turkish accent.
> They asked the school principal to change the teacher,

even. Nonetheless, since their voices were not heard, they have adopted another strategy, i.e., mimicking the teacher. As a teacher [in a private language school], sometimes we have to comply with what our customers are expecting of us!!!!!!!!

As a part of my dissertation, I interviewed a sample of teachers and it came to light that the "majority of them were of the opinion that you can attract more students by adopting a native-like accent". I do know that this is not in keeping with the current status of English as a Lingua Franca, yet a noticeable number of teachers and students hold positive attitudes towards native-like competency.

Zahra: My supervisor a couple of times has come to me complaining that "Zahra, your students no longer have that beautiful accent they had last semester. Their previous teacher spoke with a decent British accent and emphasized on students' accent, too. What's happened to them now?"

On the other hand, every one of us would agree that merely sounding nativelike is certainly not sufficient to be a good language teacher. We can say that overall, changing perceptions concerning pronunciation in the field of TESOL mean that non-native speaker teachers should try not to be hung up on or feel anxious about non-nativeness or accent, if that goes beyond basically intelligible or approximating to a locally-acceptable standard.

WHAT ARE SOME EXAMPLES OF PRACTICE IN THIS AREA?

We turn now to an example report of a small intervention in this area, carefully described by a senior figure in critical language pedagogy, Brian Morgan. One of a number of reasons why his work is important for us is that he writes in both a theoretically and practically-informed way, giving clear practical accounts of his teaching. These are collected (Morgan, 1998) in his accounts of ESL classroom practice in an adult education program in Canada, teaching mostly older Canadian immigrants from China. So that might make some of his ideas a little harder to transfer to EFL contexts.

In a chapter in his 1998 book (and compressing the account to a minimum here), Morgan reports on a series of class meetings in which intonation and stress developed as important.[4] His students were retired Chinese some of whom had immigrated to Canada late in life, and some husbands had very traditional conventional ideas about the role of their wives (i.e., to stay home and be home-makers). In the lesson (which continued over a couple of class meetings) Morgan first used textbook material to present a case (invented) in which a husband and wife, rather like his students, are disagreeing about continuing ESL classes. He then had the class brainstorm solutions. In the next class meeting, he brought in a short "scripted" dialogue (that he had written), in which a husband and wife, like his immigrant students, discuss such a matter. As the class discussed, then practiced the scripted dialogue, intonation "became the unplanned focus of our lesson" (p. 77). A crucial part of the dialogue is

Chian [the   Yuen, you're speaking English. How did you learn
husband]:   those words?

Yuen [the   Oh, I've been studying at a community centre for
    wife]:   several months. I really enjoy it, and the teacher is very
              good.

Morgan (1998) reports that he identified that his students needed to pay careful attention to developing a moderately powerful style of speech. He had them focus just on the interjection "Oh," as it signals a lot depending on its intonation patterns. If "fast-rising," that could be uncertainty; if "slow falling," it might indicate confidence, indeed power. In the problem situation as a whole, conventional gender-role-based expectations (we can call them "patriarchal"), could have been negatively affecting the wife's development. It was late in her life, but as a result of the differing circumstances in the couple's new country, the wife had the opportunity to have a more equal relationship with her husband, but this clearly would depend also on her own agency in the new country, which in turn depended on her continuing to learn English (through Morgan's class). For that to work out, at least in this constructed example, a more powerful style of speech, signaled in this case through intonation work, would be advantageous. And this was the focus of this somewhat extended section of the class. In the full report it is clear that the teacher did not didactically teach this point and associated examples, but rather the matter emerged from exploration, discussion, and dialogue between teacher and students. This reflected students' likely problem situations in their real life, as then handled and developed by the teacher, and then worked back into detailed and focused student practice, based on teacher-developed locally-relevant material (in this case).

Well, that's it, basically. If you think this is a rather small example, you may say "That's it?!", and you may say the phrase with a fast-rising tone of incredulity or disappointment. But look at it this way—when does power come into a language class? Usually never. When do we start with the immediate communicative needs of the least-powerful members of the class? Again, almost never. Does the teacher normally draw on the rest of the class for input, and have them also coach the learner or provide content for the class? (Not normally, or indeed, usually only in a highly democratic classroom.) And is it what you say, or how you say it? How does power get transferred or transmitted, in oral language? Some of it is content, but some of it is style, or paralanguage, but when do you see this sort of thing in the (pronunciation) textbooks?

The next quote shows how Shuang, one of our teachers, took a key point of Morgan's work and extended it. That is, although the question of a powerful way of using intonation came up in a case where the issue was gender, shouldn't all students be enabled to use their L2 in a powerful way?

> Brian Morgan's (1997) "Identity and Intonation" is a great article to read.
> Identity and power are quite influential factors to language learning.
> "Men's language is the language of the powerful. It is meant to be direct,
> clear, succinct, as would be expected of those who need not fear giving
> offence, who need not worry about the risks of responsibility. It is the lan-
> guage of people who are in charge in the real world" (Lakoff, 1990,
> p. 205). With application of the intelligibility principle, teachers could help
> students to build and negotiate their second language identity to achieve
> confidence and be free from worries of risks of making mistakes.

But going on one step further, we think that intelligibility needs to be put in a critical context. As instructors, we can work to legitimate the English used by an L2 user, whether it is a learner variety or a local variety. We can also focus on whose responsibility it is, in an interaction, to achieve intelligibility. In an interaction among equals, presumably this is shared. Where there is a power differential, it will be the less powerful interlocutor who has to make the most effort. Imagine if Graham is using English in negotiating a book contract with a rich Chinese publisher, who speaks a non-standard variety or Chinese English. Graham is not going to be correcting the publisher! It will be Graham (speaker of RP) who will be apologizing for not making himself clear, asking for permission to repeat himself, and so on!

Zahra commented similarly:

> In order to prepare them for encountering inner-/outer-/expanding circle
> speakers with various L1 backgrounds, what type of listening instruction is
> needed? Are our students the only interlocutors responsible for being com-
> prehensible? [But also] What is the degree of expertise that a NNS teacher
> needs to make students aware of upcoming challenges of this kind?

Finally, having a similar accent and expectations as do other L2 users from the same area is also likely to be important, both cognitively and personally. As Zahra continued,

> In our classroom contexts, i.e., EFL or expanding circle, in which the same L1 is shared, our students find it far less cognitively demanding to be mutually intelligible. Thus, they have a more successful communication.

For more accomplished users of L2 English, how they speak English is as much a part of who they are as is their first language. Levis (2005) refers to work by Jenkins which suggests that "same-L1 NNS pairs pronounce English with a greater number of deviations than do pairs of speakers from different L1s [resulting in a] tendency toward convergence, even when it means speaking English with more deviant pronunciation.... Speakers who are too accurate risk being seen as disloyal to their primary ethnic group" (p. 375). The point is, a learner's identity needs to be maintained or perhaps extended, as opposed to being lost, when L2 learning is taking place. This can and should be done through pronunciation as well as through other aspects of the L2. Unless there are exceptional power-related matters at stake (such as high-stakes oral exams to be taken), L2 learners want to be themselves (however they define that) when they are actually using their L2; very often that means accepting that they have, or indeed wanting to maintain, some aspect of their original culture and language at the same time as they use the second one.

IN CONCLUSION

This is an area that continues to develop (as Tupas's recent 2015 collection makes clear). It is tied up very directly with issues of identity and status. Not only students, but teachers themselves are affected by the topic, especially non-native teachers (and even native speaker teachers who have a non-standard variety too). Perhaps given the significance of the topic, this chapter is too short, though on the other hand we feel that there is less published material on this than there should be. We look forward to the possibility that readers of this chapter will themselves contribute to this small but important area of practice through writing about their own work in the area.

NOTES

1. English-speaking countries were at one level among the exceptions (though consider the long-standing existence of Welsh, Irish, and Scottish, in Britain; or the many Native American languages in the United States). But these

days we recognize that multilingual countries like India, Nigeria, and Malaysia, are more typical of nations in their language profile, and we are more aware of the linguistically diverse nature of even apparently monolingual countries like China or Mexico.

2. This useful term was coined by Cook (2002); it emphasizes the role of the person who has learned a second language, not necessarily to "native speaker" competence, but to a level at which they can use the language for practical purposes. It provides a more agentive and respectful term than L2 *learner* for such an individual. Only referring to them as an L2 learner emphasizes deficit rather than ability.

3. This would certainly be true in Graham's home base, where the airport bus driver will address you in Hawai'i Creole English, and the taxi driver may be a Korean or a Vietnamese (immigrant) with quite limited and strongly accented English. As an Iranian expatriate living in Australia, Arman attests to the comparative incomprehensibility of Australian English (Strine), upon first exposure.

4. For a later return to the topic, see Morgan (2001).

CHAPTER 9

DEMOCRATIC ASSESSMENT

INTRODUCTION

Assessment is a particularly challenging area for a teacher who is beginning critical language pedagogy practice. One obvious reason why the area is challenging is that it runs up against the most power-laden aspects of schools and classrooms—tests and examinations. First, there are familiar local institutional pressures, such as from one's own school administration, telling us what to do, in an area they (not to mention the students) are usually particularly concerned about (grades, tests, even graduation). Second, if you are working in the public sector, national entities like the Ministry of Education (or equivalent institution) usually have detailed prescriptions or require national tests following national curricula. Third, and more seriously, somewhat new here in the early 21st century, *supranational* entities such as major international publishing companies with interests in language testing (e.g., Pearson; see Hogan et al., 2016), or nation-based entities with international reach, such as the U.S. Educational Testing Service (ETS; cf. Nordheimer & Frantz, 1997) and the British Council (BC), have a direct effect on many ordinary English language teachers and their teaching and curriculum. This happens because these entities, too, design and administer language tests and teacher education tests (e.g., Cambridge Assessment's "Teaching Knowledge Test" [TKT], administered worldwide

Starting Points in Critical Language Pedagogy, pp. 173–194
Copyright © 2022 by Information Age Publishing
All rights of reproduction in any form reserved.

through the British Council), as well as through their indirect effects on national educational policies through their test level specifications.[1]

In addition, in many countries English language students themselves, particularly high school students and private language school students, have come to believe that they must do what the tests and testing authorities want. In fact, one of the major obstacles to practicing critical language pedagogy in the classroom is that the content and procedures of classroom language teaching are largely determined by the tests that students have to take (which is often referred to as "washback"). Students, teachers, and parents expect the teaching-learning process to prepare students for tests. And since tests are usually developed based on a non-critical view of language, critical language pedagogy may be resisted, or seen as marginal, since it is likely to be perceived as not helping us achieve winning scores on tests.

A number of specialists, recognizing the power-laden nature of language testing, have provided critical perspectives on language testing (McNamara, 2008, 2011; Shohamy, 1998, 2001a, 2001b; see Yoo & Namking for an EFL-specific view). But their discussions mostly concern the testing institutions themselves and national and international level practices.[2] The question we should address, in this chapter, is how to make the ideas of critical language testing specialists applicable at the classroom level.

The teachers that Arman and Graham have been dialoguing with admit that this is not an area where they have explored much. Focusing on the importance of dialogue and negotiation as central to critical pedagogy, for example, Jing wrote,

> For negotiated tests, if informal and small tests could be counted, I have [done] some. As for formal tests, such as the final exam and similar, I don't.

And it is also true that this is quite an undeveloped area in the classical literature of critical language pedagogy. Back when Auerbach and Wallerstein (1987) were writing that very productive ESL-oriented textbook we have often referred to here, their ideas about assessment were primarily confined to the idea that students should do it themselves. They referred to using "the concepts of self-evaluation and group evaluation with specific questions for students to evaluate the curriculum and their actions" (p. 7). And that is about as much as they had to say. So, from a critical point of view, we have to think about whose role it is to do assessment, and (as we will see) what responsibilities participants might have for assessment.

We had a chat room discussion on this topic with one of our groups of teachers interested in critical language pedagogy. We share here some of the participants' comments, which range over a number of directions, strategies, pros, and cons. In sharing them we want to suggest that even though assessment is a particularly challenging area for starting critical language pedagogy, even teachers working under difficult circumstances are willing to consider it. Shiva wrote,

> Simply involving students in the decision of when to have a test and what should be included would be good. [And] I think students need to know firstly the aim of the course, and they need to be highly involved through the course so that they can contribute to testing ideas as well.

Theresa wrote,

> I rarely have negotiated tests with my students because they don't have enough knowledge or [are not] mature enough to understand about tests and what it could be like. Also, all assessments are moderated and mandated.

> [Students] would need to know and understand levels of comprehension and testing types such as why and when multiple choice questions should be used instead of short answer.

Theresa later added,

> I taught my students Bloom's Taxonomy and levels of comprehension. Then I gave them all an information sheet about how rice is harvested (rice fact sheet). Students had to come up with a question per level of comprehension and swap with the person next to them. They were then to answer each other's questions. When I do this—no two persons had the same set of questions even though they all had the same fact sheet.

A strategy was suggested by Elahe:

> How about asking students to develop a question of each lesson during the course and using the collection of their own questions in achievement tests?

A positive outcome of student participation in testing was suggested by Shiva:

> I think this way (asking students to develop questions) students are gonna be more active through the course, and look at the material from a teacher's perspective as well, which helps them to learn the material more deeply. I think knowing the answers of the questions is not always a negative quality. They have already learned what is the aim of the course — what's wrong with it?

Jing pointed out the necessity of some basic training of students to develop test items:

Then the comprehension questions raised by students, can we be sure of these questions' validity and reliability?

One area where student involvement seems common, if overlooked, is *after* tests. In this regard, Arman pointed out,

Even regarding final tests, the least I would do to make it assessment FOR learning would be to discuss the answers after the test is over. This sometimes even results in the students helping me identify my mistakes in developing the test items and understand that alternative responses are possible, which maximizes the fairness of the test.

And Jing replied,

We discuss the answers after every monthly exam ss take. When discussing the answers, we do find a lot of problems.

And Shiva wrote,

Discussing the questions after the exam will also help both teachers and students understand each other's views on tests better. So, it will reduce the gap existing between their understanding

If we move towards taking ownership, as students and teachers working together, of assessment activities in our classrooms, what would that look like? A little later in the mainstream (non-language) critical pedagogy literature than the early brief remarks by Auerbach and Wallerstein we find the following from Shor (1992, p. 144):

The instruments used to test and measure students should be based in a student-centred, cooperative curriculum. This means emphasizing narrative grading, portfolio assessments, group projects and performances, individual exhibitions, and essay examinations that promote critical thinking instead of standardized or short-answer tests.

This is consistent with the increasing availability and use of the area of so-called "alternative assessment." This began to show up in the general (non-critical) literature of our field a few years further on from Shor's use of it, for example, a discussion of it by prominent TESOL testing specialists Brown and Hudson (1998, cf. Brown, 2013). In it they use the term to mean a number of ways of doing testing which aren't norm-referenced multiple choice tests. The most well-known of these alternatives would be portfolio assessment; others include teacher-student conferences, and peer assessment. Although they are "alternatives," these testing options are not thereby inherently critical. Or contrariwise—the stereotypical multiple-choice format, providing it is jointly-constructed, is not inconsistent with a critical or at least participatory point of view or philosophy of teaching and testing.[3] Also, there is some guidance in the mainstream education literature. Consider the title of this work: "Involving Students in The Classroom Assessment Literature" (Davies, 2007; see also Ainsworth & Christison, 1998). Mainstream teachers of quite young (elementary age) students have been doing this for a long time—at least 30 years according to these publications, and that usually means that in some (progressive) schools it has been going on since the beginning of the progressive era (near the beginning of the 20th century).

As part of our discussion with our teachers about how we could sum up a critical perspective in L2 assessment, Arman wrote:

> In critical everything, different aspects of that thing should match each other. So perhaps if an assessment task is methodologically critical (e.g., interactive and dialogical), it is best to make its content critical (e.g., choosing topics which are critical and relevant to students' real life, even perhaps introduced by the students themselves). However, this is not always possible since teachers work within constraints, not all of which are bad though. This means that they need to assess students' grammar, vocabulary, basic comprehension skills, accurate pronunciation, etc. And at low levels of language proficiency, it is very difficult to assess grammar critically for example. So, the content of grammar assessment will be, for instance, "present progressive" evaluated through very basic form-focused tasks. There is perhaps nothing critical about this, but it is essential to gauge students' grammar knowledge. Yet, teachers can still approach the *process* of testing critically, and this is where negotiated assessment comes in. To start with, teachers can ask students when, how often, and how they would like to take grammar tests, and how many of them. In addition, they should be transparent about the nature of the test, which is an important factor in test fairness. And, depending on their students' language level, they can ask them to contribute to the test by developing questions.

So perhaps we can begin by agreeing that this sort of thing is rarely done, though go-ahead teachers might also have a sense that in some of their classes, with the right students and the right circumstances, some baby steps might be taken, and that careful inspection of a relatively small literature is warranted. Let us proceed.

FIRST STEPS TOWARDS MORE DEMOCRATIC CLASSROOM LANGUAGE TESTS

The oldest meanings of the word *critical* (in English) concerns inspecting unexamined assumptions.[4] So from a critical point of view, language teachers should first think about what they are doing, when testing. "Critical" also means, among other things, always being sensitive to issues of power. One way to do this is to think about the students as themselves having rights, both in general, and in the educational situation in particular. So, we could think about the rights of the students, as they are the individuals usually with the least power, in the circumstances in which they are subjected to tests. We can ask ourselves what *we* would want, if we were going to take a classroom (or institutional) test. Think of yourself now, not as a teacher, but as a test-taker. Probably you would want to know what the test would be on, what the questions will look like, and ideally you would really like to know how the teacher will mark the test. In a traditional school, students may only have a general idea what classroom or school-based tests will be about. Students normally don't get any idea about the marking practices or procedures the teacher is going to use. How can this be changed? Possible watchwords here are transparency, communication, dialogue, and participation. Since we as teachers have no direct control over what we are calling institutional tests, let us just (for now) think about classroom tests that we ourselves as teachers are primarily implementers of.

A very preliminary step suggested by our participants is to recognize that all class activities can contribute to assessment, or can be assessed in some way, as contributing to a course grade. As one of our teachers, Shiva, put it:

> Focusing on just test papers means that the teacher is ignoring all class activities and oral work that students have done through the course.

Traditional language tests focus on just paper-and-pencil and isolated language points, but that is far from where we could be, if oral activities, presentations, group projects, creative work, and so on were included in what we assess. Of course, it is not necessarily easy to assess those, but for that matter, classroom paper-and-pencil tests are often made by teachers who have not received training on how to make reliable and valid tests, so they are not inherently better, nor totally easier to make when that is done carefully and professionally. Thus, we will emphasize a participatory (Auerbach, 1992) or participative (Reynolds & Trehan, 2000) approach here.

STUDY GUIDES

As ever, we will try to suggest simple first steps, initially. For example, a teacher could begin to make substantial use of "study guides."[5] The use of study guides allows students to be clear about, and potentially provides input on, the content of what is to be studied and tested. With study questions (questions in the study guides that directly reflect likely test questions, content, and format), students should get a clear model of the form of the questions themselves. Again, under good conditions students could even have input on those forms. This has to be done skillfully, and with some degree of sympathy as well. Jing commented,

> If we use the questions students raise, wouldn't they know the answer already?

Our answer is, we don't want students to arrive at the answer without study, but we do want them to have plenty of test-wiseness about the forms the questions will take, so that they will be able to bring their knowledge to bear and not fail to demonstrate their understanding as a result of mis-understanding the structure or format of a particular test question. We also want students to have not only studied but also revised the general area which will be assessed. If students don't have a relatively focused idea of the likely content of a test, their responses will not adequately reflect their knowledge. That is an argument from efficiency, about one impor-tant way to support the reliability or validity of a test. But beyond that is our own (critical) ethical argument, that test-takers should be treated in a respectful and humane manner, and as rights-holding participants in the educational process, who should have as much egalitarian and democratic participation in testing and assessment as can be achieved consistent with the overall effectiveness of test delivery and administration. To reiterate, and to separate some of the elements here: First, we recommend at least disclosing and clarifying, and providing examples of, the nature and types of test items mentioned. Second, transparency in regard to marking pro-cedures should be aimed at.

The next step, broadly, is student participation: getting students to par-ticipate in test development. There seem to be two main ways to do this, and which you take (first) depends on what kind of student work or assess-ment practices you do most of, perhaps. Discrete-point tests are those that assess students' knowledge of individual items. They have numerous items, and typically include true-false, fill in the blanks, and multiple-choice for-mats. Global or holistic tests require the production and assessment of a broader product, most obviously a piece of writing such as an essay. We will next consider how to assess essays and such like in a participatory way, and then go on to consider how student participation in discrete-point tests can be developed.

RUBRICS

The use of a "rubric" makes it possible to be transparent about marking practices for matters like essays, and also to involve students. A rubric is a guide for individuals engaged in assessing a product (item, object, etc).

In our field rubrics are widely used in the marking of, for example, exam essays. They typically take the form of a table with short prose entries stating the qualities of a good, medium, and poor example of the product or item under assessment. In many cases, the product is initially determined to have several important features that would guide any overall assessment of it. Thus an essay will be assessed in terms of its structure and its content, and probably also features of individual sentences and words, such as grammatical and spelling accuracy. Statements of good, medium, or bad performance in each of those categories can be arrived at. A subscore can be assigned to each level, allowing a grand total to be arrived at systematically and by reference to guiding statements for each subcategory.

The classroom instructor who uses a rubric to guide their marking of essays (or other written products) is already performing in a more professional (and ethical) way than the one who simply, quickly, and subjectively assigns a "global" mark out of 10. The teacher who distributes their preferred rubric to students before they write an essay is also doing well, because now the students know in a very concrete way what their writing is supposed to be shaped towards. The more radical step is to invite the students, in some way, to contribute to, discuss, dispute, and perhaps change, aspects of a rubric.

This participatory development or revision of a rubric is discussed by Ainsworth and Christison (1998). These mainstream authors from the field of education do not affiliate themselves explicitly with critical approaches. They simply state (p. 16), that "how student work will be assessed" should be "share[d] with students *before* they begin working. The best way to do this is to have students create the grading standards with you.... Task-specific rubrics, authored collaboratively by students and their teacher, clarify the criteria used to evaluate the project. Because students are directly involved in establishing these criteria, they understand them thoroughly and can apply them."

The work of Ainsworth and Christison, now 20 years old, is one of the most teacher-friendly, step-by-step expositions we have come across, so we will quote at greater length their "Steps in Building the Rubric with Students" (1998, pp. 16–17):

> When generating rubrics with students, we typically follow these steps to create a class-authored rubric. ...
>
> 1. Explain and clarify the performance task and how it matches the focus questions.
> 2. Show sample student projects from prior years (if available).
> 3. Explain the benefits of a task-specific rubric.
> 4. Show a prior year's rubric (if available).

5. Begin writing the rubric. Use task requirements as baseline criteria.

6. Elicit student suggestions for quality and content descriptors.

7. Ensure, through teacher-student discussion, that students understand the rubric language.

8. Record student responses, and facilitate classroom consensus of rubric terms. Clarify any terms that seem subjective or ambiguous.

9. Follow the process for each score point.

10. Review, revise, and edit the final rubric.

11. Publish the rubric.

The authors' further guidance is absolutely consistent with the overall position we've taken in this book, that teachers developing a critical language pedagogy should start with small initiatives and proceed cautiously, with plenty of advance planning. Their advice includes starting with simple rubrics, not attempting to do this with more than one project or activity (and not making it the only way you do assessment). They advise: "Be patient.... Give yourself and your students permission to experiment with this process" and "It is easier the next time around" (Ainsworth and Christison, 1998, pp. 16–17). We (the authors) did not experience this kind of assessment when we were students and we suspect that our readers likewise did not. Given this, and in the absence of workshop-based professional development in this area, teachers are not likely to find it easy to smoothly work this into instructional practices at first. (If it were easy and common, we would not be writing this book!)

PARTICIPATORY TEST DEVELOPMENT

A long time ago, noted L2 teaching expert Tim Murphey (1989, 1994) published a couple of short and simple accounts of how he involved his Japanese university students in making their own vocabulary tests.[6] These were simple classroom tests, conducted in pairs, in English. Part of Murphey's goal was to make the test itself a pedagogical task, in which English would be used interactively. But also he wanted to motivate students by giving them more control over the test. The basic sequence of activities he used was as follows. First, he got the class as a whole to generate vocabulary items (lexis and idioms) for study. (These came from the unit of material the class was studying.) Students had several days to prepare for the test. They prepared or studied the items that they identified as previously not being sure about. Then during the first phase of the test itself, students were paired up and they exchanged their study lists. There is a natural "jigsaw" element to the task because students may realize that their partner knows some vocabulary items that they don't, or one has focused on some items that the other has not. According to Murphey's report, students naturally shared their understandings, or asked each other about specific items that the other had studied. The basic test item is to explain the vocabulary item, in English, to the partner. In Murphey's context (a Japanese university), he was also able to have the students grade each other. (Each student gave the other a point for a good explanation and another mark for use of English.) But in a less relaxed classroom context, obviously the teacher can provide the mark or grade.

In a discussion of Murphey's (1989, 1994) ideas, some of our teachers were positive about them but also wanted to caution about the institutional context. Zahra wrote,

> Murphey considers student-made tests as a source of communicative-oriented fun and variety in the classroom. That's mostly right. But in terms of his justification that it's efficient for teachers in terms of time and energy on tests, I'm not sure. I think in our context it can't replace the mid-term and final tests; maybe just classroom quizzes. At the best, it can be done as an interactionist aspect of dynamic assessment. The interventionist part cannot be easily challenged.

> At [my] school, we usually assign students to design a test or a few questions as a task. It is to check and direct their awareness towards the important parts of the lesson and their own problematic areas. We sometimes assign a unit to a group of students; sometimes ask each student to individually work on the whole unit or some pages. Sometimes we randomly choose some of the items and add those of our own and administer it. But this practice meets the instructional side of the learning, and the evaluative side is left to department-made test administrations.

We're sorry to say that these two early reports by Murphey haven't often been cited or used in our professional literature. However, one exception is Ashtiani and Babaii (2007), two researchers who drew on Murphey and other critical assessment specialists in a meticulously-designed and implemented experiment in which senior high school Iranian English learners were helped (by their teacher) to construct their own tests for a module or section of a course. The students did better on the tests that they constructed themselves than a closely matched comparison group, taking the same test, but who hadn't had the chance to put it together themselves. It's a very interesting and encouraging report, that would provide good guidance and encouragement to teachers wanting to explore this possibility.

GROUP EVALUATION, SELF-EVALUATION, PEER, AND SELF-ASSESSMENT

Let us just reiterate a key point: Conceptually, the basic idea is that to move towards critical language assessment, we must move to sharing the responsibility for assessment between teacher and students, rather than have it be all the teacher's responsibility. This means that the role of students in groups, and jointly or separately assessing their own work, must eventually be considered. This is usually termed peer and self-assessment. Actually, considering the long-term nature of L2 learning, developing one's ability to self-assess and alter, intensify, change, and so forth, one's own learning practices (whether in a classroom or outside it) is very important. The problem comes because inside a conventional school or classroom, assessment is very much *not* associated with the student role, and the higher the stakes, the more contradictory the role of student is when assessment is associated with the power of the system over the individual.

We have sometimes delved into quite unfamiliar historical aspects of education with the thought in mind that if something apparently difficult and unusual can be shown to have been done in the distant past, its implausibility in the present is inherently thereby lessened. So let it be noted that the idea of "self testing" was used, 100 years ago, within the influential, highly individualized curriculum model known as the Dalton Plan, internationally popular in the 1920s and 30s (Boud, 1995; Parkhurst, 1921; van der Ploeg, 2014). Also, participatory understandings of course evaluation had been in use in U.S. high school curricula during the Social Reconstructionist era. Brameld (1956) claimed that during that period, "the most modern techniques of measuring achievement and progress are [or were] utilized, *students themselves sharing in the selection, administration and evaluation of these examinations as helpful aids to learning* (p. 250, emphasis added; see also Michaelis, 1950). Russell (1953, p. 561) referred to "the rise of informal self-appraisal in the learning activities of many schools, plus the conviction that a major goal of education is to have pupils become increasingly independent in planning, executing and evaluating."[7] Self-evaluation probably moved further into educational contexts by way of the influence of humanistic psychology in the adult and vocational training sectors from the late 1950s on (cf. Boud's 1995 personal account). Eventually it surfaced in our field, with Oskarsson (1978), at the beginning of the communicative era, and at a time when self-directed learning (later called *learner autonomy*) was having some influence. However, the literature of our field offers almost no examples of these ideas in use at that time. The practice may be slightly increasing now. Arman has tried this out:

In an undergrad writing class, I asked the students to do two types of self-assessment, one at the end of each writing assignment where they were expected to evaluate their own performance based on that assignment and the other one a general self-assessment halfway through the course where they were asked to write about their general progress and what else they thought would have to happen in classroom for them to make more progress.

Despite its existence in educational systems for 100 years, self-assessment is still quite unfamiliar to most students. At a practical level (separate from critical pedagogy considerations, perhaps), it is highly desirable to get second language learners used to the idea, because learning a second language is a long-term process which, when successful, continues, in an often mainly self-driven manner, outside the classroom. As second language learners ourselves, we may assess our abilities and judge, perhaps, that our own command of the L2 is still not adequate, and in what areas, and act (or study) accordingly. This kind of self-assessment will be needed if our efforts are to be successful and result in advanced L2 learning. Some recent ESL textbooks do incorporate a short self-assessment component where learners are asked to reflect on what they learned from each lesson of the book (e.g., *Interchange, Top Notch*, and *Four Corners*). This is of course completely low-stakes, but to the extent that students have already experienced some self-assessment legitimated by conventional classroom (and textbook) practice, critically-minded language teachers could build on this.

Any critical language teacher exploring these options will be relieved when reflecting on the fact that multiple assessments are needed if some degree of reliability and validity is to be found in any final (end-of-course) grade. Thus one (challenging) self-assessed assignment would in most cases be balanced by some other peer and even teacher-based assessments (ideally negotiated, of course).

STUDENT ASSESSMENT OF TEACHERS, OR JOINT ASSESSMENT OF A COURSE

In many EFL settings, student evaluation of teachers is not the norm. A moment's thought will confirm us in thinking that it goes naturally with a critical perspective, since it goes hand in hand with a desire to even up the power imbalances across teacher and student. It is also consistent with the position on shared evaluation of a class, mentioned as the initial position of critical pedagogy. This may be rare, but has it not been done before?

Once again, the historical record is salutary. In medieval universities, students (with administrative oversight) evaluated their professors, partly because students paid their teachers directly (Rashdall, 1936). Then, in modern times,[8] reflecting the ideas of Progressive Education in the U.S. in the 1920s, student evaluation of teachers was both done and researched at Purdue University (Remmers, 1930). There was a brief upsurge of interest in this (as a by-product of the growth of national and international student organizations) immediately after World War II (see Riley et al., 1950; Schwartz, 1950), but it was not until the dramatic social changes of the 1960s that it became, and has continued to be, a standard practice in universities in the English-speaking world (Centra, 1993). In the early developments (e.g., Remmers, 1930), teachers received the evaluations directly from the students, and retained control over them.

The topic was picked up and reviewed for TESOL specialists by Pennington and Young (1989), drawing on the mainstream education literature that had by then developed substantially (Aleamoni, 1981, 1987). A caveat made by Pennington and Young was simply that at that point there had been no cases in which the reliability and validity of faculty evaluation instruments, as used by ESL students, had been established. Their piece was then the subject of critical comment by Pennycook (1989) who pointed out the lack of attention to matters of power in it. Not long after, Wennerstrom and Heiser (1992) reported on bias in student evaluation of teachers in a TESOL context (a US university IEP). Problems with the use of student evaluation of teachers occur when they are required by administrations and not owned by teachers, and are then used unilaterally, as instruments of administrative control (and possibly as one of the only sources of information for administrative decision-making). Student evaluations of teachers have become more widely used, unfortunately, in this way. For example, Burden (2009) discusses its introduction and use (by administrations) in Japanese universities (and specifically, in EFL classrooms there), where it became mandatory around 2000. He draws mainly negative conclusions because teachers have no control over the processes, and no input into the questions, and no opportunity nor encouragement to utilize the information for formative purposes; the information is more likely to be used (by administrators) for summative purposes, he reports.

Thus, the short version of the message of this section seems to be, consider involving students in giving you feedback on your teaching, but handle with care. The more you can do this in an informal way, strictly between yourself and the students, the better and indeed the more useful it will be.

LANGUAGE ASSESSMENT LITERACY

Zahra: If we want to implement practices similar to that of Murphey in language classrooms, what knowledge do we need? Are we prepared for test construction? If we all have studied language relevant majors, is the testing material we have studied enough? Did we receive instructions for test construction during pre- and in-service courses? I can't remember receiving any instruction regarding tests in my Teacher Training Courses. Did you get any? If so, in which direction, to improve learning or to support institutes' marketing policies?

Now, what are the areas of knowledge needed to practice Murphey's tests at institutes and schools? What are the areas of knowledge needed to evaluate high-stakes standardized tests? What can be done to improve teachers' language assessment knowledge? If teachers' are equipped with such knowledge, what happens to the institutes' demands? Can we go further than mini-quizzes in the classroom? I know it's a good first step, but is it enough?

With Zahra, Arman, and Graham suspect that in most, perhaps all countries, the training of many second language teachers lacks formal content concerning test development practices and implementation criteria, by comparison with almost any other area of formal knowledge of English language teaching. Thus they do not have sufficient Language Assessment Literacy (LAL), a term which has come into use in our field recently. For studies of this specifically in EFL contexts see Al-Marooqi et al. (2017), especially Ismael (2017; on Kurdish education). Accordingly, a critical approach to language testing must also begin by critiquing our own orthodox practices and understandings. If we don't know how to make a test reliable and valid in a conventional sense, shouldn't we make the effort to find out how to do this? Where a critical language teacher's knowledge and practice would be different from a regular language teacher's in this area is that they would have a better understanding of the limitations of conventional language tests; they would also be transparent with regard to their knowledge and practice, and would be likely to share their information and views in this area with students. This would put students in a more knowledgeable and active role, able (under favorable conditions) to call for information about test reliability and validity to be shared with them, not hidden.

A small part of the problem is that conventional test design certainly does require engaging with the domain of statistics, and too many language teachers are math-phobic! However, in practice (in our opinion), the most important concepts are just that—conceptual. Understanding what reliability and validity are is an essential base for critiquing tests. Calculating reliability is a good way to get a hands-on understanding of it, and this is a matter of routine, using the increasingly foolproof and user-friendly record-keeping software that are now part of our daily life as teachers (such as Excel or other similar spreadsheets, or more dedicated apps).

Graham notes: "With Excel, anyone can easily calculate the split-half reliability of a classroom test. I pushed myself to do this with a regular midterm exam a few years ago. The test I had written wasn't very reliable (about 0.6) but combined with other forms of assessment, it was serviceable. I was also able to share the information about the test with my students."

If we do try to implement some of the alternative forms of testing referred to earlier in this chapter, we can expect to be asked, or indeed challenged, as to whether they are reliable. A first response is to turn the question back to those asking: Do you calculate the reliability of your classroom tests? If so, how reliable are they? How reliable *should* a classroom test be? (What other criteria should be used to determine the pedagogical desirability of a test? Tests, after all, also teach, and motivate.) Or for rubrics, for example—there are of course ways to determine the reliability of rubric scoring practices (various forms of inter-rater reliability, as a start). It is reasonable to ask that a teacher starting to use rubrics should acquire information about associated marking practices and concepts, particularly so as to be able to defend them.

PREPARING STUDENTS FOR INTERNATIONAL TESTS CRITICALLY

As critical second language teachers, we need to be aware of our students' real life needs. Therefore, it makes a lot of sense to have an adequate focus on helping students develop the skills they need to get a winning score on the international tests like the IELTS, PTE, or TOEFL. However, we can still fulfill the critical responsibility of raising their awareness of how these tests, as implemented in practice, have many ethical failings. A key point is to work against the normalization of these tests, despite the fact that because they are ubiquitous and institutionally-mandated and supported, they are taken for granted.

A review in this area is provided by Templer (2004). Let us note some of his main points. First, there is the simple fact that it is indeed the case that international testing of English is dominated by a handful of organizations, such as those mentioned earlier in this chapter. An EFL teacher who wishes to use other internationally-recognized products, looking around, has few options.[9] It really is an oligopoly. That alone should alert us to danger. As Shohamy (2001) says "the entrenched global proficiency exams in effect control the students, and how knowledge of English is defined" (as cited in Templer, 2004, p. 191).

Second, we could tell our students that there are indeed some testing experts who are concerned about this sort of thing. It is not just the student's critical and worried teachers; Templer (2004) identifies Hamp-Lyons, Spolsky, McNamara, and above all Shohamy, as second language testing specialists who have expressed their concerns. As Templer says, however, most of this expression of concern is directed by language testing specialists to the rest of their immediate professional community (of specialists), and one can see little effect on the testing establishment of these critiques.

Third, although not particularly motivating to our students perhaps, we should identify for them the actors, the organizations, who otherwise in their vague anonymity seem even more powerful, and (as good critical scholars), historicize them, locating them in their time and place and with regard to their origins. Yoo and Namkung (2012) locate their origins in the domain of U.S. philanthropic foundations which played a major role in U.S. higher education and, implicitly, promoted the interests of their founders (such as industrialists Henry Ford and Andrew Carnegie). TOEFL is developed and implemented by Educational Testing Service (Princeton, NJ), and yes, broadly speaking it is indeed "the world's largest private educational testing and measurement organisation" (as Templer, 2004, says). And IELTS "is jointly managed by the University of Cambridge ESOL Examinations, the British Council and IDP Education Australia." ETS is a non-profit organization in the US, but as such it is allowed to operate for-profit subsidiaries. With annual income of almost $1bn, it has been criticized: "Americans for Educational Testing Reform (AETR) claims that the ETS violates its nonprofit status through excessive profits, executive compensation, governing board member pay, by directly lobbying legislators and government officials, and refusing to acknowledge test-taker rights" (Yoo & Namkung, 2012, p. 238). It is intriguing that for most of the last decade or so, ETS was run by Kurt Landgraf, a chemical company executive with no experience as teacher or educational administrator, let alone test designer. *Caveat emptor* [let the buyer beware] holds, particularly in cases of monopoly capitalism. In some circumstances where a buyer is obliged to purchase a necessity (such as water, or power, from a utility), the organization is subject to tight government control which includes oversight boards with political and community representation. We might question how well oversight is working in the present cases.

Templer (2004) (working in Laos at the time he wrote his paper) was particularly sensitive to the costs of these tests, usually a burden borne by students themselves. We think not much has changed in the decade since his paper. The cost of these tests is still high if you are from the "two-thirds world" (the global South); basically the nominal price is identical every-where. It is the same in rich as in poor countries, and across urban or rural areas, even though rural students suffer greater burdens, needing to travel to regional centers; and for students from poorer countries, the price may be equivalent to or far more than a month's salary. Basically the pricing mechanism, like other aspects of international English, works to reproduce rich-poor distinctions within countries around the world whose students wish to study in English-using countries or institutions.

And does it seem unfair to your students that a test score that is two years old is no longer valid? It certainly guarantees a continual stream of income for the companies. And does it seem unfair to your students or to you that the versions of English acceptable are those two most powerful "standardized" versions? Perhaps that is just taken for granted, but should it be? This might be more obviously problematic if you were working in India, or the Caribbean, or the Gulf (as Khan, 2009, found, for his Saudi Arabian students, who found the kind of English in the TOEFL test "not the English everyone uses"[10]). Critical language teachers should be in a position to confirm, to their students, that their students' misgivings about these tests are not just their own worries, but real issues and indeed cri-tiques, shared around the world.

Templer (2004, p. 201) asks, "Do such weightings compress and repress space in EFL instruction for critical thought or discussion about alterna-tive futures—and indeed 'meaning-making,' which should be central in any language classroom ... TOEFLising of EFL teaching at certain levels may serve to rob teachers of the best part of our time on the job: creative interactive time with students as we discuss and inquire into issues and problems that command our authentic interest!...." (Brosio, 2003). Even while we work to prepare our students to attain the test scores they need, as the opportunity arises we should suggest to them that an overall nega-tive effect is being incurred by their language education and their teacher.

Finally, students should know that, conceptually, there are alternatives (though given the nature of concentrated international power, they may never really be effective). For example, at national level, there is the pos-sibility of some greater national control: the Malaysian University English Test (MUET), the Test of English Proficiency (TEPS: the Korean alternative to TOEFL), and, from Japan the EIKEN (Jitsuyō Eigo Ginō Kentei). Test in Practical English Proficiency). Better still, it is a matter of a university's discretion what "mosaic" of test scores, portfolio components, and in-house testing, and so forth it uses, and to what extent it prioritizes them over the two main international tests of English we have discussed. A few universities can be counted on to buck the trend. What is needed is support and interest in their procedures.

CRITICALLY ASSESSING OUR
OWN ASSESSMENT BELIEFS: MERITOCRACY

Finally, we should probably review our own perhaps ingrained attitudes towards national tests. It is quite possible that we have taken in, at an early age, the reasons generally produced, part of conventional thinking, concerning why there is national, state-level testing in academic subjects. (So, this is as distinct from the international tests of English we discussed earlier.) We may have unexamined ideas about the nature of intelligence, as many teachers are themselves success stories in their immediate circle of family and friends. We may have become teachers partly because we did better in formal classrooms than many of our peers, and for us, education may have been a means of some (perhaps small) degree of social advancement or status, so it would be natural for us still to look with favor (consciously or unconsciously) on the main instruments that appear to produce or legitimize the formal outcomes of education, namely, that national exams simply and correctly reward effort and intelligence or aptitude and appropriately reward this with social advancement, rewarding merit with a position in a meritocracy. A critical view of national-level tests in education would dissent from such a position.[11] The general critical position on educational systems is that they tend to reproduce class, race, and gender inequalities (as classically articulated by Bowles & Gintis, 1976, 2002). Whereas in the past it did so quite openly (separate schools for black South Africans; no schools at all for women; etc.), these days it does so through a variety of less overt or even unintentional processes. School operates largely on dominant values, and this disadvantages those not from the mainstream. In addition to this, when it comes to exams, there is an additional ideology in many countries, that exams are required so that the best and the brightest can be identified, encouraged, and rewarded (through advancement up the educational ladder) and so they can best contribute to society and (again) be rewarded for that (through some degree of income disparity, usually). Thus, the idea of social mobility is linked to that of meritocracy,[12] as justifying exam regimes. So, let us just take a moment to consider these two things from a critical view of education and society.

The idea of a meritocracy, "the belief that institutions should be governed by people chosen on the basis of merit, perhaps as defined by education and ability, rather than other factors, such as wealth or social class, is one that seems to resonate with the public" (Liu, 2011, p. 385). It was implicit in the establishment of national exam regimes from the Chinese imperial bureaucracy onward. As the concept of national exams became broadly spread throughout industrializing Western nations during the 19th century, as an antidote to corruption and the domination of bureaucracies by aristocracies, the ideal (of a meritocracy) became more and more visible, eventually acquiring the name in a satire written by the British politician Michael Young (1958). Liu summaries Young's views as follows:

> Young's (1958) dystopic vision of a meritocratic society stemmed from his belief that widespread acceptance of meritocracy would extinguish the cause of social justice [because] meritocracy is a justification for inequality.... [Later] Young [2001] claimed that meritocracy breeds "insufferably smug" meritocrats who feel entitled to whatever rewards "they arrogate to themselves" because they believe they advanced on their own merit and achievement. The meritorious become so self-assured as to "actually believe they have morality on their side." The others are left "morally naked" having been judged as not having merit and having been "looked down on so woundingly by people who have done well for themselves." Left without a voice, they become "disengaged" and "disaffected" citizens. General inequality becomes more "grievous," yet accepted as time progresses and the cause of social justice dwindles. This may sound extreme, but if our recent history of lower taxes for the wealthy, widening income inequality, and skyrocketing salaries and bonuses for top corporate executives despite their gross abuses of power are potential indications of meritocracy run amok, then Young's views are perhaps not quite so polemic.

The idea was not confined to Britain or to English-speaking nations. In Europe, the other country earliest committed to this idea was France; outside of Europe another notable country to build the legitimation of a national exam system on the idea of a meritocracy has been Singapore. But critical observers may question whether there is now as much less social mobility in developed nations (such as these) as there was in the previous 50 years. So what is really going on? In answering this, critical pedagogy, as a field of empirical study, goes well beyond the matter of what we do, as critical teachers, in the classroom, and develops critical analysis of educational systems in specific societies and periods. Liu (2011, p. 393) does this in considering meritocratic ideas and practices in regard to the US university system in the post-World War II era. She comments:

> The perception of the US system of higher education as a meritocratic one that also holds firm to ideals of universal access is a powerful impression that serves to reify higher education's significance in a meritocracy..... Karabel (2005) argues that a prominent reason for the symbiosis of meritocracy and higher education is because "the legitimacy of the American social order depended in good part on the public's confidence that the

pathways to success provided by the nation's leading universities were open
to individuals from all walks of life" (p. 543). However, such optimism is
misguided ... access to these institutions has been enshrouded in a history
of battles between status-groups.

It will take us too far away from the primary content of this book to
summarize these analyses, but they are extensive, detailed, and cover substantial periods of time and both specific institution-based analyses and a
number of societies (e.g., Arrow et al., 2000; Bell, 1973; Leeman, 1999; for
Singapore see Lim, 2016; Bowles & Gintis, 2002; Karabel, 2005; for France
see Goux & Maurin, 1997).

A close examination of specific institutional practices undercuts the
hopeful idea that educational institutions do in fact work fairly to identify
and reward "merit" (here identified again as something like educational
ability, or even intelligence, and effort). Important for our purposes is
to note the views of scholars such as Liu (see also Karabel, 2005, p. 551)
that "A commitment to social justice therefore requires that we carefully
consider all the underlying facets of meritocracy, including the definition
of merit, distributive justice, equal opportunity, and social mobility." Liu
continues:

> In the present day it seems largely taken for granted that meritocracy is a
> positive and preferred system in which society functions. As a principle of
> distribution, one might find it agreeable that those with greater skill should
> be more highly compensated. After all, why should not the most talented
> enjoy greater successes and rewards, especially if there was an equal op-
> portunity to earn them? This may sound like a harmless ideal to hold onto,
> but at best it is naïve.... Furthermore, the idea of equality of opportunity is
> far more elusive than it would appear and requires that we duly consider
> how power and privilege are often embedded into opportunity structures.
> One of the strongest arguments for meritocracy is that it subverts factors
> of heredity and substitutes achievement for ascription. This proposition is
> an overreaching one as Bell (1973) so simply notes, "There can never be a
> pure meritocracy because, invariably, high-status parents will seek to pass
> on their positions either through the use of influence or simply by the cul-
> tural advantages their children would possess. Thus, after one generation a
> meritocracy simply becomes an enclaved class." (p. 427)

In short, as Liu (2011) says,

> The rhetoric of meritocracy can be persuasive and it holds much allure,
> but it is also a myth that serves to detract from the work of social justice....
> Most importantly, we cannot allow the myth of meritocracy to overshadow
> the cause of social justice for those who have faced discrimination and have
> systemically accumulated disadvantages. (p. 393)

IN CONCLUSION

Relative to the importance of the topic, this is our shortest contribution. As we stated, this is a highly important domain of practice within which critical language pedagogy has much work yet to be done. Rather than recapitulate what we have written, we once again urge teacher readers to tackle this area and share their findings as teacher-researchers. And if some readers are academics, we also encourage them to pursue work at the classroom level while still engaging the field and the powerful institutions.

NOTES

1. For example, the Common European Framework of Reference for Languages: Learning, Teaching, Assessment [CEFR], whose development was partly supported by the BC (Taylor & Jones, 2006) and has been also promoted by them outside Europe.
2. For a few recent discussions, see Al_Mahrooqi et al. (2017), Serrano et al. (2018), and Becker (2016).
3. But Elahe said,
    I could never consider [multiple-choice tests] fair enough for the purpose of class achievement tests, although they are preferred for their objectivity and ease of correction by many colleagues.
4. "Given to judging" (Shakespeare's Midsummer Night's Dream, around 1600), and "involving or exercising careful judgment or observation" (Browne, 1650, p. 68: "Herein exact and critical triall should be made by public enjoinment; whereby determination might be setled beyond debate: for since thereby, not only the bodies of men, but great Treasures might be preserved, it is not only an error of Physick, but folly of State, to doubt thereof any longer." Critical, adj. (2020). The term was in due course made of major theoretical importance by Kant (e.g., 1781/1998).
5. These are increasingly emphasized in some disciplines as supporting student-centered learning (e.g., Khogali et al., 2006).
6. Very recently, he has returned to this general area: Murphey (2017), in which he emphasizes that language testing, in classrooms, should be social in nature, just as language learning is.
7. Primarily using the term self-evaluation, he draws on a number of empirical studies suggesting varying degrees of reliability for such measures.
8. Doyle (1975, p. 19) cites Kratz (1896) as "the first reported instance in North America of students rating teachers," but in fact, this is an example of various groups of elementary students writing about their ideal teacher, drawing on their recollections over some years.
9. Japan's EIKEN, Korea's TEPS, are accepted at some international universities. But this does not alter our main point.
10. ETS, responding to criticisms, diversified the range of accents it uses from 2008 on.

11. For a general review, a reference that Shohamy used is Broadfoot (1979); now dated, but prescient concerning the future of national accountability regimes.
12. The term was coined in 1958 but was intended pejoratively and used satirically (Allen, 2011; Liu, 2011; Young, 1958); Young (1958) defines it as "intelligence and effort together make up merit (I + E = M)" (p. 252).

CHAPTER 10

DEVELOPMENT OR SELF-DEVELOPMENT AS CRITICAL L2 TEACHERS

INTRODUCTION

An introductory book like this one obviously can't cover all aspects of critical language teaching, though we hope it contributes to developing your knowledge and practice substantially. How extensive the teacher's knowledge in this area becomes depends a lot on the individual teacher (as opposed to depending on the authors of this book). However, as we near the end of the work, we want to open up the matter of a teacher's further growth in critical language teaching by considering teacher development.

What we regard as the best forms and perspectives in language teacher education have always considered teachers as reflective practitioners, who have the ability to theorize about their practices and practice their personal theories. This would go back at least to the ideas of John Dewey (1933). In recent decades you can find this articulated and advocated more and more.[1] But in actual practice too much teacher education has addressed the developing teacher in a banking style, as if the teacher were just a passive technician (Griffiths, 2000). Nevertheless (as you would expect by now), a key position underlying a critical approach to language teacher development is that developing teachers (like their students) are not

---

Starting Points in Critical Language Pedagogy, pp. 195–207
Copyright © 2022 by Information Age Publishing

empty vessels to be filled with knowledge and skills of teaching by teacher educators or workshop leaders. Rather, they are individuals who are already equipped with prior experiences and personal beliefs which inform their teaching knowledge and practice. They are capable of working together to grow, or for that matter working together with a teacher educator to jointly inquire into, and pose and solve problems in the area of critical language teaching.

Within the broad area of TESOL teacher education, after some early small reports (e.g., Crookes & Lehner, 1998) we can find a few more voices articulating a critical and sociopolitical approach. Teacher educators in critical language teaching have questioned the more recent constructivist-oriented reflective models of teaching, seeing that they fail to factor in the political, ethical, and emancipatory dimensions of teaching (Akbari, 2007). They need to go beyond the conception of teachers as "reflective practitioners" and embrace the idea of teachers as "transformative intellectuals" (Giroux, 1992) and "cultural workers" (Freire, 2005) who can think critically and act transformatively (see also Hawkins & Norton, 2009).

In this chapter, we are trying to help teachers think, first, about the shortcomings of a training approach to teacher education, and then consider what they should be looking for in any teacher development experiences they may encounter. To add a practical flavor to the discussion, we will discuss feasible ways in which teachers can improve their own critical thinking abilities and transformative potential. The real-life examples incorporated into the discussion are meant to shed light on how this daunting goal has been attained by many teachers in developed and developing countries (Abednia, 2012).

FORMAL, COURSE-BASED TEACHER DEVELOPMENT

Teachers experience two main forms of professional development—first, that occurring during pre-service education, usually in the form of coursework from a university or some similar institution of post-secondary education, and second, through various intermittent short courses provided by their places of work, generally known as in-service education. Of course, these are valuable and indeed necessary, but they have their limitations, which generations of teacher educators have struggled with.

Pre-service education's limitation is to be found indicated in its name and in the dominant form of the pedagogy of higher education. Professors of education, or instructors in applied linguistics, typically attempt to *transmit* what they consider foundational knowledge both of teaching and of content (in this case, language), through what Freire would call banking education, to mostly young people who have no direct experience as teachers and do not usually know where they are going to teach (and in some cases, are not even sure they want to be teachers). Young pre-service teachers also are rightly more concerned about the problems they face carrying off the role of teacher as one of their first main roles as an adult, and less about, say, the values of the teaching profession or the theories of learning and language they are being instructed in.

In-service education's limitations are also in the name. That is, busy teachers temporarily look away from their day-to-day concerns in their regular service and attempt to pay attention to, or are required to attend, short programs that will supposedly increase their effectiveness or knowledge as (language) teachers. The programs must inevitably be short because the teachers are "in post." But can short-term programs have much effect? And are they designed to reflect teachers' actual real-world needs? And are they delivered by teacher educators who really understand and sympathize with those needs? All too often the answers will be no, no, and no.

For critical language teacher education, we must be looking for some rather different features. First, since critical language teaching arises out of a teacher's own values, there must be some disposition or willingness on the part of a teacher to consider them, possibly even with a view to shifting in this area to some extent. (And a course leader must allow them to be articulated and provide supporting content in this area.) Second, there are issues of validity. That is, walking the walk, not just talking the talk. One would want a critical teacher education course to manifest at least some of the features of a critical language class, such as a (partially) negotiated syllabus, participants in active and inquiring roles, and an emphasis on dialogue. As Nuske (2018) indicates, we must avoid any "risk that critical consciousness raising [could] lapse into a traditional and repressive banking mode of learning due to the inherently lopsided power dynamics of classrooms. Teacher-educators would therefore be well advised to avoid positioning critical concepts as fixed directives independent of context or self-evident principles of the enlightened, lest some students be intimidated into silence rather than asking questions and opening dialogues" (p. 4516)

It is possible that teachers may attend one of the (few) critically-oriented teacher development courses that have been run or exist, largely on the basis of curiosity. They may by no means be familiar with any of the tenets of critical pedagogy before attending the first meeting of such a course, and may be attending for a variety of reasons. In a recent report of one such course (Abednia, 2012), Arman described several of his teachers having (as a result) quite conventional views about their role, that it was to dutifully follow all of the instructions of the administrators of a private language school (or "institute") and further seeing their role as fairly mechanical deliverers of textbook content.

Features of that course which are important to highlight here, and which teachers considering such courses should look out for, included a substantial use of teacher diaries or journals with prompts so as to focus student teachers' reflections on the role of power, the substantial presence of student initiative or autonomy, and of course analysis of the social rather than merely instrumental aspects of the very same real-world teaching these in-service teachers were engaged in.

Arman notes that he expected these in-service teachers, when presented with some conventional academic material to engage with (e.g., basic applied linguistics writings on the topic of Methods) to probe and question the material. In fact, however, initially some of them attempted to memorize it with the expectation that they would be simply tested on it as if it were a set of accepted facts. So critical language teacher educators, on their side (or any reader of this book who as a teacher is about to take on that role) must remember not to move too fast and work with the initial expectations of teachers, establishing their confidence in the role of the teacher educator, before moving on into more challenging critical topics and practices.

Arman reports, on the basis of teacher journals, specific and in some cases fairly rapid changes in perspective. He reports that teachers showed a fairly quick willingness to articulate alterations in their attitudes to their administrations, their desire to plan their own lessons (not previously allowed or expected) and their willingness to question their previously taken-for-granted circumstances. He asked participants to write and talk about why they were teachers and how they came to be teachers in the first place. We think that pre-service teachers may be asked this, but in-service teachers are less likely to find it a central part of courses. Yet pre-service teachers hardly know why they are entering the profession (and may not always be doing so for the right reasons). In-service teachers, in contrast, may have acquired the time in position to see the limitations of their conditions of employment, but are unlikely to have been asked to reflect on the contradictions they now face. Yet we believe this is a very important aspect of teacher development with a critical dimension. Indeed, encouraging professionals to consider the contradictions between what is actually happening and why they decided to become teachers in the first place, or between what administrators and ministries of education expect and the provisions they provide teachers with to achieve such goals, can in fact lead them to take a more critical position.

CRITICAL TEACHER DEVELOPMENT GROUPS: NETWORKING

Elahe: I have been thinking about Critical Pedagogy [more] generally [and] I guess the most important role of us who are involved and a bit familiar with critical teaching is to

> develop it or spread it, I mean at least among our own
> circles. This way we may live in a less biased society and
> work in more enlightened environments.
>
> **Hoda:**   I do agree Elahe. At least we can have a community of
> English teachers who are less biased and might be able to
> spread the critical ideas in their classes and among their
> colleagues.

In the previous section we were rather swiftly dismissive of the possibilities for formal language teacher education courses to support the development of critical language teachers. Of course, we exempt our own courses from this! But not only are there few university professors or teacher educators in our field actually teaching from this perspective, so too are there few such courses. (And where they exist, because of the institutions in question, they may be expensive or require a commitment of time that is not feasible.) So, it is more important for us to think here about a teacher's role in their own self-development in critical directions. And immediately we should suggest that this is hard to do alone. We strongly encourage teachers reading this book (who have made it this far) to look out for like-minded teachers and link up with them for mutual aid in professional development. This leads straight away to the long-standing idea of the teacher development group.

Teacher development groups have been discussed in our literature for many years (e.g., Oliphant, 2003; Sithamparam & Dhamotharan, 1992), and in mainstream education literature as well of course. Structurally and conceptually the matter is simple. Like-minded teachers, recognizing the futility of isolation, arrange to meet regularly, and informally, to discuss topics and read professional literature as well as share practical problems and possible solutions in a spirit of mutual aid, resulting in professional development. However, there are a couple of aspects to critical language teacher's circumstances that require a little careful reconsideration of that literature while the idea is nevertheless advocated here.

It has probably been clear throughout this book that teachers who are implementing or attempting to develop a critical language pedagogy may be doing so somewhat alone precisely because they may be going against the grain of dominant practice in their school or their area or their country. Establishing a teacher development group means contacting others, and explaining what the topic or focus of a proposed group is, but that means, to some extent, going public about an idea one may not yet be confident about or understand. It is a Catch-22. One is in the position of inviting a colleague to share one's ignorance about a topic that is perhaps sensitive. If we were confident, it would be easier to invite others, but if we were confident, we would not need to do so anyway! And also, though this is insufficiently recognized in our literature, in actuality, schools in many cases are not unitary in the values they manifest, and they cope with this by avoiding conflict, most obviously in the sense that teachers have of teaching by themselves, so that when they close the door, they can under some conditions operate as they would prefer (cf. Achinstein, 2002). Thus, existing structures discourage even the adventurous from grouping together with others.

If one is the only teacher in the vicinity with somewhat critical views, one might wish to advertise for others, or announce the formation of a teacher develoment group that would explore and develop them. But once again, there is a Catch-22, or a risk. By going public (and indeed, about an area one would have to admit one is uncertain about), perhaps one would expose oneself to challenge or sanction. Certainly being visible, while at the same time ignorant, in connection with a sensitive topic is not what most of us would advocate, particularly in an era in which, with increased availability of technology, both central government and local administrative control has been increased, to the extent that surveillance now characterizes some schools (Taylor, 2013). The technology that would make any kind of long-distance group of teachers that could get together online, thereby mitigating the problem of isolation, is also the same technology that could be used to identify them. Nuske (2018), having engaged with this problem during his employment in Saudi Arabia, comments:

> Critical peer groups can inquire into the situational appropriateness of critical imperatives that are often presumed to be universal necessities, such as making overt references to issues of social justice in the classroom. For practitioners working within austere institutional cultures that prohibit references to political topics, such mandates may not only be unrealistic but also irresponsible. Instead, educators and mentors can open conversations about possibilities for more surreptitious forms of critical action, including using ambiguity or implication and masking socially conscious discussions as purely mechanical skill-building activities. (p. 4517)

And indeed, it is noteworthy that when in the 1980s, the military dictatorship in South Korea made the state teachers' union an illegal organization (Synott, 2002, 2007), key members of that union regrouped under the heading of a (nationally-organized) Teacher Development Group (cf. Cho, 2005).

If, like us, you are continuing to explore this area, perhaps it is also useful to think (and search) under the term "networks." This is, after all, a defining feature of the internet era. Unfortunately, what we have too often in the internet is not a normal net, with its left-to-right and up-and-down connections in two dimensions (or three), but rather, a spoke-and-hub network, which fails because all messages must pass through the hub to go out to a different spoke, and thus can be turned off at the hub, or center. It is well-known that when the internet was first established, as DARPANET, it was to make U.S. defense communications robust in the event of a nuclear attack. That is, it was indeed to make use of the capacity of a multiply-connected network to continue to transmit communications even if many individual links had been destroyed or a central communications site (like the Pentagon) had been knocked out by a major strike. We have to return to this model, with "mesh" networks being the target.

We note, from the literature on networks in social movements, that having a positive attitude towards, say, in this case critical language pedagogy, does not in itself lead to being involved in a network that would support this.

> Motivation is a necessary but insufficient condition of participation. Individuals have to be motivated and also become the target of mobilization attempts.... Informal networks are crucial for the arousal of motivation to participate, as well as for the activation and coordination of motivated individuals.... Those who are supportive of a movement also have to be targeted.... The more often [individuals] received requests to participate ... the more active they were. (Tindall, 2015, pp. 233–234)

So readers who are hoping to build a small group of likeminded teachers should not hesitate to ask others they think might be sympathetic, and ask more than once! But to reiterate, this should be done carefully.

THE PROFESSIONAL LITERATURE

Something we (your authors) have been grappling with during the writing of this book has been how much to reference—that is, how extensively to support our opinions with citations to articles and books that are part of "the professional literature." As you know, academic writing tends to be quite heavily referenced. The authors are supposed to show where they got their ideas from, refer to how concepts have been used before, indicate empirical support for their claims, and so on, all by referring to published sources, which are usually academic journal articles and books. But isn't this potentially frustrating for ordinary readers? Many language teachers reading this book might find it quite difficult if not in fact impossible to find those references, even if they had the time to do so.[2]

Many teachers indeed do not have time to engage in professional reading. And besides time, access is the most obvious other issue in the utility of professional literature for one's development as a critical language teacher. Leaving aside the matter of time for the moment, we feel a responsibility to say something useful—that is, critical!—on the topic of accessing the professional literature of our field and of critical language pedagogy.

First of all, the overall access situation has changed and is continuing to change, strikingly and rapidly, because of the internet, open source publishing, and related developments. In the past, academic authors were accustomed to, and had a professional responsibility to respond to, mailed requests for copies of their papers.[3] These days it does not take many minutes to identify the email address of an author of an article you would like to read, and if you email that person directly, it is quite likely they will send it to you. Many academic authors regularly place copies of their articles onto their website or personal blog, so you don't even have to contact them. You can just go to the site and download it. Many readers of this book will also be aware of systems like ResearchGate and Academia.edu, which foster the archiving and accessing of articles. I (Graham) regularly receive reminders from ResearchGate to upload articles or respond to requests for copies of my papers that are relayed to me by that system.

Anyone who has internet access can use Google Scholar. When I (Graham) search on a topic I am interested in, I sometimes find immediate access to an article of interest signaled there, and when I click on the link, I find myself directed to the piece that has already been made available through Academia.edu, or in some cases other archiving entities. You can set an alert in Google Scholar so that as new items are entered into it that correspond to your key terms or alert phrase, you will receive notification by email. However, we also have to recognize that for political reasons, Google is now, perhaps increasingly, not accessible in certain countries, is censored (or self-censored), and in many locations, internet access is itself slow, expensive in local terms, or actually not available. The disconnection of all internet access has increasingly been a tool that central governments are utilizing in emergencies to control the population from informing the rest of the world, and in some countries governments' explicit goal is to develop an independent internet that can be disconnected from the outside world, or at least a search engine (such as Baidu in China, Yandex in Russia, or even Naver or Daum.net in South Korea) that is locally sufficient, autonomous, and delivers the search results central authorities would prefer.

Returning to a positive and more intense procedure for obtaining publications, there is publishers' contents alerts. If you have identified a journal whose topic area is of interest to you, carefully review the webpage for that journal. Somewhere on it will be a link or button or box to check so that you can be notified by email when a new issue is published; you will receive an automatic email with the contents page, that is, a list of the articles in the issue. You are still faced with the problem of obtaining the actual article, of course.

Academic books are a little more problematic. They are expensive (if new) and for copyright reasons they are not likely to be found on the author's own websites! Older works are actually not too hard to find secondhand on booksellers' websites, but their effective price can still be high because of mailing costs. Or they may just still be relatively expensive if they are priced in dollars and one is earning the relatively small salary of an English teacher in the global South. Google Books allows partial access to many books of course. Intriguing are book archives outside of the grasp of the international copyright regime, perhaps nominally located in countries like Russia and China, which provide copies of academic and other books for very low rates or completely free with a donation requested. Although these sites may be unethical from a copyright legality standpoint, they are actually helping the world and particularly third world critical language teachers by facilitating access to important scholarly work that is otherwise too expensive to be used by the very people who need to use it. In some countries, there is still the old-school equivalent of these sites: photocopies of academic books bound by small booksellers and photocopy shops and sold without respect of copyright payments. But these will usually only be of the most common and therefore mainstream titles.

This last point brings us on to the literature of critical language pedagogy. Basically, how can you read more about what others in this area think and are doing? If we answer that question in terms of the academic journals in this area, the answer is a short one. There are just a handful of places where critical language pedagogy reports can be found concentrated. The journal *Critical Inquiry in Language Studies* is the most likely and, in a sense, dedicated source. This is the house journal of the professional society the *International Society for Language Studies*, which favors critical perspectives in language study. So, if you *are* going to spend any money, this is where it should be spent. As with most professional associations, membership comes with a subscription to the association or society's journal.

Within the field of education more broadly, just as this is a vastly larger area than applied linguistics, the critical part of it is much larger too. Nevertheless, the number of journals that are exclusively dedicated to critical pedagogy is not great. We could mention the *Journal of Critical Education Policy Studies* and one or two others (e.g., *Critical Studies in Education, Radical Education,* and *Critical Education*). Of course, the problem then is, these are unlikely to provide many articles that focus exclusively on language teaching matters. Journals in our field that are sympathetic to critical positions are many, but only one or two regularly and consistently publish articles with that orientation in each issue of the journal in question, let alone each article in an issue. Instead what we find is critically-oriented articles are scattered through the increasingly vast array of journals in our field. That is why a Google Scholar alert is probably a good way to tackle the problem of keeping up in the area, as opposed to searching for a specific matter.

And as for publishers, yes, there are one or two that may be more sympathetic to critical matters in education and in applied linguistics. Our own publisher, IAP, Routledge, Multilingual Matters, Springer … are all worth keeping an eye out for.

Now, having read an article or even a book, who will you discuss it with?

EXPLORATORY TEACHING AND WHAT FOLLOWS

Obviously, the point of this whole book is to encourage and support you in your early efforts to develop your own critical language pedagogy. The previous subsections on support from peers suggests that doing so with people is better than doing so alone. And as you will have noticed, while we have drawn from some case studies and the past publications of well-placed and dedicated individual teachers and scholars, it remains a fact that the literature of critical second language pedagogy is small. We, you, and people like us need far more reports of attempts in this area and we also will be better able to develop when we have friends providing us with feedback. And as data is collected to provide teachers with feedback, it is one more step from the informal feedback to the beginnings of more formal analysis. Once you are ready to share an informal report with fellow-teachers at some get-together, you are on the way to a publication. Not only do we need articles, we also could use published textbook materials, of course.

So, in this subsection we want to introduce you to the idea of "exploratory teaching," which as the name suggests, is the kind of teaching that reflective teachers do as they are developing. It is closely related to the ideas of action research and teacher research, and could serve as a stepping-stone to the kind of small-scale reports of (critical) language teaching practice that we are suggesting we need more of.

The term was coined by ELT researcher and teacher educator Dick Allwright. He had been promoting the idea of teachers doing research, or bringing a research perspective into their teaching, but as he worked particularly with EFL teachers in Brazil, Cuba, and Spain, he became concerned that it was inappropriate for him, as a well-resourced professor with good working conditions, to urge classroom English teachers with particularly poor working conditions to do something "extra", when they were already doing about as much as they could under the circumstances. Instead, he reformulated the action research approach:

> Exploratory teaching's emphasis on thought and discussion with colleagues, rather than on initial wide reading, and on the exploitation of

already familiar pedagogic classroom activities rather than unfamiliar research techniques, should effectively minimize the time commitment, and
therefore be less off-putting to any teacher wondering if it is all going to be
worth it. (Allwright, 1992, p. 110)

This quote suggests key aspects of this perspective. The teacher begins with
what is puzzling them about their teaching, and then starts reflecting and
possibly discussing the matter with colleagues. They then identify "familiar
pedagogic activities that you might be able to use to explore your puzzle"
(Allwright, 1992, p. 108), and here Allwright (1992) refers to common classroom activities, such as group work discussions, pair work, surveys, diaries,
reading and reporting, and numerous others. The learners themselves,
through some of these activities, may contribute to solving the problem,
or provide the data through which some aspect of (in this case a teacher's
critical language pedagogy teaching could be improved). (They may even
provide a formulation of the original problem or puzzle.) If the investigation needs to continue, Allwright recommends bringing in other teachers,
and finally, if necessary, seeking out an academic researcher. Almost more
important than that, for Allwright, is the possibility that teachers start to
work with one another on these puzzles, thereby building their professional
development through a network of advice and potentially collaboration,
building community and "broadening the atmosphere of collegiality" (p.
115). In this line of thinking, sharing ideas among fellow-teachers is the
most important way of disseminating findings. We think that teacher to
teacher communication is indeed very important. With critical language
teaching the space between teachers is often large, in terms both of time
and space, so nevertheless, a written record, that can be picked up much
later and far away, is quite valuable. We ourselves are continuing to learn
from the writings of specialists around the world, and not everything that
was published 10 or 20 years ago is irrelevant to present-day critical language pedagogy by any means! So with exploratory teaching as a start, we
would encourage dedicated teachers to think of eventually contributing to
the professional literature, as and when circumstances are favorable (and
safe).

For many of us, actually almost the first puzzle in critical language pedagogy is to put together a lesson plan and find or create the materials or
central content (realia, perhaps) through which we can actually teach. In
that sense we are a long way from exploratory teaching, and the practical
need is immediate. That is also the position this whole book has been taking, starting from the immediate interests and needs of teachers who are
beginning to explore critical language pedagogy. Another repeated theme
(also found in Crookes, 2013) is the need for materials. Let us phrase that
more in terms of beginnings, namely lesson plans. If critical language

pedagogy teachers had more examples of how other teachers have run a lesson, it would be easier to start. So let us note that a few websites hospitable to critical pedagogy have a section on "lesson plans."[4] These could well be a first stop for an exploring teacher. But having done one (successfully), we urge you to then support other teachers by polishing your lesson plan and finding a site that will take it. Some blogs or personal websites on aspects of education allow comments to be posted, and that would allow such work to get visibility and some discussion.[5]

IN CONCLUSION—
ALTERNATIVE SOURCES OF INFORMATION

A final thought for this chapter—It is remarkable how concentrated the ownership of mainstream international newspapers or news sites in the English-speaking world is. Major wire services and reporting agencies, and newspapers, such as Reuters, United Press International, the *New York Times*, *The Wall Street Journal*, *The Times* (of London), Fox News, Sky News, and so on, are increasingly owned by the same groups or even individuals. Major national-level (but internationally-oriented) news publications (in English) such as *Japan Times*, *Vietnam Times*, *China Daily*, and so on, not owned by international business enterprises, have their own biases and inevitably will produce a strongly patriotic, nation-centered version of the news, in many respects just as biased as the organs owned by a handful of rich and powerful business people.

Psychologically, it is harder to implement a critical language pedagogy and maintain an equivalent philosophy of teaching if it seems like not many you talk to and not much you read view local and world events the way you do. So it is a matter of psychological good sense and mental health to seek out so-called "alternative" news sources. What are your most relevant non-mainstream news sources, we (Arman and Graham) can't tell, of course, and it will vary greatly by your location. So having made this general point, we leave it to the reader to decide what to read, outside of our own professional literature! But we urge you to do so in connection with a group.

NOTES

1. We can get to this position by way of the term "constructivist"—the active learner constructs his or her own knowledge (cf. Freeman & Johnson, 1998), though this is not inherently critical in nature. And for a fairly recent book-length treatment of reflection in language teacher development, see Farrell (2007).

2. We are glad to say, though, that in a few cases, critical language scholars (e.g., Janks) have themselves made their sources publicly available on their own homepages, which should be turned to as a first resource. (Graham has put almost all his papers on his blog.)

3. Ok, only Graham is old enough to remember this. Arman does not.

4. For example, http://www.freireproject.org/resources/in-the-classroom/lesson-plans/

5. For example, at time of writing, http://maljewari.blogspot.com/2013/03/how-does-critical-pedagogy-look-like-in.html. One potential problem is such websites may not be active and/or links will become outdated.

CHAPTER 11

THE CRITICAL LANGUAGE TEACHER BEYOND THE CLASSROOM

INTRODUCTION

We will not do the concept of critical language pedagogy full justice if we consider only classroom-bound issues and practices. Having focused mainly on the classroom in most of our book thus far, in this final chapter we write, relatively briefly, about the difficult topic of going beyond classroom boundaries, or the idea of doing so. In some contexts, possibilities exist for L2 teachers and their students to contribute to social improvement through action at different layers of society, whether institutional, cultural, economic, or political. In this chapter, we will describe some options for this. We will also attempt to think about how critical language teachers can avoid the risks involved in doing this while at the same time remain committed to their critical vocation.

An immediate caveat: Obviously, it is not easy to experiment with one's teaching in educational institutions where there is tight and unsympathetic administrative control. Similarly, it is not easy to experiment with action beyond the classroom or school where the sociocultural and political contexts are highly oppressive. Accordingly, teachers should consider their

Starting Points in Critical Language Pedagogy, pp. 209–217
Copyright © 2022 by Information Age Publishing
All rights of reproduction in any form reserved.

employment and social circumstances carefully, and only do what they think helps them fulfill their critical responsibilities while at the same time does not unreasonably jeopardize their employment or careers, or their safety and that of their students.

In opening a discussion about action, following from education, that would move towards social change or addressing practical social issues, we are consistent with the position that school alone cannot change society. This is, or was, a point where the Freirean tradition departed from its antecedents in the progressive philosophy of education of Dewey not to mention his colleagues in the Social Reconstructionists wing of progressive education. Freire was clear that schools alone cannot change society; the Social Reconstructionists were not. Perhaps this should be considered more as a hypothesis, which would find empirical support, or not, depending on different cultural and historical circumstances. Consider the past century—it would be safe to say that progressive and alternative schools (and their students, upon graduation) did *contribute* to positive changes in various countries at various times between 1900 and 2000. Certain educational traditions we are particularly familiar with, such as progressive education in the U.S. in the 1920s and 30s, or "informal schools" and "open classrooms" in the U.K. in the 1960s, aided or supported sociocultural and political shifts that benefited and continue to benefit previously marginalized groups. Freire would have understood the practical benefits of other traditions he drew upon (such as Freinet and *l'education nouvelle*, in Europe in the 1930s: Taylor, 1991). In Brazil he had at first benefited from local political support and then suffered from its withdrawal (being forced into exile), so in (Freire 1972, p. 128) he realistically commented that, at a particular period or location, "A critical analysis of reality may ... reveal that a particular form of action is impossible or inappropriate *at the present time.*" And further, a point that will help beginning critical language pedagogy teachers operating under difficult circumstances feel a sense of relief: "Those who through reflection perceive the infeasibility or inappropriateness of one or another form of action (which should accordingly be postponed or substituted) cannot thereby be accused of inaction. Critical reflection is also action" (Freire 1972, p. 128).

Along with that cautious advice, and consistent with the idea that schools can't do everything, he advises that critical teachers should have a foot in both camps: "In terms of tactics, we all have one foot inside the system, and strategically we have the other foot outside the system" (Shor & Freire, 1980, p. 178). That is, they should implement a critical pedagogy in the classroom and engage with social movements outside it. He also writes, "For me, the best thing possible is to work in both places simultaneously, in the school and in the social movements outside the classroom.... I think if it were possible for lots of teachers who work just inside school, following the schemes, the schedules, the reading lists, grading papers, to expose themselves to the greater dynamism, the greater mobility you find inside social movements, they could learn about another side of education not written in books. There is something very important outside formal education, which the people are creating. It would be for teachers an experience of opening windows. Nevertheless, I respect teachers when they say they prefer to stay here in the schools, but even there it is necessary to be critical inside the system" (Shor & Freire, 1980, p. 39).

So, after reviewing some simple examples based in the classroom, we will spend a bit of time with the matter of social movements.

SIMPLE EXAMPLES

We will begin with ideas and examples that come mainly from explicitly democratic environments. Of course, many countries and locations cannot be so described, and many states that claim to be democracies in fact limit citizen participation in government in many ways. Throughout this book we have been holding out some possibility for critical language pedagogy in less democratic circumstances. Nevertheless, it is easier to provide an exposition by starting with conventionally democratic contexts.

The beginnings of critical language pedagogy in the U.S. were with adult immigrant students, who were expected to live, work, and have all regular legal entitlements of being a permanent resident, and in due course a citizen, in a democracy. The latter role obviously includes voting and other forms of conventional political participation, which include expressing opinions through means other than the ballot box, and the use of public media (newspapers and such like) and other forms of expression. It also includes acting within one's place of employment (if a worker) and school (if a student).[1]

If as a teacher you are employed by the state, or by a state agency receiving funds intended to benefit public welfare, and you are working with adults who have a recognized right to express themselves in the above ways, then as a teacher you have legitimized access to options for action that follow directly from your critical pedagogy. The key point, as Auerbach (1992, p. 17), says is to "enable learners to become active participants in shaping their own realities."

So while it is not absolutely an everyday matter, teachers in democracies do express themselves, supported by or together with their students, through engaging in actions and activities that have socio-political engagement. While this is not a complex matter in itself, like many other things in critical language pedagogy it may be hard to imagine (because we ourselves have not experienced it or seen it), so some simple examples may be helpful.

At a preliminary level, we can outline the steps necessary to begin to include a topic from outside the classroom in a course, through using language itself to investigate the topic, both by way of what can be found already written about it, and through using language to talk with people or otherwise investigate the matter. Bringing the details back to class is normally part of what critical language teachers and their students would do with a topic of interest or concern. Thus, under the general heading of "Investigating," we could group the following steps (which would have to be planned for, time across several weeks of class meetings allocated for, of course):

- Listening (and some speaking): Students interview people in the vicinity —within the school or community—who are affected by the topic, issue, or concern. Inviting a local political (or issues) representative to their classroom to ask and answer questions about a topic of concern or interest
- Inviting a newspaper or TV reporter to the class to share their views
- Reading: Find, read, summarize articles on the topic
- Writing: Report findings
- Speaking: report findings in various venues, beginning with the classroom but possibly encompassing, for example, giving a speech at a speech contest

All this can be individual work, though in pairs or groups would be better.

Then, some "actions" can be completed in-class. It is not unusual for critical pedagogy reports to include mention of some basic actions involving written work, such as writing to a newspaper: ("letter to the editor"), writing to a local political representative ("letter to the mayor"), or writing an article in the school newsletter, or writing directly to the school administration ("letter to the principal"). Written work can encompass a range of genres: petitions, letters, press releases, posters, pamphlets, flyers, poems, songs, stories, webpages, and in this age of easy multimedia literacy, and short videos.

Specific actions that have been mentioned in the literature include in-school actions, such as those documented by West (2014) in his report of (critically) teaching English in a private language school in South Korea. Children in his school were allocated rewards in the form of coupons that could be spent in the school snack shop. After discussing a recent unwelcome change in policy around this topic, the students (some quite young) put up posters outside their classroom calling for change in the way their rewards were allocated.

Flowerdew (2005) reports on critical EAP in a Hong Kong university. Students had to do a small-scale investigation of issues affecting their own curriculum and provide a report on it. Some of these reports had resulted in curricular change. In one case

> a group of biology majors investigating the mismatch between the under-graduate biology curriculum and future career prospects of biology students recommended that more compulsory Mandarin courses be included to give biology students a competitive edge when applying for business-related posts. The students reported that in their interview with the professor concerned, he agreed in principle with their recommendation and said he would raise this issue at a higher level. (p. 145)

An example of a more challenging end-point of action is given in a report of a US community college teacher (Ferguson, 1998). The teacher provided a simple account of how she helped her adult ESL community college students to "lobby" local lawmakers when faced with the threat of cutbacks to funding for her program and related ESL programs. The students wrote letters to the newspapers and visited local politicians in their offices. They got the money that would have been cut to be restored. This was, in a sense, simple, as the teacher and students both understood the problem, related to it directly, and would have been seen by legislators as entitled to make representations about it. On the other hand, this was and is fairly unusual and some teachers, not to mention ESL students, would have neither the courage, disposition, nor skills to do this. Furthermore, there are many places in the world where this is barely feasible or is in fact outright dangerous.

A slightly more overarching perspective is suggested by "service learning." Service learning is a widespread curricular perspective within schools and universities that suggests that valuable learning (deserving of curricular credit) can occur when students, under educational supervision, engage with community members or groups that deserve, or need, "service." Less structured, many institutions simply require students to accumulate a certain number of hours volunteering, as part of their curricular requirements. Classic or stereotypical examples are helping the poor, volunteering in "soup kitchens" or with homeless outreach programs, or helping the elderly or infirm, again through volunteering with existing organizations, whether state, official, governmental or charitable and non-governmental in nature. In a recent interview-based study of critical pedagogues working in Canadian universities (Shahsavari-Googhari, 2017), several framed this approach as part of their critical pedagogical out-of-class practice. Service learning is not without its critics and needs careful attention not to mention preparation if it is to be effective, particularly if it is to be effective in coordination with critical pedagogy. Brown (2001) includes a detailed set of steps to maximize this integration.

Let us conclude this section by asking the paradoxical question, "What is done when nothing can be done?" It is, after all, the case that under conditions of extreme oppression people still talk quietly among themselves when they think no one is listening. Forms of covert resistance have been discussed by some specialist researchers such as Scott (1985, 1990). There may be a range of stances and activities that are not usually theorized as action in the context of educational practice under conditions that inhibit the kind of in and out of classroom practices we have discussed here. One example (Priti Sandhu, personal communication) is from a teacher who was teaching in an all-boys school in a country where (at that time) girls were simply not allowed to take classes. Her form of resistance was to teach with the classroom door open. Girls gathered silently in the corridor and listened. This is a poignant example, but it suggests to us that creative (critically-minded) teachers will find ways under even the most challenging circumstances

SOCIAL MOVEMENTS

Social movements are "a type of group action. They are large, sometimes informal, groupings of individuals or organizations which focus on specific political or social issues. In other words, they carry out, resist, or undo a social change" (Wikipedia).[2] For Paulo Freire and other critical pedagogy specialists, they were and are important. Here again is Freire, talking to Shor:

> For me, the best thing possible is to work in both places simultaneously, in the school and in the social movements outside the classroom. But, one thing you must avoid is to be ineffective in both places, to do both poorly because you try to do too much ... I think if it were possible for lots of teachers who work just inside school, following the schemes, the schedules, the reading lists, grading papers, to expose themselves to the greater dynamism, the greater mobility you find inside social movements, they could learn about another side of education not written in books. There is something very important outside formal education, which the people are creating. It would be for teachers an experience of opening windows. Nevertheless, I respect teachers when they say they prefer to stay here in the schools, but even there it is necessary to be critical inside the system. (Shor & Freire, 1980, p. 39)

We think that Freire's suggestion to teachers, that they participate in social movements, is an important one, not to be dismissed out of hand by beginning critical language pedagogy teachers, but neither can it be embraced wholeheartedly by all who might like to, given the conditions of many countries. But by engaging with it, and analyzing it, we (teachers) can educate ourselves and then decide what is feasible. In this section we will first present a couple of Freire quotes and then go on to think through the matter. Note that at this point, there is a possibility that the teacher's involvement in social movements is to some extent distinct from their classroom work (cf. Marshall & Anderson, 2009).

First, what are some examples of social movements?[3] There have always been upsurges of popular opinion and protest (see Tilly, 2003, 2004). In modern times and following the industrial revolution, in developed countries one of the most significant has been the "labor movement": the activities of organized labor. Anti-war movements must have occurred many times but after World War One there were more sustained and international efforts which have now, much later, become "the" peace movement. By the middle of the last century we can find so-called "single-issue" movements, such as those for women's rights, gay rights, the U.S. Civil Rights movement (closely associated with the broader anti-racist movement) and so on. Some have an explicitly domestic or even local focus; others are international in reach, scope, and membership. The more recent single-issue ones have been labelled the "New Social Movements." And some newer ones ("21st century social movements," Jobin-Leeds & AgitArte, 2016) add prisoner rights and immigrant rights movements to revitalize older movements (such as *"Occupy"* in the United States).

There are or have also been "educational movements" in various countries in recent times, that had features of social movements. Swain (2005) reviewed cases from Bosnia/Herzegovinia, Colombia, India, Malaysia, Peru, South Africa, and the United States, and concluded that

> social initiatives in the educational domain have originated either when states have failed to fulfill their role in providing facilities and opportunities for their citizens to receive basic education and/or when a certain section of the society feared losing its identity due to nation-building projects of the state through educational curriculum machination. (p. 209)

But we can think beyond cases where minorities were underserved by educational systems, to a broader social movement intended to raise public awareness and pressure any government (local or national) into developing educational programs. Anyon (2005, 2009) analyzed the U.S. civil rights movement for its implications for education, and called for a social movement for schools (in the United States) because she feared (rightly, we think) that without greater public support for public education, the U.S. public education system would be gradually defunded (which is indeed happening).[4]

One feature of social movements is that they often involve public demonstrations. We may (naïvely?) suppose that in a democracy there is freedom of speech and thus no harm in expressing an opinion in this way. But even under the freest circumstances, should a teacher do this? Public protest, in the past, and particularly in urban environments, might have been supposed to be anonymous. But this is not the case in small towns, villages, and rural areas, and increasingly, with face recognition technology and increased surveillance everywhere, anonymity is not an option.

However, this is certainly not the only way of being involved in a social movement. A supporter of a movement could be involved in organizing public debate or protest; could be involved in fundraising; could be involved in writing press releases (if there is a press); and so on. Part of the rationale here is simply that democracy (or politics) should not be confined to the ballot box. Even in so-called democracies, the ballot alone may have relatively little effect (Fuller, 2015) if it is the only force operating for social change. Where there is conventional representative democracy and conventional party politics, most people do not get involved and democracy of any kind is thus the weaker. If one of the goals of critical pedagogy is to foster active citizenship, it is probably a good thing for a teacher to speak from experience.

IN CONCLUSION

In concluding this chapter, we can point out that it is shorter than most. This reflects the state of play, the development of the field. The action element arising from critical language pedagogy is the part of this area of curriculum theory and practice about which least is known. Not only may it happen comparatively rarely, it would be quite hard to investigate. More than that, we do not know when the seeds of action will ripen. The effects of an emancipatory education, on a young person or even a non-traditional student, may not be apparent until years later, or until circumstances arise that make some actions either possible or essential. But we would also encourage language teachers to think about the most minimal or more conventional forms of action legitimately or normally associated with critical speech or writing, and plan for them accordingly.

NOTES

1. The idea that politics is somehow confined to formal political institutions (e.g., legislatures, parliaments, provincial governments) and processes (e.g.,

voting) is mistaken. For some lines of political theory, doing politics within one's workplace, community, or home (the personal is political) is more important than confining it to the ballot-box.

2. The term can be used broadly, as Freire did. For specialists, it is one of several kinds of organizing: social movements focus on a single issue; community organizing focuses on the issues of a community, and broad-based organizing takes up a range of issues over time, usually with networks of organized groups (Stout, 2010).

3. For a popular review, see Jobin-Leeds and AgitArte (2016).

4. And if you distrust the state, but wish to have schools that would be critical or radical, you will certainly have to get organized and do most of the things a social movement does, on a local scale, if you are to get anywhere.

CHAPTER 12

ENVOI—CLOSING REMARKS

Thank you for joining us on this introductory sally into the world of critical language pedagogy. Please also join us in thanking our teachers-in-development who worked with us on the free on-line courses that have given rise to the various comments we were able to share with you throughout the book. As we have been saying all along, despite this piece of writing, in the end having a fairly long list of references, still this is not a well-developed area of research and practice. So, it is one in which the work of teacher-researchers, that is, teachers who are willing to communicate about their efforts, in systematic ways, to other teachers, are particularly needed.

Over the period of some years since this book was first conceptualized, and the on-line courses run, the perceptions your authors have of the world have changed somewhat. One of the most obvious global features that is more visible now than when we began the work is global heating (though as we close this writing, the world is also grappling with a pandemic). Another is the ever-increasing gulf between rich and poor in many countries. The rise of populism is a political development that was not very visible (it seems to us) five years ago. Continuing growth in indigenous sovereignty movements also seems a clearer part of the international scene than it was, and that perhaps is one of the global developments which is more positive though very much a site of struggle. The anti-racist struggle has recently gained a sudden upsurge in attention and energy.

Finally, we could say that the steadily increasing (if small) visibility of critical language pedagogy *is* a feature of the last few years. We are happy

Starting Points in Critical Language Pedagogy, pp. 219–220

if this book in some small measure contributes to it. But it will actually be for the readers of this work to really make it count. We do not expect substantial changes overnight, or even over a year or two. But if readers were to take seriously some of the suggestions about networking, for example, perhaps some networking of like-minded readers of this book would make its capacity to aid beginners in critical language pedagogy even more of a possibility. We would be happy to communicate with any readers with ideas about this area, or indeed on any aspects of the work as a whole. In that spirit of dialogue, we bid readers what we hope is just a temporary "Farewell!"

REFERENCES

Abednia, A. (2012). Teachers' professional identity: contributions of a critical EFL teacher education course in Iran. *Teaching and Teacher Education, 28*, 706–717.

Abdenia, A. (2015). Practicing critical literacy in second language reading. *International Journal of Critical Pedagogy, 6*(2).

Abednia, A. & Izadinia, M. (2013). Critical pedagogy in ELT classroom: exploring contributions of critical literacy to learners' critical consciousness. *Language Awareness, 22*(4), 338–352.

Achbar, M., & P. Wintonick. (producers) (1992). *Manufacturing consent: Noam Chomsky and the media* (Videotape). National Film Board of Canada.

Achinstein, B. (2002). Conflict amid community: The micropolitics of teacher collaboration. *Teachers College Record, 104*(3), 421–455.

Ainsworth, L., & Christison, J. (1998). *Student–generated rubrics: An assessment model to help all to succeed.* Dale Seymour.

Ajoke, A. R., Shapii, A. B., & Hasan, M. K. (2015). Co–curricular activities and achievement in language learning of secondary students in Nigeria. *ABAC Journal, 35*(2), 18–31.

Akbari, R., (2007). Reflections on reflection: a critical appraisal of reflective practice in L2 teacher education. *System, 35*,192–207.

Aleamoni, L. M. (1981). Student ratings in instruction. In J. Millman (Ed.), *Handbook of teacher evaluation* (pp. 110–145). SAGE.

Aleamoni, L. M. (1987). Typical faculty concerns about student evaluation of teaching. In L. M. Aleamoni (Ed.), *Techniques for evaluating and improving instruction* (pp. 25–31). Jossey-Bass.

Alexander, L. G., Vincent, M. C., & Chapman, J. (1978). *Talk it over: Discussion topics for intermediate students.* Longman.

Alexander, L. G., Kingsbury, R., & Chapman, J. (1978). *Take a stand: Discussion topics for intermediate adults*. Longman.

Alexander, L. G., & VIncent, M. C. (1975). *Make your point: 30 discussion topics for students at secondary level*. Longman.

Alford, J., & Kettle, M. (2017). Teachers' reinterpretations of critical literacy policy: Prioritizing praxis. *Critical Inquiry in Language Studies, 14*(2–3), 182–209.

Allen, A (2011). Michael Young's 'The Rise of the Meritocracy: A Philosophical Critique'. *British Journal of Educational Studies, 59*(4), 367–382

Allwright, D., Coleman, H., et al. (1989). *Reports from the language learning in large classes research project*. Overseas Education Unit, School of Education, University of Leeds, UK.

Allwright, D. (1992). Exploratory teaching: Bringing research and pedagogy together in the language classroom. *Revue de Phonetique Appliquée, 103*, 101–117.

Al–Marooqi, R., Coombe, C., AL–Maamari, F., & Thakur, V. (Eds.). (2017). *Revisiting EFL assessment: Critical perspectives*. Springer.

Anyon, J. (2005). *Radical possibilities: Public policy, urban education, and a new social movement*. Routledge.

Anyon, J. (2009). What is to be done? Toward a rationale for social movement building. In S. Shapiro (Ed.), *Education and hope in troubled times* (pp. 47–63). Routledge.

Arnold, M. (1868). *Schools and universities on the Continent*. Macmillan.

Arrow, K., Bowles, S., & Durlauf, S. (Eds.). (2000). *Meritocracy and economic inequality*. Princeton University Press.

Ashtiani, N. S., & Babaii, E. (2007). Cooperative test construction: the last temptation of educational reform? *Studies in Educational Evaluation, 33*, 213–228.

Auerbach, E. R. (1992). *Making meaning, making change*. Center for Applied Linguistics.

Auerbach, E. R., & Wallerstein, N. (1987). *ESL in action*. Prentice-Hall.

Avrich, P. (1980). *The Modern School movement: Anarchism and education in the United States*. Princeton University Press.

Ayers, W., Kumashiro, K., Meiners, E., Quinn, T., & Stovall, D. (2010) *Teaching toward democracy: Educators as agents of change*. Paradigm.

Barnes, D. R. (1971). *Language, the learner and the school*. Penguin.

Barnet, S., & Bedau, H. (2013). *Critical thinking, reading, and writing. A brief guide to argument*. Bedford/St. Martin's.

Bartlett, L. (1990). Teacher development through reflective teaching. In J. C. Richards & D. Nunan (Eds.), *Second language teacher education* (pp. 202–214). Cambridge University Press.

Bell, D. (1973). *The coming of post–industrial society*. Basic Books.

Benesch, S. (1996). Needs analysis and curriculum development in EAP: An example of a critical approach. *TESOL Quarterly, 30*(4), 725–738.

Benesch, S. (2006). Critical media Awareness: Teaching resistance to interpellation. In J Edge (Ed.), *(Re)locating TESOL in an Age of Empire* (pp. 49–64). Palgrave Macmillan.

Becker, A. (2016). Student-generated scoring rubrics: Examining their formative value for improving ESL students' writing performance. *Assessing Writing, 29*, 15–24.

Birk, N., & G. Birk. (1995). Selection, slanting, and charged language. In G. Goshgarian (Ed.), *Exploring language* (pp. 113–121). HarperCollins.

Boal, A. (1992). *Games for actors and non-actors.* Routledge

Boler, M. (1999). *Feeling power: Emotions and education.* Routledge.

Bosompen, E. G. (2014. Materials adaptation in Ghana: Teachers' attitudes and practices. In S. Garton & K. Graves (Eds.), *International perspectives on materials in ELT* (pp. 104–120). Palgrave Macmillan.

Boud, D. (1995). *Enhancing learning through self-assessment.* RoutledgeFalmer.

Bowles, S., & Gintis, H. (1976). *Schooling in capitalist America.* Basic Books.

Bowles, S., & Gintis, H. (2002). Schooling in capitalist America revisited. *Sociology of Education, 75*, 1–18.

Brameld, T. (1956). *Toward a reconstructed philosophy of education.* Dryden Press.

Brandenberg, A. (1998). *Marianthe's story: Painted words and spoken memories.* Greenwillow.

Breen, M., & Littlejohn, A. (2000). *Classroom decision-making.* Cambridge University Press.

Broadfoot, P. M. (1979). Communication in the classroom: A study of the role of assessment in motivation. *Educational Review, 31*(1), 3–10.

Brookfield, S. D., & Preshkin, S. (1999). *Discussion as a way of Teaching: Tools and techniques for democratic classrooms.* Jossey-Bass.

Brosio, R. (2003). High-stakes tests: Reasons to strive for better Marx. *Journal for Critical Education Policy Studies, 1*(2), 1–29.

Brown, D. (2001). *Pulling it together: A method for developing service–learning and community partnerships based in critical pedagogy.* Corporation for National Service, National Service Fellowship Program.

Brown, J. D. (Ed.). (2013). *New ways of classroom assessment* (Revised ed.). TESOL.

Brown, J. D., & Hudson, T. (1998). The alternatives in language assessment. *TESOL Quarterly, 32*(4), 653–675.

Browne, A. (1987). *Piggybook.* Alfred & Knopf.

Browne, A. (1998). *Voices in the park.* DK Publishing.

Browne, T. (1650). *Pseudodoxia epidemica* (2nd ed.) A. Miller for Dod & Ekins.

Bruneau, B., Rasinski, T. V., & Shehan, M. (1991). Parent communication in a Whole Language kindergarten: What we learned from a busy first year. *Reading Horizons, 32*(2), Article 4 (unpaginated).

Burbules, N. C. (1993). *Dialogue in teaching: Theory and practice.* Teachers College Press.

Burden, P. (2009). A case study into teacher perceptions of the introduction of student evaluation of teaching surveys (SETs) in Japanese tertiary education. *The Asian EFL Journal Quarterly, 11*(1), 126–148.

Canagarajah, S. (2002). *Critical academic writing and multilingual students.* University of Michigan Press.

Centra, J. A. (1993). *Reflective faculty evaluation.* Jossey-Bass.

Cho, H. S. (2005). " Although we still have a long way to go, I don't think we will ever stop." A grassroots EFL teacher development group in South Korea. *University of Hawai'i Second Language Studies, 23*(2), 70–101.

Chou, H.-Y., Lau, S.-H., Yang, H. C., & Murphey, T. (2007). Students as textbook authors. *ELT Forum, 45*(3), 18–21.

Chun, C. (2016). Critical literacy writing in ESP: Perspectives and approaches. In J. Flowerdew & T. Costley (Eds.), *Discipline–specific writing: Theory into practice* (pp. 181–195). Routledge.

Clark, J. L. (1987). *Curriculum renewal in school foreign language learning*. Oxford University Press.

Clarke, D. F. (1991). The negotiated syllabus: What is it and how is it likely to work? *Applied Linguistics 12*(1), 13–28.

Coelho, E., Winer, L., & Olson, J. W.-B. (1989). *All sides of the issue*. Alemany Press.

Connell, W. F. (1950). *The educational thought and influence of Matthew Arnold*. Routledge and Kegan Paul.

Conteh, J. & Meier, G. (Eds.). (2014). *The multilingual turn in languages education: opportunities and challenges*. Multilingual Matters.

Cook, V. (Ed.). (2002). *Portraits of the L2 user.* Multilngual Matters.

Cook, V. J. (2001). Using the first language in the classroom. *Canadian Modern Language Review, 57*(3), 402–423.

Cowhey, M. (2006). *Black ants and buddhists*. Stenhouse.

Crawford, L. M. (1978). *Paulo Freire's philosophy: Derivation of curricular principles and their application to second language curriculum design* (Unpublished doctoral dissertation). University of Minnesota, Minneapolis, MN.)

Crawford–Lange, L. M. (1981). Redirecting second language curricula: Paulo Freire's contribution. *Foreign Language Annals, 14*(4), 257–268.

Critical, adj. (2020). In *Oxford English Dictionary*. OED Online. March 2021. Oxford University Press. https://www.oed.com/view/Entry/44592?redirectedFrom=critical (accessed April 4, 2021).

Crookes, G. (2003). *A practicum for TESOL*. Cambridge University Press.

Crookes, G., & Arakaki, L. (1999). Teaching idea sources and work conditions in an ESL program. *TESOL Journal, 8*(1), 15–19.

Crookes, G. V. (2013). *Critical ELT in action*. Routledge.

Crookes, G., & Lehner, A. (1998). Aspects of process in an ESL critical pedagogy teacher education course. *Tesol Quarterly, 32*(2), 319–328.

Cullen, R. (2008). Teaching grammar as a liberating force. *ELT Journal, 62*(3), 221–230.

Crystal, D. (2003). *English as a global language* (2nd ed.). Cambridge University Press.

Dam, L. (1990). Developing awareness of learning in an autonomous language learning context. In R. Duda & P. Riley (Eds.), *Learning styles* (pp. 189–197). Nancy, Presses Universitaire.

Davies, A. (2007). Involving students in the classroom assessment process. In D. B. Reeves (Ed.), *Ahead of the curve: The power of assessment to transform teaching and learning* (pp. 31–57). Solution Tree Press.

Day, R., Shales, J., & Yamanaka, J. (2009). *Impact issues*. Pearson Education Asia.

Dewey, J. (1910a). *How we think*. D. C. Heath.

Dewey, J. (1910b). Science as subject–matter and as method. *Science, 31*, 121–127.

Dewey, J. (1933). *How we think: a restatement of the relation of reflective thinking to the educative process*. D. C. Heath

Doyle, K. O. (1975). *Student evaluation of instruction*. D. C. Heath.

Duker, S. (1962). Basics in critical listening. *The English Journal, 51*(8), 565–567.

Duncan-Andrade, J. M., & Morell, E. (2008). *The art of critical pedagogy: possibilities for moving from theory to practice in urban schools*. Peter Lang.

Dresser, R. (2012). The impact of scripted literacy instruction on teachers and students. *Issues in Teacher Education, 21*(1), 71–87.

Eastman, L. (1998). Oral discussion in teaching critical literacy to beginners. In A. Burns & S. Hood (Eds.), *Teaching critical literacy* (pp. 22–28). NCELTR.

Edelsky, C., & Johnson, K. (2009). Critical whole language practice in time and place. *Critical Inquiry in Language Studies, 1*(4), 121–141.

Ellis, R. (1994). *The study of second language acquisition*. Oxford University Press.

Estes, E. (1944). *The Hundred Dresses*. Harcourt, Brace & World.

Fairclough, N. (2003). *Analysing discourse: Textual analysis for social research*. Routledge.

Farrell, T. S. C. (2007). *Reflective language teaching: From research to practice*. Continuum.

Feeney, D. (2016). *Beyond Greek: the beginnings of Latin Literature*. Harvard University Press.

Ferguson, P. (1998). The politics of adult ESL literacy: becoming politically visible. In T. Smoke (Ed.), *Adult ESL: Politics, pedagogy, and participation in classroom and community programs* (pp. 3–16). Lawrence Erlbaum Assocs.

Flowerdew, L. (2005). Integrating traditional and critical approaches to syllabus design: the 'what', the 'how' and the 'why? *Journal of English for Academic Purposes, 4*, 135–147.

Foucault, M. (1988). Technologies of the self. In Martin, L. H. Gutman, H., & Hutton, P. H. (Eds.), *Technologies of the self: A seminar with Michel Foucault* (pp. 16–49). University of Massachusetts Press.

Freebody, P., & Luke, A. (1990). 'Literacies' programs: debates and demands in cultural context. *Prospect, 5*(3), 7–16.

Freeman, D., & Johnson, K. E. (1998). Reconceptualizing the knowledge–base of language teacher education. *TESOL Quarterly, 32*(3), 397–417.

Freire, P. (2000). *Pedagogy of the oppressed*. Penguin Books. (Original work published 1972)

Freire, P. (1973). *Education for critical consciousness*. Seabury.

Freire, P. (1985). Reading the world and reading the word: An Interview with Paulo Freire. *Language Arts, 62*(1), 15–21.

Freire, P. (1994). *Pedagogy of hope: Reliving pedagogy of the oppressed* (R. R. Barr, Trans.). Continuum.

Freire, P. (2005). *Teachers as cultural workers. Letters to teachers who dare teach*. Westview Press.

Fuller, R. (2015). *Beasts and gods: How democracy changed Its meaning and lost its purpose*. Zed Books.

Garcia, O., & Wei, L. (2013). *Translanguaging: Language, bilingualism and education*. Palgrave Macmillan.

Gebhard, M., Harman, R., & Seger, W. (2007). Reclaiming recess: learning the language of persuasion. *Language Arts, 84*(5), 419–431.

Ghahremani–Ghajar, S. S., & Mirhosseini, S. A. (2005). English class or speaking about everything class? Dialogue journal writing as a critical EFL literacy practice in an Iranian high school. *Language, Culture and Curriculum, 18*(3), 286–299.

Giroux, H. A. (1981). *Ideology, culture & the process of schooling*. Falmer Press.

Giroux, H. A. (1983). Theories of reproduction and resistance in the new sociology of education: A critical analysis. *Harvard Educational Review, 53*(3), 257–293

Giroux, H. A. (1992). *Border crossings: Cultural workers and the politics of education*. Routledge.

Goddu, J. Q. (2011). Listening effectively. In *Public speaking: The virtual textbook*. The Public Speaking Project.

Goldmark, R. I. (1918). Studies in the influence of the classics on English literature (Vol. 39). Columbia University Press.

Goodwin, J. (2001). Teaching Pronunciation. In M. Celce–Murcia (Ed.) *Teaching English as a second or foreign language* (pp. 117–133). Heinle & Heinle.

Gorlewski, J. A., Porfilio, B. J., & Gorlewski, D. A. (Eds.). (2012). *Using standards and high-stakes testing for students: Exploiting power with critical pedagogy*. Peter Lang.

Goux, D., & Maurin, E. (1997) Meritocracy and social heredity in France: Some aspects and trends. *European Sociological Review, 13*(2), 159–177.

Gray, J. (2001). 'The global coursebook in English language teaching,' In D. Block (Ed.), *Globalization and language teaching*. Routledge.

Griffiths, V. (2000). The reflective dimension in teacher education. *International Journal of Educational Research, 33*(5), 539–555.

Grigoryan, A., & King, J. M. (2008). Adbusting: Critical media literacy in a multi-skills academic writing lesson. *English Teaching Forum, 46*(4), 2–9.

Habulembe, S. H. (2007). A classroom response to HIV/AIDS: Project proposal writing. *English Teaching Forum, 45*(1), 36–42.

Hammond, J., & Macken–Horarik, M. (1999). Critical literacy: Challenges and questions for ESL classrooms. *TESOL Quarterly, 33*(3), 528–544.

Harrison, C. (2013). *The art of listening in the early Church*. Oxford University Press.

Hartse, J. H. & Dong, J. (2015). *Teaching English at colleges and universities in China*. TESOL Press.

Hawkins, M., & Norton, B. (2009). Critical language teacher education. In A. Burns & J. C. RIchards (Eds.), *Cambridge guide to second language teacher education* (pp. 30–39). Cambridge University Press.

Hayik, R. (2015). Diverging from traditional paths: Reconstructing fairy tales in the EFL classroom. *Diaspora, Indigenous, and Minority Education, 9*(4), 221–236.

Hobbs, R., He, H., & Robbgrieco, M. (2015). Seeing, believing, and learning to be skeptical: Supporting language learning through advertising analysis activities. *TESOL Journal, 6*(3), 447–475.

Hogan, A., Sellar, S., & Lingard, B. (2016). Corporate social responsibility and neo-social accountability: The case of Pearson plc. In A. Veger, C. Lubienski,

& G. Steiner-Khamsi (Eds.), *The global education industry* (World Yearbook of Education 2016). Routledge.

Hoover, R. L., & Kindsvatter, R. (1997). *Democratic discipline: Foundation and practice.* Merrill/PrenticeHall.

Howatt, A. P. R. (1984). *A history of English language teaching.* Oxford University Press.

Huh, S. (2016). Instructional model of critical literacy in an EFL Context: Balancing conventional and critical literacy. *Critical Inquiry in Language Studies, 13*(3), 210–235.

Ismael, D. A. (2017). Kurdish tertiary EFL teachers' assessment literacy in alternative assessments and its influence on the ethicality of their assessments. In R. Al-Mahrooqi, C. Coombe, F. Al-Maamari, & V. Thakur (Eds.), *Revisiting EFL assessment: Critical perspectives* (pp. 29–45). Springer.

Izadinia, M., & Abednia, A. (2010). Dynamics of an EFL reading course with a critical literacy orientation. *Journal of Language and Literacy Education, 6*(2), 51–67.

Jackson, E. (1994). *Cinder Edna.* Mulberry Books.

Janks, H. (1991). A critical approach to the teaching of language. *Educational Review, 43,* 191–199.

Janssens, F. J. G., & van Amelsvoort, G. H. W. C. H. (2009). School self-evaluations and school inspections in Europe: An exploratory study. *Studies in Educational Evaluation, 34,* 15–23.

Jefferson, T. (1954). *Notes on the State of Virginia.* H. C. Carey and I. Lea. (Original work published 1785)

Jenkins, J. (2000). *The phonology of English as an international language.* Oxford University Press.

Jenkins, J. (2003). *World Englishes.* Routledge.

Jhaly, S. (Producer). (2002). *Killing us softly 3: Advertising's image of women* (Videotape). Media Education Foundation.

Jin, L., & Cortazzi, M. (2011). Re–evaluating traditional approaches to second language teaching and learning. In E. Hinkel (Ed.), *Handbook of research in second language teaching and learning* (Vol. 2, pp. 558–575). Taylor and Francis.

Jobin–Leeds, G., & AgitArte. (2016). *When we fight we win: Twenty-first social movements and the activists who are transforming our world.* The New Press.

Jones, L. (1992). *Communicative grammar practice.* Cambridge University Press.

Jones, P., & Chen, H. (2016). The role of dialogic pedagogy in teaching grammar. *Research Papers in Education* (Talking to Learn: Dialogic Teaching in Conversation with Educational Linguistics), *31*(1), 45–69.

Kant, I. (1998). *Critique of pure reason* (P. Guyer & W. Wood, Trans.). Cambridge University Press. (Original work published 1781)

Karabel, J. (2005). *The chosen: The hidden history of admission and exclusion at Harvard, Yale, and Princeton.* Houghton Mifflin Company.

Kärkkäinen, L. (2013). *An English language club on global education for 6th graders: A teacher's handbook.* (Master's thesis) Department of Languages English, University of Jyväskylä.

Kayi, H. (2006). Teaching speaking: Activities to promote speaking in a second language. *The Internet TESL Journal, 12*(11), 1–6.

Khan, S. Z. (2009). Imperialism of international tests: An EIL perspective. In F. Sharifian (Ed.), *English as an International Language: Perspectives and pedagogical issues* (pp. 190–205). Multilingual Matters.

Khogali, S. E. O., Laidlaw, J. M., & Harden, R. M. (2006). Study guides: A study of different formats. *Medical Teacher, 28*(4), 375–377.

Kilbourne, J. (Producer). (1987). *Still killing us softly* (Videotape). Cambridge Films.

Kilbourne, J., & R. Pollay. (Producers). (1992). *Pack of lies: The advertising of tobacco* (Videotape). Media Education Foundation.

Kim, S. J. (2014). Possibilities and challenges of early critical literacy practices: Bilingual preschoolers' exploring multiple voices and gender roles. *Journal of Early Childhood Research,* 1–14.

Kohn, A. (1996). *Beyond discipline: From compliance to community.* ASCD.

Kratz, H. E. (1896). Characteristics of the best teacher as recognized by children. *Pedagogical Seminary, 3,* 413–418.

Kuo, J.-M. (2013). Implementing critical literacy for university freshmen in Taiwan through self-discovery texts. *Asia-Pacific Educational Research, 22*(4), 549–557.

Kumaravadivelu, K. (2003). *Beyond methods: Macrostrategies for language teaching.* Yale University Press.

Kuo, J.-M. (2014). Critical literacy in the EFL classroom: Evolving multiple perspectives through learning tasks. *The Journal of Asia TEFL, 1*(4), 109–138.

Lagonegro, M. (2005). *A dream for a princess.* Random House/Disney.

Lakoff, R. (1990). *Talking power: The politics of language.* Basic Books.

Laman, T. T., Jewett, P., Jennings, L. B., Wilson, J. L. & Souto–Manning, M. (2012). Supporting critical dialogue across educational contexts. *Equity & Excellence in Education, 45*(1), 197–216.

Larsen–Freeman, D. (2001). *Teaching language: From grammar to grammaring.* Heinle & Heinle.

Lau, S. M. C. (2012). Reconceptualizing critical literacy teaching in ESL classrooms. *The Reading Teacher, 65*(5), 325–329.

Lee, Y. J. (2017). First steps toward critical literacy: Interactions with an English narrative text among three English as a foreign language readers in South Korea. *Journal of Early Childhood Literacy, 17*(1), 26–46.

Leeman, N. (1999). *The big test: The secret history of the American meritocracy.* Farrar, Straus and Giroux.

Levis, J. M. (2005). Changing contexts and shifting paradigms in pronunciation teaching. *Tesol Quarterly, 39*(3), 369–377.

Lim, L. (2016). Analysing meritocratic (in)equality in Singapore: Ideology, curriculum and reproduction. *Critical Studies in Education, 57*(2), 160–174.

Liu, A. (2011). Unraveling the myth of meritocracy within the context of US higher education. *Higher Education, 62,* 383–397.

Luke, A., & Freebody, P. (1999). A map of possible practices: further notes on the four resources model. *Reading Online, 4,* 5–8.

Lundsteen, S. W. (1966). Critical listening: An experiment. *The Elementary School Journal, 66*(6), 311–315.

Lutz, W. (1995). With these words I can sell you anything. In G. Goshgarian (Ed.), *Exploring language* (7th ed., pp. 73–87). HarperCollins.

Machin, D., & Mayr, A. (2012). *How to do critical discourse analysis: A multimodal introduction*. SAGE.

Macknish, C. J. (2011). Understanding critical reading in an ESL class in Singapore. *TESOL Journal, 2*(4), 444–472.

Marchel, C. A. (2007). Learning to talk/talking to learn: teaching critical dialogue. *Teaching Educational Psychology, 2*(1), 1–11.

Marshall, C., & Anderson, A. L. (Eds.). (2009). *Activist educators: Breaking past limits*. Routledge.

McCafferty, S. G., Jacobs, G. M., & Iddings, A. G. D. (2006). *Cooperative learning and second language teaching*. Cambridge University Press.

McNamara, T. (2008). The social-political and power dimensions of tests, in E. Shohamy & N.H. Hornberger (eds.), *Language Testing and Assessment* (Encyclopedia of Language and Education, 2nd ed., Vol. 7, pp. 415–427). Springer.

McNamara, T. (2011) Measuring deficit. In C. N. Candlin & J. Crichton (Eds.), *Discourses of Deficit* (pp. 311–326). Palgrave Macmillan.

Menzel, P. (1995). *Material world: A global family portrait*. Sierra Club Books.

Menzel, P. (2007). *Hungry planet: What the world eats*. Ten Speed.

Michaelis, J. U. (1950). *Social studies for children in a democracy* (Chapter 15: Evaluation of learning in the social studies). Prentice-Hall.

Miri, M., Alibakshi, G., & Mostafaei–Alaei, M. (2017). Reshaping teacher cognition about L1 use through critical ELT teacher education. *Critical Inquiry in Language Studies, 14*(1), 58–98.

Morgan, B. (1997). Identity and intonation: Linking dynamic processes in an ESL classroom. *TESOL Quarterly, 31*(3), 431–450.

Morgan, B. (1998). *The ESL classroom: Teaching, practice, and community development*. University of Toronto Press.

Morgan, B. (2001). Language, identity and ESL pronunciation: An integrated approach. *Contact, 27*(2), 41–48.

Morgan, B. (2004). Modals and memories: a grammar lesson on the Quebec referendum on sovereignty. In B. Norton & K. Toohey (Eds.), *Critical pedagogies and language learning* (pp. 158–178). Cambridge University Press.

Morgan, B. (2009). Revitalising the essay in an English for academic purposes course: critical engagement, multiliteracies and the internet. *International Journal of Bilingual Education and Bilingualism, 12*(3), 309–324.

Moyer, B., & Tuttle, A. (1983). Overcoming masculine oppression in mixed groups. In *Off their backs… and on our own two feet: Men against patriarchy* (pp. 25–29). New Society.

Murdoch, K., & Le Mescam, N. (2006). Negotiating the curriculum with students: A conversation worth having. *EQ Australia 1*, 42–44. http://exhibitionworkshop2013.weebly.com/uploads/1/6/8/2/16822980/negotiating_curriculum.pdfMurphey, T. (1989). Student–made tests. *Modern English Teacher, 17*, 28–29.

Murphey, T. (1994). Tests: Learning through negotiated interaction. *TESOL Journal, 4*(2), 12–16.

Murphey, T. (2017). Provoking potentials: Student self–evaluated and socially mediated testing. In R. Al–Mahrooqi, R., C. Coombe, F. Al-Maamari, & V.

Thakur (Eds.), *Revising EFL assessment: Critical perspectives* (pp. 287–317). Springer.

Nation, I. S. P., & Macalister, J. (2009a). Negotiated syllabuses. (Ch. 10 of *Language curriculum design*; pp. 149–158). Rouledge.

Nation, I. S. P., & Macalister, J. (2009b). Adopting and adapting an existing course book. (Ch. 11 of *Language curriculum design*; pp. 159–181). Routledge.

Neill, A. S. (1927). *The problem child*. McBride.

Nolasco, R., & Arthur, L. (1994). *Large classes*. Phoenix ELT/Modern English Publications/International Book Distributors.

Nordheimer, J., & Frantz, D. (1997, September 30). "Testing Giant Exceeds Roots, Drawing Business Rivals' Ire". *New York Times*, Section A, Page 1.

Numrich, C. (2003). *Consider the issues*. Pearson.

Nuske, C. (2018). Critical friends: How to develop effective critical friends PD groups. In J. I. Liontas (Ed.), *The TESOL encyclopedia of English language teaching* (Vol. 7: Organizational and administrative issues & teacher training professional development) (pp. 4514–4519). Wiley.

Oliphant, K. (2003). Teacher development groups: Growth through cooperation. In G. Crookes, *The practicum in TESOL* (Appendix A, pp. 203–214). Cambridge University Press.

Osborn, T. (2006). *Teaching world languages for social justice* (Ch. 4 – The politics of grammar and vocabulary; pp. 57–70). Lawrence Erlbaum Associates.

Oskarsson, M. (1978). *Approaches to self-assessment in foreign language learning*. Pergamon Press/ Council of Europe.

Parenti, M. (1986). Methods of misrepresentation. In M. Parenti (Ed.), *Inventing Reality* (pp. 213–227). St. Martin's Press.

Park, Y. (2011). Using news articles to build a critical literacy classroom in an EFL setting. *TESOL Journal, 2*(1), 24–51.

Parkhurst, H. (1921, August 6). The Dalton Plan. *Times Educational Supplement*.

Pennycook, A. (1989). Comments on Martha C. Pennington and Aileen L. Young's "Approaches to Faculty Evaluation for ESL". A Reader Reacts. *TESOL Quarterly, 24*(3), 555–559.

Pennycook, A. (1997). Cultural alternatives and autonomy. In P. Benson & P. Voller (Eds.), *Autonomy and independence in language learning* (pp. 35–53). Routledge.

Pennycook, A. (1999). Introduction: Critical approaches to TESOL. *TESOL Quarterly, 33*, 329–348.

Pennington, M. C., & Young, A. L. (1989). Approaches to faculty evaluation for ESL. *TESOL Quarterly, 23*(4), 619–646.

Pereira, A. H., Ismail, K., & Othman, Z. (2013). A model for the Malaysian English Language Club activities. *Procedia—Social and Behavioral Sciences, 90*, 48–56.

Pessoa, R. R., & Freitas, M. T. De U. (2012). Challenges in critical language teaching. *TESOL Quarterly, 46*(4), 753–776.

Peterson, B. (1994). The complexities of encouraging social action. In W. Au, B. Bigelow, & S. Karp (Eds.), *Rethinking our classrooms: Teaching for equity and justice* (pp .40–41). Rethinking Schools.

Phillipson, R. (1992). *Linguistic imperialism*. Oxford University Press.

Plutarch. (1969). *On listening*. In *Moralia* (Vol 1., pp. 201–262; trans. F. C. Babbitt). Loeb. (Original work published circa AD 75)

Rashdall, H. (1936). *The universities of Europe in the Middle Ages* (F. M. Powicke & A. B. Emden, Eds.). The Clarendon Press.

Remmers, H. H. (1930) To what extent do grades influence student ratings of instructors? *Journal of Educational Psychology, 21,* 314–316.

Reveal the Real You!: 20 Cool Quizzes All About You. (1999). Troll Publications/ Petersen Publishing Company.

Reynolds, M., & Trehan, K. (2000). Assessment: A critical perspective. *Studies in Higher Education, 25*(3), 267–278.

Richards, J. C., & Bohlke, D. (2012). *Four Corners* (Level 3). Cambridge University Press.

Riley, J. W., Ryan, B. F., & Lifshitz, M. (1950). Rutgers University Press.

Rogers, C. R., & Farson, R. E. (1957). *Active listening.* Industrial Relations Center, University of Chicago.

Rosenthal, L. (2004). Do school inspections improve school quality? Ofsted inspections and school examination results in the UK. *Economics of Education Review, 23,* 143–151.

Rost, M., & Wilson, J. J. (2013). *Active listening.* Routledge.

Rousseau, J.-J. (1938). *Emile, or on education.* Dutton.

Roy, L. (2017). "So What's the Difference?": Talking about race with refugee children in the English language learner classroom. *TESOL Journal, 8*(3), 540–563.

Russell, D. H. (1953). What does research say about self-evaluation? *Journal of Educational Research, 46*(8), 561–573.

Sadeghi, S. (2008). Critical pedagogy in an EFL teaching context: An ignis fatuus or an alternative approach. *Journal for Critical Education Policy Studies, 6*(1), 277–295.

Salas, S., Fitchett, P. G., & Mercado, L. (2013). Talking to learn across classrooms and communities. *English Teaching Forum, 51*(1), 18–25.

Say, A. (1993). *Grandfather's journey.* Scholastic.

Sayer, P. (2012). *Ambiguities and tensions in English language teaching: Portraits of EFL teachers as legitimate speakers.* Routledge.

Schein, E. (1993). On dialogue, culture, and organizational learning. *Organizational Dynamics, 22,* 40–51.

Schneider, J. (2005). Teaching grammar through community issues. *ELT Journal, 59*(4), 298–305.

Schwartz, E. G. (1950). *Faculty rating: An intercollegiate program for the evaluation of faculty instruction* (R. J. Medalie, Ed.). United States National Student Association.

Scott, J. C. (1985). *Weapons of the weak: Everyday forms of peasant resistance.* Yale University Press.

Scott, J. C. (1990). *Domination and the arts of resistance: Hidden transcripts.* Yale University Press.

Seidlhofer, B. (2001). 'Closing a conceptual gap: the case for a description of English as a lingua franca'. *International Journal of Applied Linguistics, 11,* 133–58.

Serrano, M. M., O'Brien, M., Roberts, K., & Whyte, D. (2018). Critical Pedagogy and assessment in higher education: The ideal of 'authenticity' in learning. *Active Learning in Higher Education,19*(1), 9–21.

Shahsavari–Googhari, R. (2017). *How do teachers challenge neoliberalism through critical pedagogy within and outside of the classroom* (MA thesis). University of Western Ontario.

Shin, H., & Crookes, G. (2005). Exploring the possibilities for EFL critical pedagogy in Korea—A two-part case study. *Critical Inquiry in Language Studies, (2)*2, 112–138.

Shohamy, E. (1998). Critical language testing and beyond. *Studies in Educational Evaluation, 24*(4), 331–345.

Shohamy, E. (2001a). Democratic assessment as an alternative. *Language Testing, 18*(4), 373–391.

Shohamy, E. (2001b). *The power of tests: A critical perspective on the uses of language tests*. Longman.

Shor, I. (1992). *Empowering education. Critical teaching for social change*. The University of Chicago Press.

Shor, I. (1987). *Critical teaching and everyday life*. University of Chicago Press.

Shor, I. (1996). *When students have power: Negotiating authority in a critical pedagogy*. University of Chicago Press.

Shor, I., & Freire, P. (1980). *A pedagogy for liberation*. Bergin & Garvey.

Shulman, M. (2004). *Thinking critically: World issues for reading, writing and research*. University of Michigan Press.

Simon, R. I. (1985). Critical pedagogy. In T. Husen & W. Postlethwaite (Eds.), *International encyclopedia of education: Research and studies* (Vol. 2, pp. 1118–1120). Pergamon Press.

Simpson, A. (1996). Critical questions: Whose questions? *The Reading Teacher, 50*(2), 118–127.

Sithamparam, S., & Dhamotharan, M. (1992). Peer networking: Towards self–direction in teacher development. *English Teaching Forum, 30*(1), 12–15.

Smith, R. (2008). Learner autonomy. *ELT Journal, 62*(4), 395–397.

Sokol, D. K. (2004). The use of ethics in the EFL Classroom. *English Teaching Forum, 42*, 2–5.

Stillar, S. (2013). Raising critical consciousness via critical writing in the EFL classroom. *TESOL Journal, 4*(1), 164–174.

Stout, J. (2010). *Blessed are the organized: Grassroots democracy in America*. Princeton University Press.

Sundqvist, P., & Sivén, L. K. (2016). *Extramural English in teaching and learning* (Ch. 3: English in schools from various national perspectives; pp. 43–74). Palgrave Macmillan.

Sung, K., & Pederson, R. (Eds.). (2012). *Critical ELT practices in Asia*. Sense.

Swain, A.(2005). *Education as social action, knowledge, identity and power.* Palgrave Macmillan.

Synott, J. (2002). *Teacher unions, social movements, and the politics of education in Asia*. Ashgate.

Synott, J. (2007). The Korean Teachers and Educational Workers' Union: Collective rights as the agency of social change. *IEJLL: International Electronic Journal for Leadership in Learning, 11* (#23).

Tajeddin, Z., & Enayat, M. J. (2010). Gender representation and stereotyping in ELT textbooks: A critical image analysis. *Teaching English Language and Literature [Iran], 4*(2), 51–79.

Taylor, P. V. (1991). *The texts of Paulo Freire.* Open University Press.

Taylor, A. (2015). Listening in the pedagogy of discomfort: A framework for socially–just listening. In L. J. Waks (Ed.), *Listening to teach: Beyond didactic pedagogy* (pp. 113–136). SUNY Press.

Taylor, E. (2013). *Surveillance schools: Security, discipline and control in contemporary education.* Palgrave Macmillan.

Taylor, L., & Jones, N. (2006). Cambridge ESOL exams and the Common European Framework of Reference. *Research Notes* [Cambridge ESOL], *24*, 1–5.

Templer, B. (2004). High–stakes testing at high fees: Notes and queries on the international English proficiency assessment market. *Journal for Critical Educational Policy Studies, 2*(1), 189–228.

Thornbury, S. (1999). *How to teach grammar.* Pearson Education.

Tilly, C. (2003). When do (and don't) social movements promote democratization? In P. Ibarra (Ed.), *Social movements and democracy* (pp. 21–45). Palgrave Macmillan.

Tilly, C. (2004). *Social movements, 1768–2004.* Paradigm.

Tindall, D. B. (2015). Networks as constraints and opportunities. In D. della Porta & M. Diani (Eds.), *The Oxford handbook of social movements* (pp. 231–245). Oxford University Press.

Tomlinson, B. (Ed.). (1998). *Materials development in language teaching.* Cambridge University Press.

Tomlinson, B. (2012). Materials development for language learning and teaching. *Language Teaching, 45*(2), 143–179.

Tupas, R. (Ed.). (2015). *Unequal Englishes.* Routledge.

Vandergrift, L., & Goh, C. C. M. (2012). *Teaching and learning second language listening: Metacognition in action.* Routledge.

Vandrick, S. (1994). Feminist pedagogy and ESL. *College ESL, 4*(2), 69–92.

Van der Ploeg, P. (2014). Dalton Plan. In D. C. Phillips (Ed.), *Encyclopedia of educational theory and philosophy* (pp. 207–208). SAGE.

Van Dijk, T. (1995). Aims of critical discourse analysis. *Japanese Discourse, 1*, 17–27.

Vasquez, V. M. (2004). *Negotiating critical literacies with young children.* Lawrence Erlbaum Associates.

Voloshinov, V. N. (1973). *Marxism and the philosophy of language* (L. Matejka & I. R. Titunik, Trans.). Harvard University Press.

Waks, L. J. (Ed.). (2015). *Listening to teach: Beyond didactic pedagogy.* SUNY Press.

Wallace, K. (2003). *Critical reading in language education.* Palgrave Macmillan.

Wallerstein, N. (1983). *Language and culture in conflict: Problem–posing in the ESL classroom.* Addison Wesley.

Wartenberg, T. E. (2014). *Big ideas for little kids: Teaching philosophy through children's literature* (2nd ed.). Rowman & Littlefield.

Weigand, E. (Ed.). (1994). *Concepts of dialogue: Considered from the perspective of different disciplines.* Niemeyer.

Wennerstrom, A. K., & Heiser, P. (1992). ESL student bias in instructional evaluation, *TESOL Quarterly, 26*(2), 271–288.

West, G. B. (2014). *Doing critical language pedagogy in neoliberal spaces: A materialist narrative analysis of teaching young learners of English in a Korean hagwon* (Unpublished MA thesis). University of Hawai'i. http://hdl.handle.net/10125/101229.

Williams, C. (1996). Secondary education: teaching in the bilingual situation. In C. Williams, G. Lewis, & C. Baker (Eds.), *The language policy: taking stock.* CAI Language Studies Centre.

Williams, C. (2002). *Ennilliaith: Astudiaeth o Sefyllfadrochiyn 11–16 oed* [A language gained: A study of language immersion at 11–16 years of age]. School of Education. http://www.bangor.ac.uk/addysg/publications/Ennill_Iaith.pdf

Wilkinson, L., & Janks, H. (1998). Teaching direct and reported speech from a critical language awareness (CLA) perspective. *Educational Review, 50*(2), 181–190.

Wilson, J. L. (2010). "They say we're the land of tolerance": Using critical dialogue to interrogate issues of immigration in a middle–level classroom. In L. B. Jennings, P. C. Jewett, T. T. Laman, M. Souto–Manning, & J. L. Wilson (Eds.), *Sites of possibility: Critical dialogue across educational settings* (pp. 15–38). Hampton Press.

Wright, T. (1994). *Investigating English.* Edward Arnold.

Wright, T. (2005). *Classroom management in language education.* Routledge.

Yoo, Y., & Namkumg, G. (2012). English and American linguistic hegemony: A case study of the Educational Testing Service. *The Korean Journal of International Studies, 10*(2), 221–253.

Young, E. (2002). *Seven blind mice.* Puffin Books.

Young, M. (1958). *The rise of the meritocracy.* Thames & Hudson.

Zhao, J. (2013). Confucius as a critical educator: Towards educational thoughts of Confucius. *Frontiers of Education in China, 8*(1), 9–27.

ABOUT THE AUTHORS

Arman Abednia received a PhD in TEFL from Allameh Tabataba'i University in 2010 and is currently a PhD candidate in Education at Edith Cowan University. His research interests are critical pedagogy, TESOL teacher education, teacher professional identity, and needs analysis. He has published in journals such as *Teaching and Teacher Education, System, Language Awareness, TELL,* and *Journal of Language and Literacy Education* and presented in conferences such as AAAL, AARE, TWN, and TELLSI. He reviews papers for Teaching and Teacher Education and System. Dr. Abednia has taught undergraduate courses such as Reading Comprehension, Advanced Writing, and Second Language Teaching Methodology, graduate courses such as Research Methodology, Teaching L2 Skills, and ESP, communicative courses of English, Business English, IELTS, and TOEFL. He has also been involved in conducting teacher education courses and designing and supervising second language instruction programs. He has also conducted workshops on critical approaches to teaching EFL/ESL skills as well as research basics, qualitative research, critical research, and grounded theory. He has worked in Iran, Australia, and New Zealand. At the moment, while doing his PhD research, he is a casual employee in Graduate Research School at Edith Cowan University where he provides consultations for higher degree by research students.

Graham V. Crookes is Professor in the Department of Second Language Studies (SLS), and previously had administrative responsibilities there as Executive Director, ESL Programs (with oversight of the English

Language Institute [ELI] and the Hawai'i English Language Program [HELP]) and subsequently as Department Chair for almost 10 years. He received his PhD in Educational Psychology and his MA in ESL from the University of Hawai'i. He also holds postgraduate certificates from the University of London, in education, and from the University of Essex, in applied linguistics. Besides critical language pedagogy Dr. Crookes's specialties include the methodology of second language teaching and teacher development (including practice teaching supervision and more recently, philosophy of teaching). Besides teaching regular graduate and undergraduate courses for the Department of SLS, he has conducted courses and workshops for teachers especially on teaching methodology, action research, and critical pedagogy, in a variety of settings around the world, including Colombia, Denmark, Korea, Kyrgyzstan, Singapore, and Vietnam. He has published in academic journals such as *Language Learning, TESOL Quarterly, Applied Linguistics, Language Teaching,* and *Studies in Second Language Acquisition.* Topics he has addressed in print include the analysis of scientific text, dyadic interaction for SLA, aspects of task-based language curriculum and task design, SLA theory, the relationship between SL theory and teaching, SL practice teaching, planning in SL speech production, discourse analysis of SL speech, SL motivation, critical action research, SL teachers' working conditions, innovation in SL curricula, critical SL teacher education, SL program advocacy, and SL critical pedagogy. He was co-editor (with S. M. Gass) of a two volume series on task-based language teaching (Tasks in a pedagogical context and Tasks and language learning) published by Multilingual Matters in 1993. In 2003 he published *A Practicum In TESOL: Professional Development Through Teaching Practice,* published by Cambridge University Press, and in 2009 he published *Values, Philosophies, and Beliefs in TESOL: Making A Statement,* also with Cambridge. Particularly related to the present work is his 2013 book *Critical ELT in Action. Foundations, Promises, Praxis* which he published with Routledge.